RAILS ACROSS CANADA

RAILS ACROSS CANADA

THE HISTORY OF CANADIAN PACIFIC AND CANADIAN NATIONAL RAILWAYS

TOM MURRAY

Voyageur Press

First published in 2006 and 2004 as two volumes by MBI, an imprint of MBI Publishing Company, 400 First Avenue North, Suite 300, Minneapolis, MN 55401 USA

Voyageur Press titles are also available at discounts in bulk quantity for industrial or sales-promotional use. For details write to Special Sales Manager at MBI Publishing Company, 400 First Avenue North, Suite 300, Minneapolis, MN 55401 USA.

To find out more about our books, visit us online at www.voyageurpress.com.

ISBN-13: 978-0-7603-4008-0

The Library of Congress has cataloged the hardcover editions as follows:

Murray, Tom, 1948–
        Canadian Pacific Railway / by Tom Murray
                p. cm.
        Includes bibliographical references.
        ISBN-13: 978-0-7603-2255-0 (hardback)
        ISBN-10: 0-7603-2255-4 (hardback)
    1. Canadian Pacific Railway Company–History. 2. Railroads–Canada, Western–History. I. Title.
        TF27.C3M87 2006
        385.0971–dc22
                                        2006001320
Murray, Tom, 1948–
        Canadian National Railway / by Tom Murray
                p. cm.
        ISBN 0-7603-1764-X (alk. paper)
    1. Canadian National Railways–History. 2. Railroads–Canada–History. I. Title.
        TF26.M87 2004
        385'.0971–dc22
                                        2004040340

Front cover photos by Tom Murray (top) and Bill Linley (bottom). Title page photo by Jim Shaughnessy. Back cover photo by Stan Smaill.

Editor: Dennis Pernu
Design Manager: LeAnn Kuhlmann
Designer: Chris Fayers
Cover designer: Simon Larkin

Printed in China

CONTENTS

CANADIAN PACIFIC RAILWAY

ACKNOWLEDGMENTS..8

INTRODUCTION..9

Chapter 1   A RAILWAY TO CREATE A NATION................................12

Chapter 2   BECOMING A GLOBAL TRANSPORTATION SYSTEM: 1885–1918.............38

Chapter 3   SERVING CANADA THROUGH PEACE AND WAR: 1918–1948..............78

Chapter 4   THE CRUMP ERA: 1948–1972.....................................92

Chapter 5   CPR'S PASSENGER TRAINS......................................114

Chapter 6   CANADIAN PACIFIC BULKS UP, THEN SLIMS DOWN: 1972–1996.......130

Chapter 7   UNWINDING THIRTY YEARS OF DIVERSIFICATION: 1996–2006........146

SOURCES..161

CANADIAN NATIONAL RAILWAY

ACKNOWLEDGMENTS..164

INTRODUCTION..165

Chapter 1   THE BIRTH OF CANADIAN NATIONAL.............................168

Chapter 2   THE FIRST QUARTER CENTURY: SURVIVING DEPRESSION AND WAR.....186

Chapter 3   POSTWAR CN: YEARS OF MODERNIZATION AND GROWTH..............206

Chapter 4   CN PASSENGER SERVICE.......................................226

Chapter 5   FROM SEA TO SEA: THE REGIONS OF CN.........................244

Chapter 6   CN'S U.S. AFFILIATES.......................................278

Chapter 7   PRIVATIZATION AND EXPANSION................................298

CN EPILOGUE...316

SOURCES...317

INDEXES...319

CANADIAN PACIFIC
RAILWAY

TOM MURRAY

Voyageur Press

Acknowledgments

To be given an opportunity to write about Canadian Pacific Railway is a great privilege. It is, justifiably, one of the best-documented companies in North America, and my bookshelves have been groaning under the weight of the books written by others about its history. I am grateful to all of them for providing material for me to draw on. I hope that readers who are not already familiar with these earlier books will be motivated, after reading this one, to dig deeper. References to several of these works are found in the text of this book, and the bibliography contains a fuller list.

Generations of photographers have trained their lenses on CPR. This made for such an abundance of archival and contemporary photos that it was a great challenge to choose the ones to appear here. I did my best to select photos that are both visually appealing and as representative as possible of the company's history and geography. I am indebted to all ten of the photographers who allowed their material to be reproduced in this book: Bruce Blackadar, Eric Blasko, John Leopard, Bill Linley, Phil Mason, Steve Patterson, George Pitarys, Jim Shaughnessy, Stan Smaill, and Pat Yough.

CPR was constructed at a time when photography was already well developed as a commercial enterprise, and technical advancements had made it possible to take photographs in the field (even under adverse conditions). The building of the railway was an event of national importance in Canada, and its early years were amply recorded. I want to thank the Glenbow Archives in Calgary and Library and Archives Canada in Ottawa, both of which provided archival photos for this book.

The California State Railroad Museum allowed the use of several photographs by Philip R. Hastings, M.D., whose collection was donated to the museum by his family in 1997. The Denver Public Library's Western History Collection, which is the custodian of the Otto C. Perry Memorial Collection of Railroad Photographs, allowed three of Mr. Perry's CPR photos to be reproduced here.

Although CPR's history has been well documented, it's possible for a writer to go astray, and to reduce that potential I had assistance from several railway veterans. Raymond L. Kennedy, who was a longtime CPR employee, provided detailed feedback on an early draft of this book and saved me from several errors. F. H. Howard, who had a long career in the Canadian transportation industry, reviewed the text and gave me the benefit of his experiences with the people of CPR. Former Canadian Pacific Chairman and Chief Executive Officer (and fourth-generation CPR employee) William W. Stinson provided a number of helpful notes and comments on the draft text. CPR veterans Phil Mason and Stan Smaill, both of whom provided photos for this book, also gave me a great deal of help in understanding the history of this company.

Despite the assistance of such knowledgeable people, errors of fact and interpretation may have found their way into this book. They are my responsibility alone.

Finally, I have been fortunate to have the support of my wife, Marcia, who has not only enabled me to devote time to this project but has actively encouraged it. For that reason, and many others, this book is dedicated to her.

INTRODUCTION

Canadian Pacific began as a railway, became a global transportation system, and then evolved into a diversified industrial conglomerate. Today it is, once again, a railway. This book is an effort to tell the story not just of the railway, but of the company that was created around it.

That story is a rich one, with many colorful individuals involved. They include George Stephen and Donald Smith, cousins from Scotland whose vision made Canadian Pacific possible; William Cornelius Van Horne, a gifted railroader who guided the company through its perilous years of construction and early operation; Thomas Shaughnessy, an administrative and logistical wizard who strengthened the railway both physically and financially; Edward Beatty, who helped the company survive the challenges of vigorous competition and demoralizing economic conditions; Norris Crump, an up-from-the-ranks railroader who forced the company to change technologically and spurred its expansion into new lines of business; and Ian Sinclair, who alienated many by his emphasis on non-rail enterprises, but whose instincts may well have been the right ones, given the economic and regulatory climate of his time.

As a railway, CPR has long had a reputation for conservatism, for not spending a dollar that was not absolutely necessary. That reputation is no accident. Its roots are in the financial challenges that faced the company throughout its early years, as it pushed across Canada, through inhospitable

An eastbound freight powered by five SD40 and SD40-2 locomotives makes its way along the Kicking Horse River on CPR's Mountain Subdivision in August 1977. The train has just left Golden, British Columbia.
Bruce Blackadar

At Cavers, Ontario, on CPR's Nipigon Subdivision, Train 411 winds along the north shore of Lake Superior, in October 1998. *John Leopard*

territory. There were no footsteps for the railway's builders to follow in, and no way to know in advance what physical challenges they would face. As the line was extended westward, the early estimates of construction costs proved over-optimistic. The fact that CPR has survived as an independent company since its incorporation in 1881 without going through bankruptcy (in an industry where corporate reorganizations have been commonplace) is testimony to the merits of its fiscal prudence.

But being tight with a dollar did not make Canadian Pacific the company that it became—one whose impact on the national life of Canada has been beyond measure. One generation of CPR leaders after another has taken an expansive view of the company's capabilities and potential, beginning with George Stephen, who saw the railway as the cornerstone of an enterprise that would link Britain and Asia. It has never been a company that shied away from new opportunities.

For a railway, geography is destiny. In February 2006, CPR observed the 125th anniversary of its incorporation. Although the company has radically changed in terms of technology, operating practices, and traffic during that time, its geography remains much the same as when it was completed

The rear brakeman has left the caboose and is getting into position to help yard his train as it arrives at the Tadanac Yard near Trail, British Columbia, in October 1972. This was a scene that would soon become obsolete as railroads eliminated roofwalks from freight cars in the interest of safety. Cabooses, too, would be phased out in the coming years. *Tom Murray*

across Canada in 1885. Every day, CPR faces challenges that George Stephen and William Van Horne would understand, as its employees move trains over Kicking Horse Pass, keep the railway operating in inclement weather on the north shore of Lake Superior, and serve the transportation needs of farmers on the Canadian prairie.

Before beginning the story, a note on style is in order. In this book, the abbreviation "CPR" is generally used to refer to the company. In conversation, and in many prior books, common practice has been to refer to "the CPR" or "the C.P.R." However, in company publications (such as annual reports)

today's Canadian Pacific Railway Limited refers to itself as "CPR." This is in line with the practice of other contemporary railroads. However, in train operations and on freight cars and other equipment, the shorter "CP" is generally used as an abbreviation or reporting mark. Therefore, in photo captions the reader will often find "CP" used, as in "engine CP 4105" or "extra CP 5856 west." In other places, the abbreviation "CP" is used in connection with the company's non-rail activities.

Also, the reader should be aware that Canadian Pacific Railway Limited did not sponsor this book, or participate in its development.

The towers of Canada's Parliament buildings can be seen in the background at Ottawa Union Station in June 1965. Vancouver–Montreal Train 8, *The Dominion*, behind CP FP7 1431, is completing its station stop. This train carries a heavy load of express and mail in addition to its passenger business. Next to it is Ottawa–Montreal Train 232. *Bill Linley*

CHAPTER ONE

A Railway to Create a Nation

Most North American railroads began their lives as local or regional

enterprises, growing larger over time through acquisition and new con-

struction. By contrast, Canadian Pacific Railway was conceived from

the beginning as transcontinental in scope. This railway would not

only provide transportation, but would also give tangible expression to

the political, economic, and social connections between Canada's east-

ern and western provinces. The history of Canadian Pacific is, in many

ways, the history of Canada itself.

The building of a railway across Canada was motivated largely by political considerations. In the United States, anti-British sentiment increased during the Civil War, and in British North America there was fear that the north-south trade on which the provinces depended would disappear. Following the United States' purchase of Alaska from Russia, there was talk among some U.S. politicians of the unification of all North American lands bordering the Pacific Ocean, or even the annexation of all the lands north of the border.

British North America, was, until 1867, a loose amalgamation of provinces. To forestall the annexation of British Columbia and other British territory by the Americans, a stronger form of union was needed. Confederation was the answer.

The first provinces to unite as Canada in 1867 were Ontario, Quebec, Nova Scotia, and New Brunswick, followed by Manitoba in 1870. While they continued to have differences politically and economically, these provinces did at least represent a contiguous territory with many common interests.

Bringing British Columbia into Confederation was more complicated. Prior to 1868, the Hudson's Bay Company controlled the central part of British North America, thus interposing a privately controlled region between east and west. The passage of the Rupert's Land Act in that year removed this obstacle but did nothing to mitigate the physical barriers between the Atlantic and Pacific regions.

By 1870, political forces within British Columbia had reached agreement on the terms under which they would agree to Confederation, and a delegation traveled to Ottawa to negotiate with the government of Canada. The agreement that emerged included a promise by Canada that a railway would be built to link British Columbia with the East. Construction was to begin within two years and completion was promised within ten years. Following ratification of the

deal by provincial and Canadian legislatures, British Columbia became part of Canada on July 19, 1871.

A railway across Canada would never have been built were it not for the vision and commitment of Sir John A. Macdonald, leader of the Conservative Party, who served as prime minister of Canada from 1867 to 1873 and from 1878 until his death in 1891. He spearheaded the confederation movement, and he understood the importance of a railway in uniting the nation.

Government subsidies would be critical in getting the railway built, since it would tap into lands that had no economic activity beyond fur trading. As John Lorne McDougall writes in *Canadian Pacific: A Brief History*, "Canadian Pacific came into existence at the time and in the shape it did because it was an answer to a basic national problem and because the government was, for that reason, ready to provide the subsidies for it. It was essential to the life of Canada as a nation, but in economic terms it was a desperately premature enterprise."

Macdonald's eagerness to get the railway built was largely responsible for the gap in his career as prime minister from 1873 to 1878. In the months prior to British Columbia's entry into Canada, Macdonald encouraged shipping magnate and industrialist Hugh Allan, then Canada's richest man, to form an enterprise to build the railway.

At this time, many believed that an all-Canada route between east and west was

The last rays of sun hit the peaks of the Sir Donald Range as a westbound coal train passes Glacier, British Columbia, having just exited the Connaught Tunnel in November 1977. Photographer Mason notes, "The peaks visible in the photo are, left to right, Eagle Peak and Mount Uto and the flank of Mount Sir Donald, visible on the right. The summit of the Rogers Pass grade is about mid-train." The mountain and the range are named after Sir Donald Smith, a founder of Canadian Pacific. *Phil Mason*

impractical due to the rugged nature of the land north of Lake Superior. American railroaders were confident that a route that dipped into the U.S. would be the only way of connecting the eastern provinces with British Columbia. Even the management of Canada's largest railway, the Grand Trunk,

shared this view; Grand Trunk steered clear of any involvement in transcontinental railway projects until the twentieth century.

This view matched well with the self-interest of the owners and operators of U.S. railroads in the northern states, from the Great Lakes westward. One of those was Northern Pacific's banker, Jay Cooke. In December 1871, Cooke and other Americans, with Hugh Allan as the sole Canadian member, formed a partnership to build the Canada Pacific Railway. They did not disclose publicly that the railway would be routed through Sault Ste. Marie, Ontario, and then across the Upper Peninsula of Michigan and northern Wisconsin to a connection with the Northern Pacific at Duluth, Minnesota.

The lack of Canadian representation made this proposal politically unacceptable, and in February 1873 a new company, to be known as Canadian Pacific Railway Company, was formed. Allan was its president, it was Canadian in character, and it was specifically chartered to run north of Lake Superior.

However, this enterprise was doomed by the disclosure of Allan's prior dealings with Cooke and the other Americans. The fact that Macdonald had encouraged the Allan group (even though he was not aware of their planned route via the United States) gave the Liberal opposition in Parliament the fuel they needed to bring Macdonald down. The resulting furor became known as the Pacific Scandal. Faced with mounting criticism over his distribution of money from Allan to Conservative candidates, Macdonald resigned on November 5, 1873.

Historian W. Kaye Lamb, in his book *History of the Canadian Pacific Railway*, describes the outcome of the scandal: "Denied financial backing, the first Canadian Pacific Railway Company quietly disappeared. Sir Hugh Allan withdrew from the Pacific railway scene, and the threat of an American takeover disappeared."

In 1885, CPR construction crews building from the east reached Revelstoke, British Columbia, on the Columbia River. A set of three SD402F units leads a westbound coal train at Revelstoke in December 1990 (part of a group of 25 such units delivered in 1988). In the background is Mount Mackenzie, named after the first Liberal Prime Minister of Canada (1873 to 1878), Alexander Mackenzie. *Phil Mason*

17

With Macdonald out, Liberal leader Alexander Mackenzie became prime minister in November 1873. Though the Liberals had been harsh critics of the Macdonald government's handling of the Pacific railway, they inherited obligations and commitments from which there was no turning back. Surveys to identify a potential route for the railway had been under way since 1871. However, no construction had taken place during the first two years following British Columbia's entry into Canada, and the country was now in an economic depression.

Mackenzie was forced to make at least a modest beginning on the project, and in 1874 he authorized the construction of the first line that would eventually become part of Canadian Pacific. This was not part of the east–west main line, but instead ran south from Winnipeg, Manitoba, to the U.S. border. In conjunction with a rail line south of the border being built at the same time, it would allow construction materials to reach Winnipeg by rail rather than by overland haulage.

Work on the Pembina Branch, as the 63-mile (101-kilometer) line south of Winnipeg was known, proceeded slowly, and the line was not placed into service until 1878. In the meantime, a contract had been signed for construction of a connecting line running 20 miles (32 kilometers) north from Winnipeg, to Selkirk, then eastward to Fort William on Lake Superior. Initial surveys had the east–west transcontinental rail route crossing the Red River at Selkirk, although the route was later changed in favor of Winnipeg.

In the national election of September 1878, Macdonald returned to power and resumed his role as prime minister. Six months earlier, a partnership of four men had acquired control of the St. Paul and Pacific Railroad, which was to be the U.S. connection for the Canadian rail line being built southward from Winnipeg. The partners were James J. Hill, Norman W. Kittson, Donald A.

Smith, and George Stephen. By December 1878, the lines both north and south of the border were completed.

Despite Canada's promise to the citizens of British Columbia in 1871 that they would have their railway within ten years, as the 1870s drew to a close, the government had awarded construction contracts for only 700 miles (1,126 kilometers) of track. These contracts

covered the building of the lines between Lake Superior and Winnipeg, and from Yale to Kamloops Lake, British Columbia.

Economic depression, political turnover, and the lack of able and willing entrepreneurs to take on responsibility for the completion and operation of the railway all led to delays. But with the economy reviving, and Macdonald back in power, two of those handicaps were overcome. The third would soon be rectified as well.

George Stephen, a Scot who had come to Canada in 1850, had served as president of the Bank of Montreal since 1876. He would soon add another presidency to his résumé: that of Canadian Pacific Railway. He was, in Lamb's words, "the heart and soul of the C.P.R. 'syndicate,' as the small closely knit

The original bridge over the Fraser River at Cisco was replaced by this through-truss design in 1909, but the piers and masonry foundations of the first bridge, dating from 1884, were used for the new structure, and remain in service in the twenty-first century. Here, a train of coal empties crosses the bridge in 1985. *Phil Mason*

group that launched the company came to be called, and in its critical first half-dozen years it was in great measure a personal enterprise."

Two other members of the syndicate were, like Stephen, also part of the St. Paul and Pacific group: Stephen's cousin, Donald A. Smith, and James J. Hill. Smith, who came to Canada from Scotland at the age of 18, was a veteran of the Hudson's Bay Company who had risen to be the company's chief commissioner in Canada; he was elected to Parliament in 1871. Hill was born in Ontario but was now a leading businessman in St. Paul, Minnesota; his principal legacy would be the building of the Great Northern Railway from St. Paul to Seattle.

In October 1880, the syndicate agreed to build the 1,900 miles (3,058 kilometers) of track needed to complete the railway (including the challenging segments north of Lake Superior and through the western mountain territory) for $25 million in cash subsidy and a

land grant of 25 million acres (10.1 million hectares). The eastern terminus of the railway would be at Callender, Ontario, near Lake Nipissing. There, it would connect with the Canada Central Railway, which extended from that point to Ottawa.

This contract was for more than construction, however. Stephen and his colleagues agreed to "for ever efficiently maintain, work and run the Canadian Pacific Railway." Following the government's ratification of the contract, the Canadian Pacific Railway Company was incorporated on February 16, 1881.

Overcoming Nature's Barriers

Three major physical challenges faced the surveyors and builders of the railway across Canada:

- The Laurentian Shield, a vast and heavily forested land of rock, muskeg, and rivers north of Lake Superior;

- The Rocky Mountains and other ranges separating the interior of British Columbia from the prairies; and
- The canyons of the Thompson and Fraser rivers, which gave the railway a path to the Pacific but presented numerous engineering challenges.

A key figure in deciding how to overcome these barriers (although some of his advice was later disregarded) was Sandford Fleming. Like many of those involved in the early development of the Pacific railway, Fleming was a Scot. He had served as the chief engineer of the Intercolonial Railway, built to connect Quebec and the Maritime provinces. In 1871, he was selected as the chief engineer of the Pacific railway. Almost immediately upon British Columbia's entry into Canada, his survey parties began their work.

The Fraser and Thompson Rivers

One of Fleming's earliest conclusions was that the most economical route through the Rockies lay through Yellowhead Pass, just west of today's Jasper, Alberta. From that point, the most favorable route to the sea would take the railway down the Upper Thompson River to Kamloops, then via the Thompson and Fraser rivers to the harbor at Burrard Inlet (where Vancouver is now located). Though some pressed for a route that would take the railway to a western terminus farther north, which

This 1881 photo, taken at Tunnel No. 8 between Yale and North Bend, British Columbia, in the Fraser River Canyon, illustrates the physical obstacles that engineer Andrew Onderdonk and his crews had to overcome as they pushed eastward. *Richard Maynard/ Library and Archives Canada/C-07660* ·

would have allowed for a relatively short ferry trip (or even, some said, a bridge) to Vancouver Island, Fleming's choice of Burrard Inlet was ultimately accepted by the government.

Although only minor progress was made in constructing the railway in the first eight years following British Columbia's entry into Canada, in 1879 the government awarded a contract that showed it was serious about the project. For $9.1 million, American engineer Andrew Onderdonk agreed to construct the 127-mile (204-kilometer) segment between Yale, British Columbia (the point at which the Fraser River became navigable) and Kamloops Lake. The completion date was set for June 30, 1885.

Onderdonk began work at Yale on May 15, 1880. Building a railway up the Fraser Canyon demanded extraordinary amounts of black powder and human muscle. In *The Pictorial History of Railroading in British Columbia*, Barrie Sanford writes that as he began the project, Onderdonk "estimated his manpower requirement at 10,000 men, nearly one-third of the entire provincial

An eastbound train winds along the Thompson River at Thompson, British Columbia, in June 1975. Behind the locomotives is a "robot" car housing remote-control equipment used primarily on westbound tonnage trains. This technology, implemented on CPR beginning in 1967, allowed longer trains to be operated with mid-train power remotely controlled from the lead locomotive. The robot cars were phased out in the 1980s as the equipment became compact enough to be mounted on the locomotives themselves. Remote control is not needed on this eastbound train; the robot car is being transported to a point such as Golden where it will be added to a westbound train. *Steve Patterson*

The original western terminus of the transcontinental railway was Port Moody, British Columbia, on Burrard Inlet. In 1885, CPR reached agreement with the province to extend the line 13 miles (21 kilometers) west to the town of Granville, which was renamed Vancouver. This 1886 photo shows a British man-of-war anchored in the harbor at Port Moody. *Photo by O. B. Buell, courtesy of Glenbow Archives/NA-4140-85*

population at the time." To help meet this need, Onderdonk imported more than 6,000 Chinese laborers.

Onderdonk was forced by his government contract into some shortsighted economies, which required reworking by Canadian Pacific after it took ownership of the Yale–Kamloops Lake segment. However, his success in building the railway through the canyons of the Fraser and the Thompson led to his being awarded two additional construction contracts. One, with the government, covered the 90 miles (145 kilometers) of railway from Yale to Burrard Inlet. The other contract, with Canadian Pacific, was for the 125 miles (201 kilometers) east of Kamloops Lake.

A Crucial Routing Decision: How to Cross the Rockies?

Fleming had recommended a route through Yellowhead Pass, which crossed the Rocky Mountains at the relatively modest elevation of 3,711 feet (1,131 meters). Weighing against this route were several considerations. Yellowhead is roughly 200 miles (321 kilometers) north of the southernmost Canadian mountain passes; keeping the line closer to the international boundary would minimize

Train 2, the eastbound *Canadian*, passes over the 484-foot (148-meter) Stoney Creek Bridge in August 1977. The original wooden bridge, on the east slope of Rogers Pass, was constructed in 1884 and replaced by a steel arch in 1893. That bridge was reinforced in 1929 through the addition of a second arch on each side, in order to accommodate the weight of the 375-ton Selkirk locomotives delivered that year. *Phil Mason*

the risk of U.S. railroads penetrating the border territory. A more southerly line would also have fewer north-south water courses to bridge. Since most of Canada's existing population centers were located within 100 miles (160 kilometers) of the U.S. border, there would also be some savings in rail mileage in comparison with a route that swung north through Yellowhead. Finally, James J. Hill

Canadian West, and whether the change was for better or worse is still a matter of debate." He also observes that the group that made the final decision in favor of a southern crossing of the mountains at a May 1881 meeting in St. Paul—Hill; Stephen; R. B. Angus, a colleague of Stephen's from the Bank of Montreal who was part of the CPR syndicate; and John Macoun, a botanist who had explored the western prairies—left no written record of their specific reasons for doing so. Yellowhead Pass would eventually host the main line of the Grand Trunk Pacific and (briefly) the Canadian Northern Railway, but not until the second decade of the twentieth century.

The syndicate's decision in favor of a southern route left open the question of precisely which passes would be used to traverse the Rockies, the Selkirks, and other mountain ranges of eastern British Columbia. However, even as the syndicate members were meeting in St. Paul, Major A. B. Rogers, a surveying engineer hired by Hill early in 1881, was in the field, seeking a route to connect the prairies and the Pacific.

By the end of the surveying season, Rogers had made a preliminary choice, which would be confirmed by more detailed surveys in 1882 and 1883. The railway would approach the Rockies from the east using the Bow River Valley and cross them at Kicking Horse Pass (elevation 5,332 feet, or 1,625 meters). It would then descend along the Kicking Horse River to what would become the town of Golden. West of that point, the route would cross and then follow the Columbia River and one of its tributaries, the Beaver River, eventually surmounting the Selkirks at a pass located by Rogers in 1882, and subsequently named for him.

Westward from the Selkirks pass, the railway would follow another water course, the Illecillewaet River, to a second crossing of the Columbia, at a point where the town of Revelstoke would be located. The Gold Range (now known as the Monashees) would

believed that a southern route would be preferable because of its proximity to coal deposits in and near southeastern British Columbia.

In the final analysis a crossing of the continental divide at Yellowhead lost out to a southern route. Lamb notes that "It was a momentous decision that altered substantially the future pattern of settlement in the

be surmounted at Eagle Pass. There, CPR would connect with the line to be constructed by Andrew Onderdonk, which would follow relatively easy topography eastward from Kamloops Lake to the Shuswap Highlands, which would be crossed at Notch Hill.

While the work of finding a route through the mountains was proceeding, a new figure entered the CPR story. William Cornelius Van Horne was an American who had risen to the position of general manager on the Chicago, Milwaukee & St. Paul Railroad. At the age of 38, he was recruited by Hill to take a similar position with CPR, and he joined the company on November 1, 1881. He was a renaissance man who devoted himself to learning not just his own job but that of every other person he came into contact with in his career. Because he understood how a railway's engineering, operations, and commercial activ-

The original crossing of Rogers Pass required an elaborate system of loops and wooden trestles to overcome the area's rugged topography. The notes with this 1886 photograph read: "Second crossing of Fivemile Creek, looking north-east. Upper track, right. Sir Donald Range in the background." *Photo by O. B. Buell, courtesy of Glenbow Archives/NA-4140-39*

Nine miles (13 kilometers) west of Lake Louise, and 3 miles (4.5 kilometers) east of the Continental Divide, Train 1, *The Canadian*, passes Wapta Lake at Hector, British Columbia, in June 1975. Hector is named after James Hector, a geologist on the Palliser Expedition of 1857–1860. In 1858, while the Hector party was exploring a tributary of the Columbia River, a horse fell into the river. In the process of retrieving the horse, Hector was kicked and knocked unconscious. The river, and the pass that it led to, came to be known as Kicking Horse. *Steve Patterson*

ities were connected, he was ideally suited to guide CPR through the completion of its east-west rail system. CPR had been a group of bankers and industrialists managing a surveying and construction operation; Van Horne's arrival transformed it into a nascent railway company.

Within a year of Van Horne's arrival, he had recruited former colleague Thomas G.

Shaughnessy to join him at CPR. Shaughnessy's title at CM&StP—general storekeeper—belied the range of his abilities. At CPR, he took charge of purchasing. This function was of considerable importance given that the ultimate financial cost of the transcontinental railway was, at its inception, largely a matter of guesswork. Cost control was of the utmost

importance, and Shaughnessy's ability to strike a hard bargain with suppliers helped keep expenses down. Equally important was his ability to keep the supply system running at a smooth and measured pace so that work crews had the right volume of materials at the right time.

During 1882, under Van Horne's leadership, CPR track was pushed westward about 575 miles (925 kilometers) from Winnipeg, and in October trains began operating between Winnipeg and Regina, Saskatchewan, a distance of 350 miles (563 kilometers). The attack on the mountains began the following year. Track crews reached Calgary in August 1883. From that point, says Lamb, "track was *continued on page 32*

continued from page 29
pushed on up the Bow River valley and thence to the Kicking Horse Pass. By November 27, it had neared the summit and there paused for the winter—almost a mile (1.6 kilometers) above sea level and 962 miles (1,548 kilometers) from Winnipeg. The two seasons had witnessed a prodigious construction feat that had never been equaled in railway history."

The pace at which Van Horne had moved west came at some cost, however. The speed of construction (combined with unrealistic cost estimates relied upon by the CPR syndicate when they negotiated their contract with the government) meant that the company was running through its available funds faster than expected. By late 1883, CPR was in financial difficulty, and in early 1884 a $22.5 million loan from the government was arranged to tide the company over. Van Horne was pressured to cut costs wherever he could and to bring the construction project to completion as soon as possible.

One way he responded was to make an exception to the general rule that CPR would be constructed with a ruling gradient of no more than 2.2 percent. West of Kicking Horse Pass, a route had been surveyed that would have complied with that guideline. However, it would have required a tunnel that would not only be expensive for the cash-strapped company, but would also have delayed completion of the line. A more economical descent of the western slope of the Rockies could be built, but it would have a grade of 4.5 percent. This was the route that Van Horne chose to use, and thus was born what became known as CPR's "Big Hill." It was described as a temporary solution, but it would last until the opening of the Spiral Tunnels in 1909.

The line from Kicking Horse Pass to Beavermouth, 22 miles (35 kilometers) east of Rogers Pass, was completed during the 1884 construction season. Rogers Pass, at 4,340 feet (1,322 meters), was almost 1,000 feet (305 meters) lower than Kicking Horse, but presented its own challenges. Several high bridges were required to cross deep gorges in the Beaver River Valley, and more trestles were required west of the summit. On the western slope, heavy snowfall and the threat of avalanches dictated long snowsheds. The severity of this crossing was mitigated by construction of the 5-mile (8-kilometer) Connaught Tunnel, opened in 1916, but in the interim it presented serious operational and maintenance challenges for CPR and its employees.

The Lake Superior Line

At the beginning of 1883, work was nearing completion on the government-built line between Winnipeg and Port Arthur, on Lake Superior, which would be transferred to CPR ownership in May of that year. But only about 40 miles (64 kilometers) of the line between Callender, Ontario, where CPR would connect with the Canada Central, and Port Arthur, had been completed. When Fleming had surveyed this area, he had settled on a route far north of Lake Superior. But George Stephen was determined to put much of the railway along the lake shore. A primary reason was to allow materials to reach the construction zone by water. By late 1883, work was well underway, with 9,500 men

One of the many snowsheds that CPR built in the early years to help keep the line open through the mountains year-round, shown as it was being constructed in the 1880s. CPR spent more than $2 million building snowsheds in 1886 and 1887. *Notman & Son/Library and Archives Canada/C-007674*

employed on construction crews east of Port Arthur. Numerous rock cuts, bridges, and fills were required.

James J. Hill had remained part of the CPR syndicate but by early 1883 he understood that Stephen and Van Horne were committed to building the line north of the lake. Until that time, Hill remained hopeful that the syndicate would come to share his view that an all-Canadian route was foolish, and so he maintained his association with CPR. His St. Paul and Pacific (now the St. Paul, Minneapolis and Manitoba) had profited from hauling construction materials north to the border, but what he really wanted was to see his railway become a link between CPR's eastern and western lines. When he saw that this was not to be, he parted ways with the syndicate.

In May 1884, Van Horne, who had been with CPR for only two-and-one-half years,

The numerous rivers and streams flowing into Lake Superior required extensive use of bridges, such as this one over the Steel River, 14 miles (22 kilometers) east of Schreiber, Ontario. *Library and Archives Canada/C-03411*

was given the title of vice president and made a director of the company. "Thereafter," says Lamb, "the executive committee consisted of George Stephen, Donald Smith, R. B. Angus, and Van Horne—a tightly knit and determined group, sharing the conviction that the company must not and would not fail."

Unlike the route west of Winnipeg, which was pushed forward in a continuous line, the trackage north of Lake Superior was finished in separate segments, dictated by the proximity of supply points and by the time required to bridge major rivers emptying into Lake Superior. During 1884, work progressed at a much more rapid pace than in the prior years, and by the end of that year only a few significant gaps remained. In May 1885, the last segment of this line was completed at Jackfish Bay, Ontario.

A bridge under construction at Nipigon River, Ontario, on the north shore of Lake Superior, 70 miles (113 kilometers) east of Fort William. *Library and Archives Canada/ C-021981*

Near Middleton, Ontario, on the north shore of Lake Superior, in September 1993, Extra 5736 West crosses the Little Pic River Bridge, a curved deck-truss structure that stands 90 feet (27 meters) above the water.
Steve Patterson

The Last Spike

Completion of the line east of Winnipeg left only one gap in the transcontinental route. In personal terms, the gap was between Andrew Onderdonk, whose crews were pushing eastward from Kamloops Lake toward Eagle Pass, and James Ross, CPR's construction superintendent, pushing westward toward the same point from Rogers Pass.

Onderdonk arrived first, in late September, and pronouncing his contract fulfilled, dismissed his crews. Ross did not arrive at the agreed meeting point until November. Given the momentous nature of the event, a ceremony might have been expected. But Van Horne was determined to keep it simple.

The meeting point was named Craigellachie, in honor of a peak in the Spey Valley of Scotland, home to the ancestors of George Stephen and Donald Smith. At 9:22 on the morning of November 7, 1885, Smith drove the last spike; it was made of iron, not precious metal. Van Horne's speech became famous for its brevity and simplicity: "All I can say is that the work has been well done in every way."

In October 1998, SD40-2 CP 5932 leads westbound Train 411 through Jackfish Tunnel on the rugged north shore of Lake Superior. The last spike on the CPR line between Montreal and Winnipeg was driven at Jackfish on May 16, 1885. *John Leopard*

Perhaps the most famous photograph from the early years of Canadian Pacific, this scene depicts the last-spike ceremony at Craigellachie, British Columbia, on November 7, 1885. The key figures shown are Donald Smith (driving the spike), Sandford Fleming (top hat, behind Smith), and William Cornelius Van Horne (to Fleming's right). The line through the mountains would soon be closed for the winter, reopening in the spring of 1886. *Alexander Ross/Library and Archives Canada/C-003693*

At Chokio, between Fort Macleod and Brocket, Alberta, CP 5712 is eastbound on the Crowsnest Subdivision, constructed in 1897 and 1898. The Livingston Range of the Rockies is in the distance. *John Leopard*

CHAPTER TWO

BECOMING A GLOBAL TRANSPORTATION SYSTEM: *1885–1918*

In the decade following the opening of the transcontinental main line,

CPR's owners were faced with a dilemma. The enterprise was, as John

Lorne McDougall observed, "desperately premature." In the near term,

there were no sources of traffic along the newly developed lines.

To complicate matters, the railway was essentially a seasonal

enterprise west of Calgary. During the long winter, heavy snowfall and

avalanches kept the line closed for extended periods. To keep the line

open, more men and equipment had to be employed during winter

Six 0-6-6-0 Mallet locomotives were delivered between 1909 and 1912 for pusher service out of Field, British Columbia, but they were hard to maintain. In 1916 and 1917 they were rebuilt as 2-10-0 Decapods. CPR Class R2B 2-10-0 5752, at Montreal in August 1956, was one of these locomotives. *Jim Shaughnessy*

than in the summer. But revenues fell during the winter, creating pressure on the company's treasury to maintain the cash flow to pay employees and suppliers.

CPR could not stand still and wait for business to develop. It had to grow its network in order to become economically self-sustaining. Between 1885 and 1896, it expanded its route miles from 3,998 (6,434 kilometers) to 6,476 (10,422), an increase of 62 percent. Much of this growth came in the East, where, unlike the area from Lake Superior west, there was a developed economy and an established need for rail service.

Truly Transcontinental:
CPR Reaches the Atlantic

Even as CPR was pushing westward, it had been extending its reach in the East. Part of George Stephen's vision for the company was that it would be the critical middle sec-

tion of a water-land-water route between Britain and Asia. To fulfill that role, it needed good access to a year-round port. Montreal, closed to shipping for much of the winter, did not meet that need.

The most ready access to Atlantic ports was via railroads already in operation in New England. In 1883, CPR acquired the South Eastern Railway, which extended through Quebec to Newport, Vermont. There, it connected with the Passumpsic Railroad, which acted as a bridge to other New England railroads serving the ports of Boston and Portland.

A trio of 1958-vintage Montreal Locomotives Works (MLW) RS-18 units is in charge of CPR Train 904 at McIndoes, Vermont, in February 1973. In another 8 miles (13 kilometers) the train will reach the interchange point with the Boston & Maine at Wells River, Vermont, but the crew will take the train another 40 miles (65 kilometers) beyond Wells River to the B&M yard at White River Junction. At right is the Connecticut River. *Tom Murray*

In the same year, CPR gained control of the Atlantic and North-West Railway, which had been chartered to build between the Atlantic Coast and Lake Superior, to construct a bridge over the St. Lawrence River near Montreal, and to build a line across northern Maine between Quebec and New Brunswick. This international route to the Maritimes was known as the Short Line. With this route in hand, CPR would be able to connect from Saint John, New Brunswick, to Halifax, Nova Scotia, via the Intercolonial Railway. In 1889, the first CPR train reached Saint John. The relationship with the Intercolonial would prove frustrating and unworkable for CPR, but the company had at least established a beachhead in the Atlantic provinces.

CPR's growth in the East was not limited to a route from Montreal to the Atlantic. In 1887, it opened a new line from Montreal to Smiths Falls, Ontario, thereby improving its Montreal–Toronto route. Three years later, it reached Windsor, where it was able to connect (via ferry) with the Wabash Railway in Michigan. With this route in operation, CPR had completed its basic network in southern Ontario.

Both CPR and Grand Trunk had their eye on Sault Ste. Marie as a way of connecting with U.S. railways that were building toward that point from the west. GT, which deeply resented CPR's aggressive push into southern Ontario, tried to forestall CPR from reaching the Sault gateway by acquiring various lines that gave it a toehold in the region northwest of Toronto. But CPR had a strategic advantage because it had already reached from Montreal to Sudbury, Ontario, where a line to the Sault would connect with its transcontinental main line. GT claimed that

Above: The line between Mattawamkeag and Vanceboro, Maine, was built by the European and North American Railway in 1871 as part of a route from Bangor to Saint John, New Brunswick, and operated by the Maine Central Railroad (with CPR holding trackage rights beginning in 1889). Here, Train 981 from Saint John to Montreal passes the station at Mattawamkeag, leaving Maine Central rails for CPR's, in October 1970. The track in the foreground is Maine Central's route to Bangor. The Mattawamkeag–Vanceboro line was purchased by CPR in 1974. *Tom Murray* **Below:** An eastbound intermodal train from Chicago to Montreal passes Newtonville, Ontario, in October 1986, with CPR and Soo Line power. In the foreground is Canadian National's Montreal–Toronto main line. *Eric Blasko*

Completion of CPR's route between Montreal, Quebec, and Windsor, Ontario, in the late 1880s made CPR a head-to-head competitor with rival Grand Trunk. Detroit–Toronto Train 516 is at Milton, Ontario, in July 1993, having just descended Campbellville Hill and the Niagara Escarpment (seen in the background). CP 4713, an MLW M-636, leads the train. *John Leopard*

it held a charter to build to the Sault, but CPR moved forward anyway, reaching Sault Ste. Marie in 1888.

CPR intended to connect at Sault Ste. Marie with the Duluth, South Shore & Atlantic Railway and with the Minneapolis, St. Paul & Sault Ste. Marie Railway. The former would give CPR access to Duluth, the latter to St. Paul and Minneapolis. CPR lacked the capital to buy these railroads, but George Stephen and Donald Smith stepped into the breach and, using their own funds, gained control of both companies in 1888.

The following year, through train service was established between Boston and St. Paul by way of Montreal and the Sault. That same year, CPR helped both companies avoid bankruptcy. In return for CPR's guarantee of their bonds they entered into "secure and permanent" traffic arrangements with CPR.

W. Kaye Lamb summarizes the nine-year period beginning with the formation of the company in 1881:

By 1890 the Canadian Pacific's entire eastern network was approaching completion.

CP 5007 was one of 12 2,500-horsepower GP35 units acquired in 1964. Here, it leads an MLW FB2 and FA2 upgrade at Campbellville, Ontario, on the Niagara Escarpment. *Bill Linley*

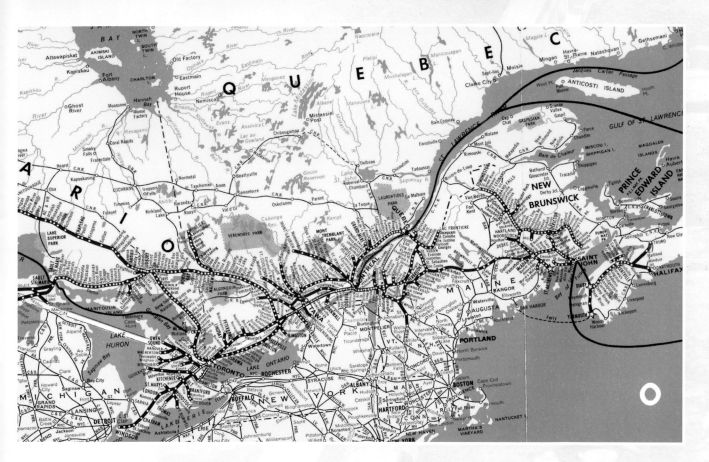

Excerpt from a 1957 map showing CPR rail lines in eastern Ontario, Quebec, the Maritime Provinces, and New England. Today, the CPR network goes as far east as Montreal, with lines east of that point having been sold, leased, or abandoned. However, as a result of the 1991 acquisition of Delaware & Hudson Railway and other U.S. transactions, CPR now serves Binghamton and Albany, New York, and Harrisburg, Pennsylvania, and reaches New York City, Philadelphia, and Washington, D.C., via trackage, haulage, or marketing rights. *Author collection*

This bridge, on the Kicking Horse River in British Columbia, shows the heavy use that CPR's builders made of the material most readily available to them: wood. By doing so, they completed the line as quickly as possible, but the railway had to replace many wooden structures within the first decade after the transcontinental route was completed in 1885. This photo was taken circa 1887–1889. *Photo by Boorne and May, courtesy of Glenbow Archives/NA-1753-6*

Extending from Saint John, Quebec, Montreal, and Ottawa to Toronto, Windsor, and Detroit, and from Sault Ste. Marie over affiliated lines to Duluth and St. Paul, it exceeded considerably in span the system of its great rival, the Grand Trunk. To have built the main line to the Pacific and acquired this network in only nine years was indeed a remarkable accomplishment.

Rebuilding the Railway

The completion of the transcontinental line in 1885 was more of a beginning than an end. "Low first cost" had been the guiding princi-

ple of the railway's builders, and while William Van Horne had ensured that the line would be safe to operate, it was neither efficient nor economical. As Lamb describes the physical condition of the CPR in 1885:

For hundreds of miles it consisted of little more than the ties and the two rails that rested upon them, with a row of telegraph poles along one side carrying two wires on a single stubby crosstree . . . it was a characteristic of pioneer railways that, having been built, they must forthwith be rebuilt, and much of the main line of the Canadian

Pacific was no exception. Solvent, but nonetheless chronically short of money, the C.P.R. had to begin this task immediately after its nominal completion.

The needs included equipment, loading platforms, warehouses, ballast, straightening of curves, widening of cuts, reduction of grades, and improvement of bridges and culverts.

Given the company's limited funds, and the emphasis on extending itself eastward, the serious task of rebuilding did not actually begin until 1890. One of the most visible—and critical—improvements was replacement

of the hastily built timber structures that dotted the CPR from one end of Canada to the other. Between 1890 and 1895, the company would replace 2,178 wooden bridges with steel, masonry arches, fill, thus allowing for the operation of heavier equipment while at the same time eliminating a fire hazard. In addition, 72-pound rails replaced the 56-pound rails used during construction, and many grades and curves were reduced.

The rebuilding of Canadian Pacific has continued right up to the present day, with the improvement of engineering and construction techniques, the growth of traffic, and the evolution of operating strategies.

Meeting the American Challenge in Southern British Columbia

George Stephen (later Lord Mount Stephen) resigned as president of CPR in 1888. He remained as a director of the company, and Van Horne moved into the presidency. One of the major challenges that Van Horne faced during his entire time in this position was the struggle for rail dominance in the Kootenay and Okanagan regions of southern British Columbia. Ironically, his foe in this struggle was a man who had been present at the creation of Canadian Pacific and had, in fact, recommended Van Horne for his first post at CPR: James J. Hill.

Although Hill and Stephen worked together to advance each other's ventures, by the time Stephen resigned as president of CPR, their diverging interests had complicated the relationship. Hill resented the fact that Stephen, along with Donald Smith, had gained control of the two U.S. railroads running westward from Sault Ste. Marie. One of Stephen's last acts as president was to arrange for CPR to purchase these properties (from himself and Smith).

Stephen and Hill continued to collaborate in the 1890s, particularly on Hill's takeover of the Northern Pacific, but Van Horne had come to view Hill as an adversary

Nelson, British Columbia, was the largest terminal on the Crowsnest Pass–Kettle Valley route through southern British Columbia. CP 5758, next to the coaling tower, is a Class R3b 2-10-0, built in 1917 at CPR's Angus Shops in Montreal. This photo is from May 1951. *Photo by Philip Hastings, courtesy of California State Railroad Museum/ negative no. 200*

who could not be trusted, and whose business interests would invariably be contrary to those of the Canadian Pacific.

Van Horne's view was confirmed by the outcome of a battle with Hill for control of a small railroad in Minnesota. In 1892, CPR, through the Duluth, South Shore & Atlantic, gained control of the Duluth & Winnipeg Railway, running northwest from Duluth. Van Horne saw this as a key link in a CPR route from Duluth to the West. But Hill wanted it for himself, and quietly bought up the railway's

debt. In 1897, Hill took control of the D&W, which would become Great Northern's route into the Minnesota Iron Range.

By the early 1890s, deposits of gold, silver, zinc, and copper had been discovered in the Kootenay area of southern British Columbia. Since the Columbia River flowed south into the United States, Washington State stood to benefit more than British Columbia from the smelting and other activities it would take to develop these resources, unless Canadians took steps to prevent this.

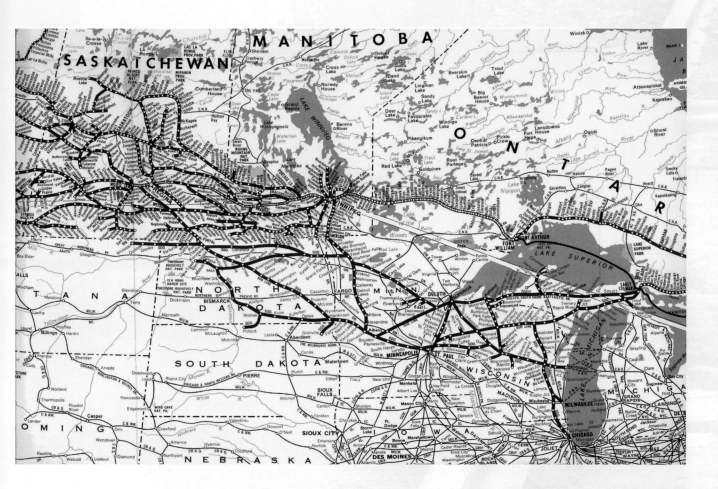

Excerpt from a 1957 map showing CPR rail lines in Saskatchewan, Manitoba, and western Ontario. The company's U.S. affiliate, Soo Line Railroad, served the upper midwestern states. Today, many Soo Line routes in Wisconsin and Michigan are part of Canadian National, and CPR's St. Paul–Chicago route consists of trackage formerly operated by the Milwaukee Road. As a result of Soo Line's 1985 acquisition of the Milwaukee Road, CPR also reached into Indiana and as far south as Louisville, Kentucky, via trackage rights. In 2005, CPR said it would sell the Louisville line to a regional carrier, Indiana Rail Road. After many years of holding a majority interest in Soo Line, CPR gained full control of the U.S. road in 1990 and has since integrated it into the CPR system. *Author collection*

Hill made no secret of his intention to reach the Kootenay region via branch lines from his Great Northern Railway. In 1892, Van Horne, seeking to establish a CPR presence in the Kootenay before Hill, opened a 28-mile (45-kilometer) line between Nelson and Robson, connecting Kootenay Lake with the Columbia River. Soon, CPR had steamer service operating on the Columbia River between Revelstoke and Robson.

The next year, the first American railway arrived in southern British Columbia, reaching the outskirts of Nelson from Spokane, Washington. It was the creation not of Hill,

but of another entrepreneur, D. C. Corbin. However, it was equally suspect from Van Horne's perspective, especially since it connected with the Great Northern at Spokane.

Development of the region's mining industry took a major step forward with the opening of a smelter at Trail Creek, next to the Columbia River, in 1896. The smelter operator built a line along the river northward to Robson and talked about plans to go farther. In 1898, CPR gained control of the railway and with it, the smelter. With this acquisition, the company found itself in the metal-refining business. The smelter at Trail

A set of five Canadian Locomotive Company (CLC) H16-44 units eases down the 3.61 percent grade of Poupore Hill, British Columbia, en route to the CPR yard at Tadanac, in October 1972. This line, along the Columbia River north of Trail, was originally constructed in 1897 by Augustus Heinze, who opened the first smelter at Trail. *Tom Murray*

Creek was the beginning of an important Canadian Pacific subsidiary, Consolidated Mining and Smelting, which would later be known as Cominco.

The ore that fed the Trail Creek smelter came from Rossland, 13 miles (21 kilometers) distant. Corbin built a second rail line into southern British Columbia, this one extending to Rossland from Northport, Washington. In 1898, this line passed into the control of Hill.

Van Horne knew that in order to be a meaningful participant in the growing economy of southern British Columbia, CPR needed an east–west line through the region, connecting with Lethbridge in the East and Vancouver in the West. But the cost of constructing a line into the Kootenay from the east exceeded CPR's financial resources. Starting in the early 1890s, CPR made various proposals for the government to subsidize this route.

These efforts came to fruition in 1897 with a pact between the company and the government of Canada, known as the Crow's Nest Pass Agreement, that was given effect by an Act of Parliament on June 29, 1897. A subsidy of $11,000 per mile would be granted to CPR, in return for which the railway would grant rate concessions on certain commodities moving to and from the Prairie provinces. It must have seemed like a sensible arrangement to the parties involved, but CPR's agreement to make permanent rate

Above: The S.S. *Rossland* was launched in 1897 as part of CPR's steamboat operations in the Kootenays. British Columbia historian Robert D. Turner has described it as "the fastest steamer on the Upper Columbia and a beautifully-proportioned vessel as well." In this 1911 photo, the *Rossland* is shown on Arrow Lake. *Canada Patent and Copyright Office/Library and Archives Canada/C-021044*

Below: Excerpt from a 1957 map showing CPR rail lines in British Columbia and Alberta. The Spokane International, running 149 miles (240 kilometers) from Eastgate, Idaho, to Spokane, was sold to Union Pacific in February 1958, but has remained an important conduit for CPR traffic destined to the western United States. The white line across the southern part of the two provinces represents Canadian Pacific Airlines' transcontinental route. *Author collection*

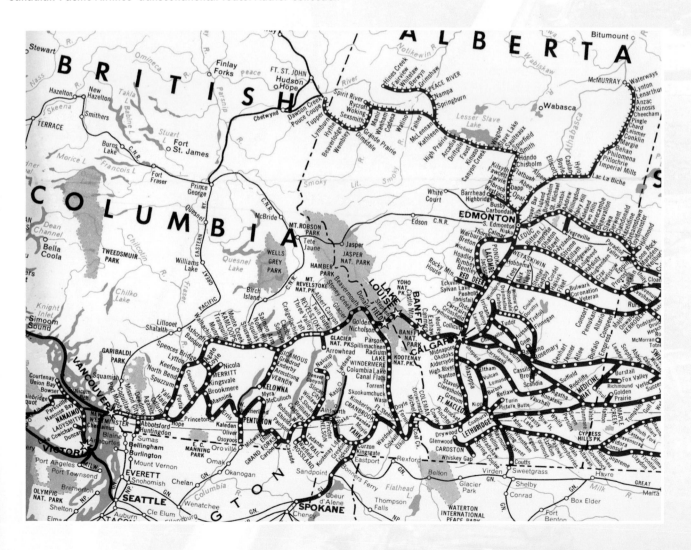

The Tadanac Yard crew waits in the clear while the crew on the freight from Nelson, British Columbia, behind CLC C-Liner 4105, yards its train in October 1972. The industrial facility behind CLC Train Master (Model H24-66) 8905 is part of Cominco's Trail, British Columbia, lead and zinc smelter complex. Cominco, originally the Consolidated Mining and Smelting Company of Canada, was controlled by Canadian Pacific from 1906 to 1986. *Tom Murray*

reductions on grain moving to Fort William and Port Arthur would become an enduring source of controversy for decades.

As it moved westward toward the Kootenay region, the Crowsnest line reached an area of southeastern British Columbia rich in coal deposits. The coal traffic generated here helped feed the energy-hungry smelter operations in the Kootenay. Longer term, coal traffic became a mainstay of CPR's western business, particularly after Canadian coal companies developed export markets in the 1970s, and Canadian Pacific itself became a major player in the region's coal business.

The objective of the Crowsnest line was Nelson, British Columbia, the eastern gateway to the Kootenay mining region, but CPR would not reach that objective for more than 30 years. When operations over the Crowsnest line began in 1898, the western terminus at Kootenay Landing was 55 miles (88 kilometers) short of Nelson, with steamer, tug, and barge service connecting the two points. Four years later the line was extended 20 miles (32 kilo-

meters) to Proctor, and finally, in 1930, construction was completed on the difficult segment along Kootenay Lake between Proctor and Nelson.

While the Crowsnest line approached the Kootenay from the East, CPR was also at work on a line westward toward the coast. It began with a line approximately 100 miles (161 kilometers) in length from Robson west to Grand Forks and Midway, which was completed in 1899.

Although CPR control of the smelter at Trail Creek (now known simply as Trail) had frustrated Hill's ambitions in that area, farther west he was more successful. He gained control of the Granby Company, owner of three major smelters in the Grand Forks area, and, via a Great Northern branch, controlled much of their rail traffic.

Even though Great Northern was an annoyance in southern British Columbia,

continued on page 58

In May 1951, a pair of 2-8-0 Consolidations, CP 3676 and CP 3626, power a northbound freight leaving the Tadanac Yard near Trail, British Columbia. The bridge crosses Topping Creek, a tributary of the Columbia River. *Photo by Philip Hastings, courtesy of California State Railroad Museum/negative no. 2523*

Above: CP 4065, a Fairbanks-Morse-designed, CLC-built model CPA16-4, began life as a CLC demonstrator and was purchased by CPR in 1951. Here, it leads the westbound Michel switcher at Elko, British Columbia, in September 1972. This unit has been preserved for possible restoration. *Stan Smaill* Opposite: CP 8723, a CLC H16-44, leads the Tadanac freight across the Topping Creek Bridge and prepares to enter the Tadanac Yard in October 1972. A sure-footed head brakeman prepares to dismount and line the switch into the yard. *Tom Murray*

In the early 1970s, the diesel shop at Nelson, British Columbia, was home to CPR's remaining fleet of Fairbanks-Morse-designed, CLC-built diesels, including both road switchers and a handful of C-Liner cab units like CP 4105. On this day in October 1972, the 4105 leads the Nelson–Tadanac turn, en route back to Nelson, just north of Trail. *Tom Murray*

Above: At Slocan City, British Columbia, in 1975, the CPR barge is loaded for the 20-mile (32-kilometer) trip across Slocan Lake to Roseberry on the isolated Kaslo Subdivision. Once the cars and engine (GP9 8637) are loaded onto the barge, it will be propelled across the lake by the tugboat. *Iris G. Steve Patterson* **Opposite:** Barge service was provided on Lake Slocan in southern British Columbia from 1897 to 1988. In August 1977, when this photo was taken, CPR provided once-weekly barge service from Slocan City (shown here) at the end of a branch off the Boundary Subdivision. *Phil Mason*

An all-General Motors consist of three GP9s and an F7B lead Train 53 west across the Kettle River Bridge at milepost 81.5 on the Boundary Subdivision, Cascade, British Columbia. Train 53 was a daily freight from Nelson to Midway. This line was abandoned in 1990. *Phil Mason*

continued from page 53

CPR continued to push westward toward its objective of a link with the main line to Vancouver. A CPR-financed company, the Kettle Valley Railway, completed the last segments in this route. As Lamb notes, "The construction, over difficult and often treacherous terrain, was a daunting task of engineering and perseverance, especially through the Coquihalla Pass, which Sandford Fleming had rejected as a possible route for the CPR main line because of narrowness, heavy snowfall and avalanches." The line required many bridges, snowsheds, and tunnels. It was opened to a connection with the main line at Hope in July 1916, "and its completion provided the CPR with another east–west route through British Columbia."

Exit Van Horne

The building, rebuilding, and expansion of Canadian Pacific during the period 1881 to 1899 represented the combined effort of thousands of individuals, but the three who played the most visible roles were its first three presidents: George Stephen, the financier and visionary; William Cornelius Van Horne, the railroader and taskmaster; and Thomas George Shaughnessy, the detail-oriented administrator.

The three complemented each other well during the construction and early operation of the railway. Once the company's foundation was in place, Stephen moved into the background, allowing Van Horne's skills as a railroad operating man, salesman, leader, and motivator to come to the fore. But as the 1890s drew to a close, the challenges of running CPR grew somewhat less daunting, and overcoming them less exciting to Van Horne. In 1899 he resigned from the presidency but stayed on as chairman. He was no longer a powerful voice in the affairs of Canadian Pacific, although even in retirement many outsiders still looked at him as the personification of the the company.

Van Horne's importance to the company was summarized by the Canadian Railway Hall of Fame:

Incredibly, while the CPR's contract with the government dictated completion of the road within a decade, Van Horne—through sheer determination—found ways to finish it in five. Even more remarkably, once Van Horne had completed the CPR, he operated it and, despite the economic malaise for most of the 1880s and 1890s, made it into a paying proposition. Surely, the Canadian Pacific's role as an instrument of Canadian nationalism would have followed a different course, had Van Horne not been at the helm.

Shaughnessy was officially in charge of purchasing for the company during its construction, but his role might today be described as "chief logistics officer." He was responsible for seeing not only that good deals were struck with the company's suppliers but that there was an efficient flow of men and materials toward the front lines as the railroad built west. His skills at managing the company's cash flow—stretching out the payment of bills to creditors,

The year is 1905, and a passenger train arrives at Innisfail, Alberta, on CPR's Calgary–Edmonton line. The water tank is of typical CPR design, with the ball at the top indicating the water level. *Glenbow Archives/NA-1709-71*

Class P1b 2-8-2 No. 5068 powers a westbound CPR passenger train near Leanchoil, British Columbia. The date of the photo is believed to be between 1913 and 1920. *Andrew Merrilees/Library and Archives Canada/PA-143158*

while insisting on timely payment of sums owed to CPR—helped the company weather the financial crises that plagued it during the years of construction and early operation.

As Van Horne became preoccupied with the Duluth & Winnipeg affair, Shaughnessy

teen years as CPR president, from 1899 to 1918, were as full of fortune as Van Horne's and George Stephen's were dogged by misfortune. It seemed as if all the gods of railway prosperity were cooperating. The company's profitability was staggering."

CPR Extends Its Presence in the United States

CPR had reached into the upper midwestern states through the 1888 acquisition of the Minneapolis, St. Paul & Sault Ste. Marie (commonly known as the Soo Line) and the Duluth, South Shore & Atlantic, both of which connected with CPR at Sault Ste. Marie. In 1893, a second link was established with the Soo Line when it built a line across North Dakota to a location in the northwestern corner of the state, which was given an appropriate name for an international rail gateway: Portal. CPR built a branch from Moose Jaw, Saskatchewan, to complete the link; the station on the Canadian side of the border was called North Portal.

During the Shaughnessy years CPR's U.S. presence was enhanced in various ways. CPR's Pembina branch, south of Winnipeg, connected with Great Northern, but GN was no longer a friendly connection. To rectify that, Soo Line built a line of its own from Glenwood, Minnesota (on the Minneapolis–Portal line), to Noyes, Minnesota, across the border from the CPR station of Emerson, Manitoba. The line was completed in 1904. Soo Line now connected with CPR at three points on the international boundary.

In 1909, Soo Line leased the Wisconsin Central, a railroad that connected the Twin Cities of Minneapolis and St. Paul with Chicago. It also had a network of lines in Wisconsin that reached as far north as the Twin Ports of Duluth and Superior, and to Ashland, Wisconsin. This gave CPR control of a continuous line of railroad extending all the way from western Canada to Chicago.

effectively became the chief operating officer of Canadian Pacific. Upon Van Horne's resignation, he received the title of president.

As David Cruise and Alison Griffiths describe it in their book, *Lords of the Line: The Men Who Built the CPR*, "Shaughnessy's nine-

continued on page 64

Top: At Portal, North Dakota, a Soo Line crew from Harvey, North Dakota, has arrived with a train for the CPR. The CP crew will tie their caboose onto the rear of the westbound train before departing for Moose Jaw, Saskatchewan. *Phil Mason* **Above:** A set of 1949-built General Motors (Electro-Motive Division) F7 units powers Soo Line Train 86 as it departs Thief River Falls, Minnesota, headed for Minneapolis, in April 1974. On the head end are several cars of grain and pulpwood from local Soo Line origins, but most of the train consists of potash, liquefied petroleum gas, and forest products from CPR origins, interchanged to Soo at the Emerson, Manitoba/Noyes, Minnesota border crossing. *Tom Murray* **Opposite:** The rear of Extra CP 5856 West passes over the head end of the train, which is exiting the lower portal of the Upper Spiral Tunnel in June 1978. *Phil Mason*

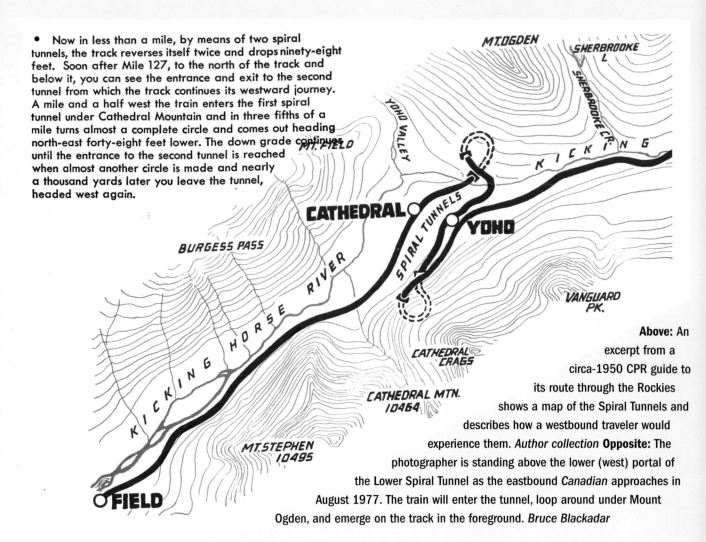

• Now in less than a mile, by means of two spiral tunnels, the track reverses itself twice and drops ninety-eight feet. Soon after Mile 127, to the north of the track and below it, you can see the entrance and exit to the second tunnel from which the track continues its westward journey. A mile and a half west the train enters the first spiral tunnel under Cathedral Mountain and in three fifths of a mile turns almost a complete circle and comes out heading north-east forty-eight feet lower. The down grade continues until the entrance to the second tunnel is reached when almost another circle is made and nearly a thousand yards later you leave the tunnel, headed west again.

Above: An excerpt from a circa-1950 CPR guide to its route through the Rockies shows a map of the Spiral Tunnels and describes how a westbound traveler would experience them. *Author collection* **Opposite:** The photographer is standing above the lower (west) portal of the Lower Spiral Tunnel as the eastbound *Canadian* approaches in August 1977. The train will enter the tunnel, loop around under Mount Ogden, and emerge on the track in the foreground. *Bruce Blackadar*

continued from page 61

CPR also extended its reach into Great Northern's backyard in Washington State. In 1906, D. C. Corbin completed the Spokane International Railway from Spokane to Eastport, Idaho (across the border from Kingsgate, British Columbia). There, it connected with a CPR branch line that in turn connected with the Crowsnest Pass route. In 1917, CPR purchased the Spokane International.

Taming the Passes: Kicking Horse and Rogers

Shaughnessy would leave his mark in many ways, but key physical improvements were among the most important and most lasting. One of the major operating obstacles that limited CPR's operations west of Calgary was the Big Hill between Laggan (Lake Louise) and Field, British Columbia. Surveys aimed at improving the route through Kicking Horse Pass, and eliminating the 4.5 percent descending grade westward into Field, began in 1902.

Although various solutions were considered, the one that was finally chosen was a pair of spiral tunnels that would provide for a substantial change in elevation in the smallest possible area, reducing the eastward ruling grade to 2.2 percent.

As George Buck describes the tunnels in his history of railways in British Columbia and Alberta, *From Summit To Sea*, "the upper, or Number One, encountered first approaching from the east, would curve through 234° in 3,255 feet, and would drop the line by forty-eight feet. The lower—Number Two—

Above: The head end of CPR Extra 5592 East has emerged from the Lower Spiral Tunnel and is about to cross the Kicking Horse River as it makes the ascent through Yoho toward the Upper Spiral Tunnel.
Steve Patterson

Right: An SD40-2/SD40 consist leads a westbound train exiting the Connaught Tunnel in June 1973.
Phil Mason

curved 232° in 2,921 feet, and would drop the line by forty-five feet to the valley of the Kicking Horse River." The tunnels opened in August 1909.

In Rogers Pass, avalanches had been a continuing problem, particularly in 1899 and again in 1910, when 62 people were killed by slides. In 1912, Shaughnessy announced a program to double-track the crossing of Rogers Pass, using a tunnel that would be 5 miles (8 kilometers) long and reduce the westbound grade to less than 1 percent.

The bore was placed into service in December 1916 and named the Connaught Tunnel in honor of the governor-general of Canada. The new line built to reach the tunnel extended from near Stoney Creek in the East to Ross Peak in the West.

Competition from Canadian Northern and Grand Trunk

In the first decade of the twentieth century, two separate plans were developed for new transcontinental railways. One was the brainchild of William Mackenzie and Donald Mann, whose Canadian Northern Railway (CNoR) was getting more than a toehold in the prairies where CPR had previously enjoyed a monopoly. They were determined to extend their railway from its Manitoba base both eastward and westward; by 1915 CNoR would connect Montreal and Vancouver.

CPR's eastern rival, Grand Trunk, was also in an expansionist frame of mind. Under the leadership of Charles M. Hays, who became the railway's general manager in 1896, a two-part plan was developed. It would extend Grand Trunk's reach from Moncton, New Brunswick, in the East to Prince Rupert, British Columbia, in the West. East of Winnipeg, a federally financed and constructed railway, the National Transcontinental, would be leased to Grand Trunk upon completion. GT would operate it as part of a through route connecting with the GT-built Grand Trunk Pacific, to be built from Winnipeg to Prince Rupert.

Both projects were born of a giddy optimism that could see no end to the country's economic expansion. Both would be undone

This 1915 profile shows the CPR route between Calgary in the east and Kamloops, British Columbia, in the west. At Rogers Pass, it gives both the original elevation (4,340 feet, or 1,323 meters) and the height of the line then being built, which would use the Connaught Tunnel (3,801 feet, or 939 meters). *Author collection*

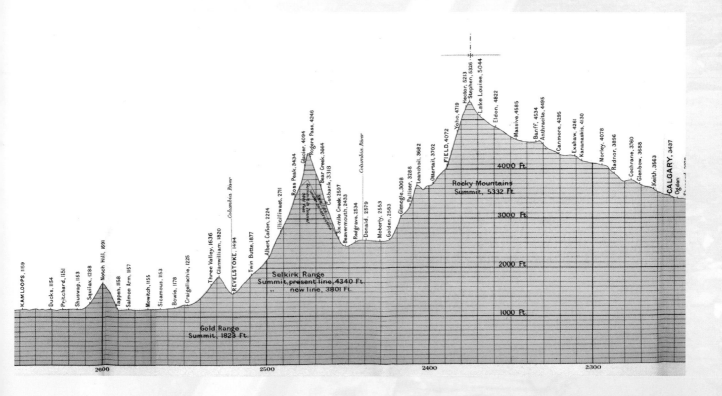

Class D10j 4-6-0 970, built by MLW in 1912, awaits the morning call on a cold night at Sutton, Quebec, in December 1955. *Jim Shaughnessy*

by economic decline and the coming of World War I.

CNoR was financed largely by debt and by cash subsidies for construction. This fragile plan quickly came undone as CNoR faced the dual challenge of building through mountainous territory to reach the Pacific and a slackening of immigration to the prairies, which had helped put traffic onto its network of main and branch lines. Mackenzie and Mann secured financial help from the government, but at the cost of surrendering much of their stock in the closely held company.

GTP's problems were somewhat different in origin but similar in results. Its lines west of Winnipeg were built to a high standard, and it had relatively few branch lines to feed traffic onto the main line. It was also obligated to lease the National Transcontinental when that line was completed across the

The 4-6-0 type was a popular and long-lived engine on CPR. This example, a Class D4g engine built at CPR's Angus Shops in 1915, was, according to photographer Shaughnessy, "the last D-4 class Ten-Wheeler in the Kingston, Ontario, engine house" when this photo was taken in July 1956. *Jim Shaughnessy*

EFFECTIVE JUNE 30 1913

In 1910, CPR obtained control of the Dominion Atlantic Railway in Nova Scotia, which extended CPR's route map eastward to Halifax. The DAR connected with the CPR through a steamer service across the Bay of Fundy, between Saint John, New Brunswick, and Digby, Nova Scotia. The cover of this 1913 Dominion Atlantic timetable advertises not only the Bay of Fundy service but also the steamer services available between Yarmouth, Nova Scotia, and Boston. *Author collection*

wilderness region between Winnipeg and eastern Canada, but construction costs had been higher than expected (and rental fees would follow suit). It, too, sought help from Ottawa, which was given at the cost of a first mortgage on the property. GTP's parent company, Grand Trunk, increased its own exposure through cash advances to the subsidiary.

CPR's view was that the financial difficulties of these companies should be worked out through bankruptcy proceedings, but with a war under way, the government was unwilling to take any chances. It continued to prop up the two railways and thus started down the road toward nationalization.

Seeing that nationalization was all but inevitable, Shaughnessy proposed that CPR itself be part of the scheme by becoming manager of a combined enterprise—CPR, CNoR, and GTP—free of government involvement. But important constituencies, particularly on the prairies, resisted any return to the monopoly that CPR had once enjoyed and (in their view) abused.

Shaughnessy proposed an alternative plan: CPR would buy CNoR, leaving the

well-constructed GTP as a competitor. However, this plan, too, was rejected. CPR was left with the specter of a rival rail system with access to the federal treasury and none of the do-or-die imperatives of private enterprise to guide its investing and ratemaking policies.

Between 1917 and 1923, CNoR, GTP, and Grand Trunk were folded in stages into a national enterprise to be known as Canadian National Railways. CNoR was the first to be nationalized, becoming part of a government system that already included the Intercolonial Railway in the Maritime Provinces, as well as the government-built National Transcontinental. GTP followed in 1919, and after considerable legal wrangling, Grand Trunk was forced into the system in January 1923.

Canadian Pacific's Navy

The builders of the CPR, and George Stephen in particular, had conceived the railway "as part of an all-British through route from Europe to the Orient." In late 1885, CPR offered to provide a mail service between Great Britain and the Far East via transatlantic steamer, railway, and transpacific steamer. Nothing came of this offer at the time, but it signaled the company's intention to make the railway the centerpiece of a global transportation enterprise. CPR was more successful two years later when it again offered to provide such a service; this time, its bid was accepted.

CPR's contract to provide the international mail service between Britain and Asia was signed in mid-1889, and three months later the company ordered three twin-screw, 485-foot (148-meter), 5,940-ton (gross) steamers—to be named *Empress of India*, *Empress of Japan*, and *Empress of China*—all to be built at Liverpool. From 1891, when the *Empress of India* left

Cruise by **Canadian Pacific**
TO
ALASKA
AND THE
YUKON

SKAGWAY
JUNEAU
PETERSBURG
WRANGELL
KETCHIKAN
PRINCE RUPERT
OCEAN FALLS
VANCOUVER
VICTORIA
SEATTLE

PRINCESS KATHLEEN

A brochure describing CPR's Alaska cruise service, circa 1950. The ship depicted is the *Princess Kathleen*. Launched in 1924, it was first used in Vancouver–Victoria–Seattle service, and, during World War II, as a troop carrier. After being returned to Canadian Pacific, it was outfitted for Alaska cruise service. It sank (with no loss of life) after running aground in 1952 while en route from Juneau to Skagway. *Author collection*

Liverpool for the first time en route to Asia, until 1971, when the *Empress of Canada* made its last transatlantic sailing, Canadian Pacific's *Empress* steamers set a high standard for ocean transportation.

After one abortive attempt at entering the coastwise trade in the late 1890s, Canadian Pacific made a more strategic move into this business in 1901 through the purchase of Canadian Pacific Navigation Company and its 14-vessel fleet, which, despite its name, previously had no corporate relationship with CPR. This became the core of CPR's British Columbia Coast Service. As CPR replaced the former C.P.N. fleet with new vessels, the

Princess fleet was born. By 1914, this fleet of 13 vessels was plying routes touching every port between Seattle and Skagway.

CPR had tried for years to reach satisfactory arrangements with existing Atlantic steamship lines for operation of a fast passenger and mail service between Britain and Canada, but to no avail. In 1902, Shaughnessy said that CPR would build its own steamers if it could receive a suitable subsidy for the mail operation. Receiving no response to this proposal, in 1903 CPR entered the

CANADIAN PACIFIC RAILWAY
STEAMSHIP LINES
Atlantic Service

MONTREAL, QUEBEC and LIVERPOOL

For Proposed Sailings see page 58 of this folder

"Taking on the Pilot"

THE EMPRESS OF THE ATLANTIC

EMPRESS OF IRELAND and EMPRESS OF BRITAIN

Finest and Fastest Steamships in the Canadian Service
Hold all Records between Liverpool and Canadian Ports

The two palatial Royal Mail steamships on the Canadian Pacific Railway Company's Atlantic service on the Quebec-Liverpool Route in summer and St. John (N. B.)-Halifax (N. S.)-Liverpool Route in winter. Length 570 feet, breadth 65 feet, 14,500 tons' register, 18,000 horse-power, and make the passage between Liverpool and Quebec in less than a week. Accommodation for 350 1st-cabin, 350 2d-cabin, 1,000 3d-class passengers.

All Canadian Pacific Steamships in the Atlantic service are equipped with Marconi Wireless Telegraphy, and also with a submarine signal system, thus ensuring perfect safety in navigation. The submarine signal acts in foggy weather in the same capacity as a lighthouse does in clear weather.

Detailed Information Will Be Given on Application to

W. B. HOWARD,
General Agent,
8 King St.,
St. John, N. B.

C. L. WILLIAMS,
General Agent,
340 Sixth St.,
Pittsburgh, Pa.

H. M. MacCALLUM,
General Agent,
224 South Clark St.,
Chicago, Ill.

WM. WEBBER,
General Agent,
Dom. Express Bldg.,
Montreal, Que.

F. R. PERRY,
General Agent,
332 Washington St.,
Boston, Mass.

A. A. POLHAMUS,
General Agent,
609 Spring St.,
Los Angeles, Cal.

H. M. TAIT,
General Agent,
232 Nicollet Ave.,
Minneapolis, Minn.

I. E. SUCKLING,
General Agent,
16 King St., East,
Toronto, Ont.

W. H. SNELL,
General Agent,
458 Broadway,
New York, N. Y.

G. M. JACKSON,
General Agent,
645 Market St.,
San Francisco, Cal.

J. J. FORSTER,
General Agent,
713 Second Ave.,
Seattle, Wash.

J. S. CARTER,
General Agent,
210 Portage Ave.,
Winnipeg, Man.

W. G. ANNABLE, General Passenger Agent,
Dominion Express Building,
MONTREAL, Que.

Atlantic trade by purchasing 15 relatively young ships from an existing operator. This fleet allowed CPR to implement both a passenger and mail service and a cargo service.

Still, the purchased ships were not as fast as those that CPR had planned to order for its own account—and the standards of speed and vessel size were being raised by the company's main competitor in the Canadian transatlantic service, the Allan Line. In 1904, CPR responded by ordering two vessels, the *Empress of Britain* and the *Empress of Ireland*, which raised the bar a notch with a top speed of 18 to 19 knots. They did not need to be as fast as the fastest ships in service between New York and Britain, because of the shorter distance on the more northerly route. Their fuel consumption and operating performance were efficient enough that CPR was able to operate them without a subsidy for carrying the mail. In 1909, Shaughnessy arranged for CPR to buy control of the Allan Line, eliminating its main competitor on the route. CPR kept the Allan name and did not even acknowledge its control of the line until 1915.

As Lamb summarizes it, "By 1914 the Canadian Pacific had become one of the world's major shipowners. Its ocean, coastal, lake, and river fleets consisted of about a hundred ships, over thirty of them on the Atlantic."

In the aftermath of the war, CPR found it necessary, both because of losses to its prewar fleet and as a way of staying competitive on both oceans, to bolster its fleet with a series of acquisitions. In 1921, it bought four ships, two of which were noteworthy. One of them became the *Empress of Scotland* and was put to work as the flagship of the company's Atlantic fleet. The other became the *Empress of Australia* and went to work on the Pacific, where it was for a time the largest liner of any ownership.

The Allan Line, which CPR had acquired but kept as a separate identity for marketing and operational purposes, was folded into the company's primary fleet during the early 1920s. In 1921, the company's Ocean Services department was given a new identity: Canadian Pacific Steamships Limited.

The Beginnings of Diversification

Having an extensive fleet of oceangoing and lake vessels was not the only way in which CPR distinguished itself from most other North American railways. The company also got into the hotel business very early. CPR began building hotels as a way to avoid moving heavy dining cars up and down grade west of Calgary. The first CPR hotels (Mount Stephen House at Field, Glacier House near Rogers Pass, and Fraser Canyon House at North Bend) began as meal stops for the passengers on CPR trains.

CPR's cash flow was aided by the sale of lots in the new city of Vancouver. Van Horne decided to use some of the proceeds from these real estate dealings to build a new hotel at Banff, Alberta, where hot springs had been discovered in 1883. The location was named by Donald Smith (later Lord Strathcona) for the county in Scotland where George Stephen was born. The hotel, CPR's first other than the original three "meal stop" locations, opened in 1888. The original building was designed by American architect Bruce Price in a château or castle style that would be emulated in other CPR hotels and stations to follow.

In 1893, CPR opened the most imposing of its château-style hotels, the Château Frontenac in Quebec City. Like the Banff Springs

The station at Glacier, British Columbia, in Rogers Pass, looking eastward toward a part of the Selkirks known as the Hermit Range. The photo was taken from CPR's Glacier House hotel. *Notman & Son/Library and Archives Canada/C-022331*

An early view of the Banff Springs Hotel. CPR president William Van Horne selected the location, and Donald Smith named it for the Scottish county where George Stephen was born. The hotel opened in 1888. *Library and Archives Canada/PA-031580*

Hotel and Windsor Station in Montreal, it was designed by Bruce Price. Between 1901 and 1914, CPR added several new hotels across Canada and expanded others.

Land was another source of diversification for CPR. As part of its agreement to build and operate a railway across Canada, Canadian Pacific received a land grant of 25 million acres (10.1 million hectares). Land served two main purposes: it could be mortgaged, giving the railway an infusion of cash to finance construction, and it could be sold to farmers willing to develop it, which would put traffic on the railway.

Unlike railroad land grants in the United States, which were typically in a checkerboard pattern adjacent to the right-of-way, CPR's

grant was limited to lands owned by the government, which effectively meant that only land in the prairie region was included (and not all of the land, because some of it was set aside for other purposes). Another limitation, designed to benefit the railway, was that it need accept only lands that were suitable for settlement. The result was that CPR designated only 5.3 million acres (2.1 million hectares) adjacent to its main line as part of the land grant. The balance was to be obtained in areas far north of the main line and as far south as the U.S. border.

Although land sales proceeded at a brisk pace through 1883, in the following years sales and development were much slower than the railway's backers had hoped. Drought and

CPR's 1898 station at Vancouver echoed the château style of its major hotels. Designed by brothers Edward and William Maxwell, the attractive structure remained in service only until 1914, when CPR opened a new, larger station in Vancouver. The Maxwell-designed station was then demolished. *Library and Archives Canada/PA-029818*

New York architect Bruce Price was hired by CPR in 1886 to design Windsor Street Station in Montreal. The building was completed in 1889, and new wings were added in 1906 and 1914. The 1914 addition included the 15-story tower shown here, which would serve as the company's headquarters until 1996. *Phil Mason*

economic hard times from the mid-1880s through the mid-1890s stalled the development of the prairies. (One bright spot in the land development picture was in British Columbia, where CPR made a deal with the provincial government for a land grant in 1885. Part of the land included in this grant was on the site where the city of Vancouver now exists. CPR did a brisk business in the sale of lots in the developing city, which reached a population of 10,000 by 1889.)

In 1897, land sales picked up and in the two-year period 1902–1903 the company's total sales were more than 3.5 million acres (1.4 million hectares), or roughly 10 percent of the 36 million acres (14.6 million hectares) the company had acquired through federal and provincial land grants. Although sales dropped off after that, the company continued to sell land at a steady pace for the next decade. Many of the sales were to immigrants from the United States.

Unfortunately, while CPR's main interest in the land was to see it developed, many buyers had other ideas. Much of the acreage ended up in the hands of speculators who did not occupy or farm their land but simply held it in hope of an eventual profit. Some of those buyers ended up defaulting on their purchases, and CPR reclaimed the land.

CPR was eager to promote settlement in the hot, dry area of southern Alberta. Captain John Palliser, leader of an early expedition into this territory, had warned it would not be hospitable to farming; his forecast proved accurate. Canadian Pacific invested millions of dollars in an elaborate canal system designed to irrigate the territory near Calgary,

using water from the Bow River. Even with the irrigation system in place, settlement of this land remained sparse. Of 1.6 million acres (600,000 hectares) sold in the areas covered by irrigation projects, sales contracts on almost 600,000 acres (240,000 hectares) had to be canceled.

CPR's land ownership would eventually generate a good economic return, but not in the way that the railway's builders had hoped. Much of the land that the company acquired in Alberta proved to have productive oil and gas reserves. When it sold this land, CPR retained mineral, oil, and gas rights, which would be major sources of income for a future Canadian Pacific subsidiary, PanCanadian Petroleum Limited.

Notes with this 1905 photo at Strathmore, Alberta, 35 miles (56 kilometers) east of Calgary, describe it as "a new town, one week old." In fact, the town of Strathmore had been settled soon after the arrival of the Canadian Pacific in 1883, but it was in the dry area of Alberta where poor growing conditions discouraged settlers. By 1905, a CPR-funded irrigation system had reached the town, lots were opened for sale, and Strathmore was moved 4 miles (6.4 kilometers) north. The town later became the site of a 2,000-acre (809-hectare) CPR demonstration farm aimed at showing new settlers how to farm. *Canada Dept. of Mines and Resources/Library and Archives Canada/PA-020553*

This 45-car eastbound freight is close to cresting the summit of Kicking Horse Pass (and the Continental Divide) at Stephen, British Columbia, in August 1938. On the head end are 2-10-2 No. 5810 and 2-8-2 No. 5364, while another 2-10-2, No. 5812, pushes from the rear. *Photo by Otto Perry, Courtesy of Denver Public Library, Western History Collection/OP-20502*

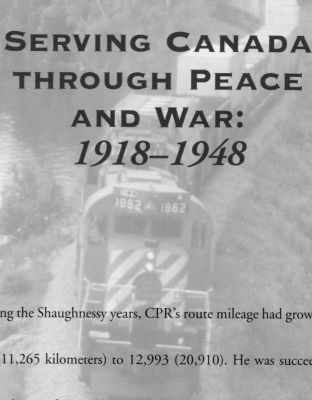

CHAPTER THREE

SERVING CANADA THROUGH PEACE AND WAR: *1918–1948*

During the Shaughnessy years, CPR's route mileage had grown from

7,000 (11,265 kilometers) to 12,993 (20,910). He was succeeded in

the presidency of Canadian Pacific by Edward Wentworth Beatty, a

man different in several respects from his three predecessors. First, he

was Canadian-born. Second, he was a lawyer. Third, he had not par-

ticipated in the construction of the railway. When the last spike was

driven at Craigellachie, he was barely eight years old, and when he

became president in 1918, he had just turned 41.

CPR predecessor Passumpsic Railroad had its repair and construction shops at Lyndonville, Vermont, 9 miles (14.5 kilometers) north of St. Johnsbury, but they were long gone by the time this local train stopped there in the late 1940s.
Photo by Philip Hastings, courtesy of California State Railroad Museum/ negative no. 2484

As described by David Cruise and Alison Griffiths, Beatty's 25-year tenure in CPR executive posts (6 as president, 18 as president and chairman, and 1 as chairman) "was radically different from the almost unbroken prosperity of the Shaughnessy years. Beatty's reign began and ended with world wars, and in between he had to cope with dramatic economic swings and the ominous spectre of a new and powerful competitor. J. J. Hill was gone, but the Canadian National Railway Co. more than took his place."

Beatty took over at a time when the economics of the railway were at an inflection point, thanks to the monetary inflation and other economic changes wrought by World War I (in which 1,116 CPR employees died). Since 1900, the company's operating ratio (expenses as a percentage of revenues) had ranged between 60 and 70, except for 1916, when it dipped to 59.7 thanks to the boom in war-related traffic.

In 1918, the year he became president, wage increases and other cost escalation pushed

that ratio to 78.1, and for the duration of Beatty's 25 years at the top of the company, the operating ratio never went below 77. His first reaction was to economize. Maintenance was deferred and every operating expense was examined to determine whether it was truly necessary.

CPR could not stand still, however. Equipment was worn out by the crush of traffic it had experienced during the war, and it needed replacement. The only way of achieving long-term operating efficiency on the railway was to modernize it. The company's other businesses, notably ships and hotels, also required investment if Canadian Pacific was to stay ahead of the competition. By the early 1920s, Beatty was ready to move ahead.

Recognizing that CPR would have to wring every possible operating economy out of its infrastructure, Beatty determined that longer, heavier trains were part of the answer to this challenge. To make this possible, he moved quickly to expand CPR's locomotive fleet with an emphasis on heavier, more

A CPR rotary snowplow at Revelstoke, British Columbia, circa 1928. *Canada Dept. of Interior/Library and Archives Canada/ PA-041142*

CPR F1a Jubilee-type 4-4-4 No. 2927 lays overnight at Sutton, Quebec, between runs on the local to Montreal, in December 1955. *Jim Shaughnessy*

Handling less-than-carload freight was a labor-intensive business, as shown by this photo taken at Dudswell Junction, Quebec, on CPR's Quebec Central subsidiary, in September 1947. *Photo by Philip Hastings, courtesy of California State Railroad Museum/ negative no. 2606*

powerful engines: 2-8-2 Mikados, 4-6-2 Pacifics, and 2-10-2 Santa Fe types.

At the same time, CPR increased the hauling capacity of its freight cars and raised its track standards. Starting in 1921, 100-pound rail replaced 85-pound as the main-line standard, and in the mountains, 130-pound rail was installed when it became available. Rock ballast, which offered better drainage, replaced gravel.

Many of these steps might have been taken anyway, but they were given special urgency by the presence of a new, nationwide competitor: Canadian National.

Coexisting with Canadian National

CN's leader in the 1920s, Sir Henry Thornton (an American who had been head of the Great Eastern Railway in Britain), was determined to build a company that could compete with CPR on almost every front, including freight and passenger rail services, hotels, and ships.

"Much to Beatty's, and the CPR's, dismay," writes George Buck, "Thornton soon

proved himself capable of turning the CNR into a serious competitor. . . . Beatty spent vast sums to upgrade the CPR both to meet and beat the CNR competition." CPR replaced wooden cars with steel and bought larger and more powerful locomotives.

As a result of this head-to-head competition, both railways invested heavily in new prairie branch lines, with CPR pushing northward into territory where new, more robust varieties of wheat were now being grown. By no coincidence, this was an area that CN (with its east–west routes lying to the north of CPR's) might have considered its own natural preserve. However, CPR had a legitimate interest in developing some of these areas, especially in Alberta, because a portion of its land grant acreage was here. In the period from 1923 to 1931, CPR built 2,121 route miles (3,413 kilometers) of new prairie trackage.

Each player matched or bettered its adversary at every turn. The result was duplication of facilities and services. In the prosperous 1920s, this could be papered over with profits from business where competition didn't drive down prices. But with the onset of the Great Depression in the early 1930s, neither company could afford to play this game any longer.

The Depression, though historically traced to the October 1929 stock market crash, was not immediately evident. In 1930, rail traffic declined but not at an alarming rate. Still, CN, which was dependent on public funds to support its investments in equipment and facilities, and which was still wrestling with the challenge of integrating the varied properties it had inherited, had little margin for error. It had the support of the Liberal government of Mackenzie King, but in 1930 power swung to the Conservatives. Thornton would be answerable for CN's financial results in a way that he had managed to avoid through the boom times of the 1920s.

GREAT LAKES

STEAMSHIP SERVICES

VIA PORT McNICOLL

Last trip September 30, 1925.
STEAMSHIPS "KEEWATIN" AND "ASSINIBOIA"

WESTBOUND

Lv Toronto					
Ar Port McNicoll	Rail				
Lv Port McNicoll		12.40 pm E.T.	Wednesday	Saturday
Ar Sault Ste. Marie	Steamer	4.15 pm		
Lv Sault Ste. Marie		4.30 pm		
Ar Port Arthur		11.00 am	Thursday	Sunday
Ar Fort William		12.30 pm		
Lv Fort William		7.00 am	Friday	Monday
Ar Winnipeg	Rail	8.30 am C.T.		
		8.05 am		
		8.15 pm		

Last trip September 30, 1925.

EASTBOUND

Lv Winnipeg					
Ar Fort William	Rail	10.00 am C.T.	Friday	Tuesday
Lv Fort William		10.25 am E.T.	Saturday	Wednesday
Lv Port Arthur	Steamer	1.30 pm		
Ar Sault Ste. Marie		1.30 pm		
Lv Sault Ste. Marie		9.00 am	Sunday	Thursday
Ar Port McNicoll		1.00 pm		
Lv Port McNicoll	Rail	8.00 am	Monday	Friday
Ar Toronto		8.30 am		
		11.55 am		

VIA OWEN SOUND

Last trip September 28, 1925.
STEAMSHIP "MANITOBA"

WESTBOUND

Lv Toronto				
Ar Owen Sound	Rail			
Lv Owen Sound		5.20 pm E.T.	Monday
Ar Sault Ste. Marie	Steamer	10.45 am	
Lv Sault Ste. Marie		10.45 am	
Ar Port Arthur		5.30 pm	Tuesday
Ar Fort William		5.50 pm	
Lv Fort William		2.00 pm	Wednesday
Ar Winnipeg	Rail	3.00 pm	
		10.55 pm C.T.	
		10.00 am	Thursday

Last trip October 1, 1925.

EASTBOUND

Lv Winnipeg				
Ar Fort William	Rail	♭ 7.50 pm C.T.	Wednesday
Lv Fort William		7.00 am	Thursday
Lv Port Arthur	Steamer	12.00ⁿ'n E.T.	
Ar Sault Ste. Marie		1.00 pm	
Lv Sault Ste. Marie		10.30 am	Friday
Lv Owen Sound		6.00 am	
Ar Toronto	Rail	6.45 am	Saturday
		11.35 am	

♭ Train leaving at 7.50 p.m. carries standard sleeping car passengers only, another train leaving at 5.40 p.m. carries standard sleeping and sleeping car passengers.

Train Equipment.—Parlor Cars between Toronto, Port McNicoll and Owen Sound. Parlor and Dining Cars on day train from Fort William to Owen Sound. Dining Cars on night trains between Fort William and Winnipeg. Sleeping and E.T.—Eastern Time. C.T.—Central Time.

CANADIAN PACIFIC

JUNE 28, 1925

CANADIAN PACIFIC RAILWAY

INDEX OF CONTENTS PAGES 104 to 114

LIST OF AGENCIES PAGES 9 to 12

THE WORLD'S GREATEST TRANSPORTATION SYSTEM

INDEX TO STATIONS
AND OTHER INFORMATION

1. **TO FIND THE STATIONS** about which information is desired:
   See index to Canadian Pacific Stations pages 104 to 112.
   See index to Stations on other Railways pages 113 and 114.
   British Columbia and Alaska Steamship schedules pages 101 and 102.
   Atlantic and Pacific Steamship schedules pages 5 to 8.

2. **THE DAYS ON WHICH TRAINS RUN** are indicated by signs placed against the leaving and arriving time of each train at the head and foot of each column of times.

3. **GENERAL INFORMATION** page 120.

4. **EXPLANATION OF SIGNS** is shown near each table of schedules, as indicated by note at foot of each page.

5. **GENERAL MAP** on pages 61 to 88. Canadian and United States Railway lines map pages 120 to 124 and sectional maps throughout the folder, are of assistance in tracing routes.

6. **EQUIPMENT OF TRAINS** carrying sleeping parlor or dining cars is indicated under EQUIPMENT near the table of schedules on which such train is shown.

7. **SLEEPING AND PARLOR CAR FARES** between principal points on page 115.

STANDARD TIME GOVERNING TRAIN MOVEMENTS, PAGE 8

W. H. SNELL, Gen'l Pass'r Agent, VANCOUVER.

R. G. McNEILLIE, Gen'l Pass'r Agent WINNIPEG.

GEO. A. WALTON, Gen'l Pass'r Agent, MONTREAL.

C. E. McPHERSON, Asst. Passenger Traffic Mgr., WINNIPEG.

H. W. BRODIE, Asst. Passenger Traffic Mgr., MONTREAL.

C. B. FOSTER, Passenger Traffic Mgr., MONTREAL.

C. E. E. USSHER, General Passenger Traffic Manager, MONTREAL.

FOLDER A

Printed in the United States

A June 1925 timetable provides sailing schedules for CPR's Great Lakes steamship services. *Author collection*

The issues of competition between private enterprise and public enterprise that Shaughnessy had foreseen during the formative years of Canadian National would now be revisited by Beatty.

In 1931, a Royal Commission was appointed to look into the state of Canada's railways and make recommendations for improvement. They were unsparing in their criticism of CN. Thornton offered only a weak defense of his record. Much of the Commission's criticism of the company related to the lack of private-sector incentives for efficiency, echoing the fears of Shaughnessy as he had watched CNoR and GTP move toward nationalization more than a decade earlier.

Beatty's proposed solution also echoed Shaughnessy. He recommended that CPR and CN be joined together under a single administration, with sufficient financial safeguards to protect the interests of CPR investors. But like his predecessor, he gave too little recognition to the view that many Canadians held of CPR: that it was a potential monopolist that could be checked only by a vigorous competitor.

Acting on the Commission's recommendation that the two national railways be

CP 2822, shown here at Westmount, near Montreal, in March 1957, was a Class H1c Royal Hudson type, delivered by MLW in 1937. Of the 65 H1 Hudsons owned by CPR, 45 were of this semi-streamlined design. After a visit to Canada in 1939 by King George VI and Queen Elizabeth, when the *Royal Train* was hauled by Hudson 2850 from Quebec City to Vancouver, CPR received permission to designate the 45 engines as "Royal Hudsons." The crown on the engine running board symbolized the designation.
Jim Shaughnessy

forced to cooperate as a means of preventing further financial drain from overeager competition, Parliament in 1933 passed the Canadian National–Canadian Pacific Railway Act. Little came of it. One of the few tangible results was the pooling of passenger trains between Quebec City, Montreal, Ottawa, and Toronto. Another was that CPR closed its hotel in Vancouver and assumed joint control with CN of the new hotel that the latter was building. Beatty continued to press for a unified rail system, but his efforts were in vain.

Ships and Hotels

Thornton made CN competitive with CPR in many ways, but not on the high seas. In this arena, CPR remained the premier Canadian operator. In the late 1920s, Beatty led the company into new investments designed to bolster its competitive position. He was motivated by the operating inefficiencies of some of the vessels acquired after World War I and by changing passenger demographics. A new market was developing among middle-class passengers who wanted something better than steerage but not as expensive as first class. Tourist class was the answer, and in 1928 and 1929 CPR put four *Duchess*-class ships into service to meet this need. They were followed in 1931 by the *Empress of Britain*, the second ship to bear this name, which was meant to serve the first-class market. It was able to make the Quebec–Liverpool roundtrip in just 14 days.

Between 1924 and 1928, CPR engaged in three major hotel projects. The first two, at the Château Lake Louise and Château Frontenac, both involved rebuilding of wings that had been damaged by fire. The third, at Banff Springs, replaced the last parts of the hotel dating to its building in 1887. Other hotel investments followed, most notably the Royal York in Toronto, which opened in 1929, and with a subsequent addition, became the largest hotel in the British Commonwealth.

Whether all the money put into hotels represented a wise investment is open to debate; their return on capital was substantially less than that generated by other parts of the CPR corporate family. Although hotels were always intended to be a sideline—something that would attract travelers to the railway and other CPR transportation services—CN's aggressive hotel-building efforts of the 1920s arguably led CPR to over-invest in this part of its business.

The Crow's Nest Rates: A Growing Problem

The Crow's Nest rates on grain became a source of increasing controversy in the 1920s. Several increases had been authorized during and soon after World War I, and the rate cap had even been suspended during the period from 1919 to 1922. Although operating economies had for a time helped keep the rates compensatory to the railway, postwar inflation in wages and other operating expenses made it increasingly difficult for the railway to make money on this traffic. The grain business was also becoming more complicated because, with the completion of the Panama Canal in 1914, grain from the far West to Europe could now move via Vancouver and the canal at a lower cost than if it were shipped via eastern ports. But the railway faced significant costs in hauling grain over several mountain ranges to reach the Pacific.

The Banff Springs Hotel reopened in 1928, following an extensive rebuilding, with 600 rooms. This photo was taken soon after the project was completed. *Photo by W. J. Oliver, courtesy of Glenbow Archives/NA-4868-277*

CP 5915, a Class T1a 2-10-4 Selkirk type built by MLW in 1929, is shown at Banff, Alberta, in August 1938. The Selkirks were designed under the supervision of Henry Bowen, who served as CPR's chief of motive power from 1928 to 1949. Historian Omer Lavallée notes that the Selkirk type was "the largest and heaviest steam locomotive to operate in the British Commonwealth during Canada's steam era." The 20 T1a Selkirks were assigned to main-line and helper service between Calgary and Revelstoke.
Photo by Otto Perry, Courtesy of Denver Public Library, Western History Collection/OP-20417

By the 1920s the Crow's Nest rate had already become an article of faith among Canadian farmers; in a business subject to the vagaries of weather and an unpredictable marketplace, stable transportation rates helped keep them in business even as the price of grain itself fluctuated from year to year. For the next five decades and more, railway rates on grain would be a subject of continuing dialogue, controversy, and friction involving the growers, their political representatives, and the railways.

Surviving the Depression

In the United States, many railroads were forced into bankruptcy during the Depression, including all four of CPR's U.S. subsidiaries (Soo Line, Duluth, South Shore & Atlantic, Wisconsin Central, and Spokane International).

CPR was able to avoid bankruptcy. For years, it had sought capital through issuance of stock whenever possible, rather than by issuing debt, making it more robust than many of its U.S. counterparts. It did suspend its dividend for a time, but that was a small price for shareholders to pay, given the alternative of having their investment wiped out in bankruptcy court.

CPR's second source of strength was its physical plant. Though operated conservatively, CPR's management had consistently worked to improve the condition of the road's equipment and track. The 1920s had been a

CP 2928 is a Class F1a 4-4-4. A 1938 product of the CLC shop at Kingston, Ontario, it has been preserved by the Canadian Railroad Historical Association at Delson, Quebec, where this photo was taken in 1972. The CRHA describes the engine as follows: "CP 2928 represents the 'Jubilee' wheel arrangement, light motive power designed by Bowen for service on secondary lines. The wheel arrangement was peculiar to the CPR in Canada and was developed to replace the older, smaller locomotives used on these lines." *Jim Shaughnessy*

time of particularly vigorous efforts to improve the property. Thus, maintenance expenses could be cut back for a time without putting the railway's employees, passengers, or shippers at risk.

Although it was financially and physically stronger than many other railways, CPR had to engage in serious belt-tightening to survive the Depression. Employment fell from 75,709 people in 1928 to 49,412 in 1933. Wages of railway operating employees were cut from their original levels in 1933, first by 10 percent and then by 20 percent. These wage cuts were reversed in stages between 1935 and 1938.

Another set of contributors to CPR's relative success during the Depression was its various non-rail operations. Hotels, ships, and the smelter at Trail, British Columbia, all earned operating profits during this period, which helped the parent company weather the economic adversity of this decade.

In World War II (as in World War I) CPR shops were converted to produce munitions. By the end of 1943, CPR's Angus Shops in Montreal had built 1,420 28-ton Valentine tanks. This shipment, being secured to railcars on December 29, 1941, was en route to the Soviet Union. *National Film Board of Canada/Library and Archives Canada/PA-174520*

Pushing the Railway to Its Limits: World War II

The beginning of Beatty's tenure as president of Canadian Pacific came shortly before the end of World War I. His service in this post would conclude as World War II began. By 1940, his health limited his participation in the affairs of the company, and many of his duties were assumed by vice president D'Alton C. Coleman, who had earlier served as vice president in the company's western region. In 1942, Coleman became president, and Beatty died the following year.

Between 1918, when Beatty became president, and 1943, when he died, CPR had grown from 12,993 route miles (20,910 kilometers) to 17,034 (27,414). Much of this growth resulted from the addition of more than 2,000 miles (3,200 kilometers) of branch line on the prairies. CPR's all-time peak Canadian mileage was attained in 1936: 17,241 miles (27,747 kilometers).

The onset of war in Europe, and Britain's growing involvement in it, was reflected in a pickup in CPR's traffic. Revenue ton-miles, which approached 15 billion in 1929, and then fell below 10 billion in 1933, grew to more than 16 billion in 1940. At the peak of the war effort, in 1944, volumes topped out at more than 27 billion revenue ton-miles.

As in the first World War, Canadian Pacific's first direct involvement with the war effort came through the takeover of its ocean-going fleet. "By the spring of 1940," W. Kaye Lamb writes, "eighteen of the company's twenty ocean liners and freighters had been taken over, and one [the freighter *Beaverburn*] had been lost. . . . The loss was the first of many, for few shipping companies were to suffer as high a proportion of fleet casualties as the Canadian Pacific." An early casualty of the war was the 42,000-ton *Empress of Britain*, which was serving as a transport. On October 26, 1940, it was attacked by German aircraft off the coast of Ireland; it sank two days later. Beatty took the news of this loss very

CP 7014 was part of CPR's first group of production-model diesel locomotives, five American Locomotive Company (Alco) S-2 units delivered in 1943. Prior to the delivery of these locomotives, CPR's only diesel locomotive was a one-of-a-kind switch engine built by National Steel Car Company of Hamilton, Ontario, using British components. In February 1968, CP 7014 is about to exchange cabooses on the rear of an eastbound freight at Farnham, Quebec. At the time, cabooses ("vans" in Canadian parlance) were assigned to individual crews. CP 7014 remained on the CPR roster until 1982.
Bill Linley

hard, since the ship was not only the pride of the fleet, but also his personal favorite.

"Six *Empresses*, four *Duchesses*, and five *Beavers* steamed a total of 3,617,000 miles (5,821,000 kilometers) and carried over a million military and civilian passengers and about a million tons of cargo. The cost," Lamb writes, "was high; by the end of the war eleven of the fifteen ships had been lost, nine by enemy action and two by marine accident."

CPR's traffic was bolstered at first by the shortage of shipping capacity, which put freight on the railway that would have otherwise moved via water. The port of Saint John became much busier, as vessel operators sought to avoid the longer cruises that calls at Montreal or Quebec City would have required. Halifax saw a similar surge, but it was served by CN; CPR's Dominion Atlantic was not a significant factor there.

Aside from the growth in freight traffic, CPR's passenger business was also swollen by both military and civilian traffic. In 1941, the company carried 9.1 million passengers. In 1944, it carried an all-time record 18.5 million.

A 1946 company publication recorded the cost of war to CPR's employees: "Over 20,000 C.P.R. people answered the call to the colors and of that number 658 were killed on active service."

The aftermath of World War II was similar to that of World War I. Inflation in wages and prices drove up the railway's operating expenses, while government control over rail rates, and the inevitable decline in volumes

CP 5313 leads a doubleheaded westbound freight crossing the St. Francis River at Lennoxville, just east of Sherbrooke, Quebec, in January 1954. The 5313 was a Class P2b 2-8-2 Mikado built by MLW in 1920.
Jim Shaughnessy

once the war effort wound down, created a squeeze on operating income. In the postwar era, labor was unwilling to abide the company's paternalistic attitude of earlier generations. They wanted higher wages, as well as working conditions more on a par with those in other industries. A strike in 1950 resulted in the appointment of an arbitrator who granted the operating unions both a wage increase and a reduction in the normal work week to 40 hours.

Limited availability of new equipment during the war meant that cars and locomo-

tives, which had been taxed to their limit during the war, needed repair and replacement. The competitive landscape was also changing, with airlines, truckers, and the automobile all competing for a slice of the railway's business.

Coleman saw Canadian Pacific through the war years and retired in 1947, at age 68. His place as chairman and president of the company was taken by William M. Neal, who would serve in the post for only one year. When Neal retired in 1948, the functions of chairman and president were split, with G. A.

Walker taking over as chairman and William A. Mather as president.

But the appointment that would have the most dramatic long-term implications for the railway was that of Norris R. "Buck" Crump as vice president of the railway in 1948. Crump started his CPR career in his hometown of Revelstoke, British Columbia, at the age of 16. He took leaves of absence to obtain first a bachelor's and then, in 1936, a master's degree, both at Purdue University in Indiana. His master's thesis was about potential railway applications of the internal-combustion engine.

CPR had been slow to adopt the diesel-electric engine, and when Crump moved to his new position, the conventional wisdom among most senior managers was that the diesel's primary role would be in the yard, not on the road. Crump brought a different perspective to the steam-versus-diesel issue. Over the next 12 years, CPR would undergo a radical change in the way it powered its freight and passenger trains.

An eastbound doubleheaded CPR freight at Lennoxville, Quebec, on the Montreal–Saint John line, on a minus-20-degree Fahrenheit day in January 1954. *Jim Shaughnessy*

A westbound train, with MLW RS-3 CP 8444 leading, enters the Belleville Subdivision at Smith Falls, Ontario, in December 1965. *Bill Linley*

CHAPTER FOUR

THE CRUMP ERA: *1948–1972*

Norris Crump held the presidency of Canadian Pacific from 1955 to 1964; during the last three years of this term he also held the position of chairman. After the premature death of his successor as president, Robert A. Emerson, he held both posts again for a short time in 1966, until Ian D. Sinclair was named president. Crump continued as chairman until his retirement in 1972, when Sinclair took over as chairman and Frederick S. Burbidge became president.

In November 1954, the local train from Sutton, Quebec, to Montreal, pulled by Jubilee (Class F1a) 4-4-4 2927, passes a pair of diesels led by Alco FA-1 4006 on a freight bound for Newport, Vermont, at West Brome, Quebec. *Jim Shaughnessy*

Although Crump's term as president amounted to less than ten years, the entire period from 1948 to 1972 can fairly be called "The Crump Era." He was the person who set in motion two major forces that irrevocably changed Canadian Pacific: the technological modernization of the railway and the broad diversification of the company's business portfolio, both within and outside the transportation industry. During the last six years of Crump's time with Canadian Pacific, his successor, Ian Sinclair, became the public face of the company and further broadened the company's business portfolio, but Sinclair was implementing ideas that had started with Crump.

The End of Steam and the Beginning of Dieselization

When Crump arrived at headquarters in 1948, CPR was still acquiring steam locomotives. The last new steam locomotive

Steam and diesel were serviced side-by-side at the St. Luc Yard engine house in Montreal, and at dozens of other CPR locations, throughout the transition period of the middle and late 1950s. The two forms of motive power are represented here by Class G1s 4-6-2 2210 (built by CPR in 1907) and FA-2 4091, a 1953 product of MLW. Dieselization of the railway would be completed in 1960. *Jim Shaughnessy*

delivered to the railway arrived in March 1949. It was a 2-10-4 Selkirk, No. 5935, assigned to operate between Calgary and Revelstoke, and while it was in many respects the pinnacle of CPR steam locomotive development, it had a short career, lasting only until 1956.

As the last steam power was arriving on the scene, so were the first diesels. Between 1943 and 1947, the company had purchased 55 diesels for yard service. In 1949, it took two additional steps on the path toward dieselization. The Esquimalt & Nanaimo, CPR's Vancouver Island operation, received a group of Baldwin road switchers that allowed steam operations to be phased out. In the East, three General Motors (Electro-Motive Division) E8's went into service as part of an equipment pool with the Boston & Maine Railroad, powering passenger trains between Montreal and Boston. Freight operations in

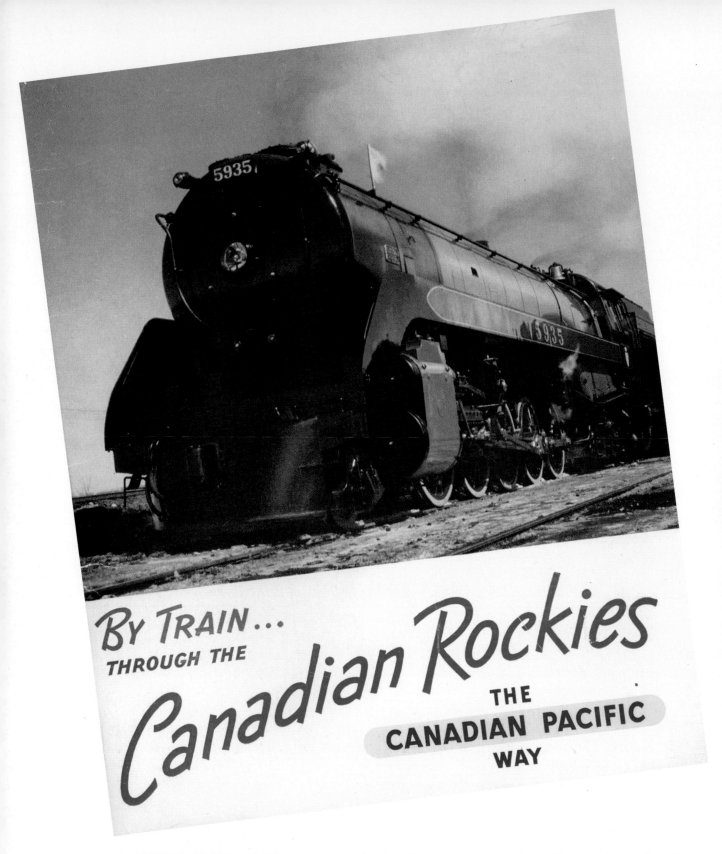

Class T1c Selkirk 5935, shown here on a CPR booklet describing the railway's route through the Rockies, was the last Canadian Pacific steam locomotive delivered, on March 12, 1949. Both the ten T1b Selkirks delivered in 1938 and the final six Class T1c engines of 1949 were semi-streamlined, carried Tuscan red side panels and gold-leaf trim, and were assigned to passenger trains between Calgary and Revelstoke. CP 5935 has been preserved by the Canadian Railroad Historical Association as part of its collection at Delson, Quebec. *Author collection*

In 1905, CPR purchased the Esquimalt & Nanaimo Railway on Vancouver Island for $1 million. CPR then expanded the railway from 78 miles (125 kilometers) to approximately 200 miles (320 kilometers). The railway's traffic base consisted almost entirely of forest products. To reach the mainland, freight cars moved via the ferry slip at Nanaimo, shown here in 1970. Baldwins 8000 and 8001 (Model DRS4-4-1000) were CPR's first road switchers, part of a group of 13 units delivered in 1948 to dieselize the E&N.
Steve Patterson

Vermont and southern Quebec, and on the north shore of Lake Superior, were the next to be dieselized.

Dieselization had to accommodate two main needs: the training of personnel (both operating crews and maintenance workers) and the development of facilities to fuel and maintain the new locomotives. Because of these factors, diesels were first introduced on a region-by-region basis. Later, as enough territories had the trained staff and the facilities to deal with diesels, certain trains were dieselized across several divisions. Steam operations were eliminated completely in 1960.

Aside from the conversion to diesel power, the railway was modernized in many other ways in the decade following World War II. In addition to automatic block signals that were installed on more than 3,000 miles (4,800 kilometers) of the railway, more than 31,000 new freight cars were added to the CPR fleet, and in 1950 a new classification yard was opened at St. Luc, west of Montreal, equipped with retarders and automatic switch controls.

One of CPR's early ventures into dieselization involved its Montreal–Boston passenger service, operated jointly with the Boston & Maine. B&M assigned EMD E7 diesels to the trains, and CPR wanted to assign similar units to the power pool for these trains. By the time CPR placed its order, the improved E8 model was available, and CP specified the newer design. Here, CP 1802, one of the railway's three E8 units, powers the daytime *Alouette* as it approaches Glencliff Summit, New Hampshire, on the B&M in May 1950. *Photo by Philip Hastings, courtesy of California State Railroad Museum/negative no. 800*

Squeezed Between Rising Costs and Regulated Rates

As much as CPR needed a technological overhaul, the program carried out under Crump's leadership in the years before he became president was a costly one. According to W. Kaye Lamb, "modernization, which had begun in 1947 and under Crump's urging had been stepped up to an intensive five-year program in 1951, had cost $600 million by the time he

assumed the presidency in 1955. . . . It had been a difficult period financially."

David Cruise and Alison Griffiths add more color to the picture, noting that when Crump became president, he "inherited the CPR's highest debt since 1941, the highest fixed charges since 1948 and the lowest return on investment since 1922. The source of the problems was the railroad itself . . . Crump faced a classic Catch 22: the railroad couldn't attract investment because it wasn't profitable and couldn't become profitable without massive investment. And there was a devilish kicker, the notorious 1897 Crow Rate . . . which froze grain rates—the largest component of rail revenue—at artificially low levels."

Costs continued to escalate, but increases in freight rates could not keep pace. The most worrisome source of cost increases, because it represented a very large percentage of operating

Above: In the early 1960s, service on the Montreal–Boston route was converted to Budd Rail Diesel Cars, freeing CPR's E8 units for other service. In June 1968, CP 1802 is on a Quebec City train about to depart Montreal's Windsor Station. At right is Canadian Pacific's Château Champlain hotel, opened in 1967. *Jim Shaughnessy* **Left:** CPR began to dieselize its freight service between Montreal and Wells River, Vermont, in May 1949, with the acquisition of twelve 1,500-horsepower road-freight units (eight FA-1 cab units and four FB-1 booster units) from Alco. The fresh paint is visible on this FA-1 as the engineer removes white flags from the unit at Wells River, the interchange point with the Boston & Maine, approximately two months after the FA-1s were delivered. *Photo by Philip Hastings, courtesy of California State Railroad Museum/ negative no. 2521*

In 1949, CPR received five Alco RS-2 road switchers. For most of their careers they were assigned out of Newport, Vermont, or Brownville Junction, Maine. In February 1977, CP 8403 is at Richford, Vermont. *George Pitarys*

expenses, was labor. Union negotiators were becoming more demanding and less willing to settle for what they considered substandard wages and working conditions.

If CPR's unions were becoming more demanding, so were the company's shippers. Rail rates were (and are) set, in large measure, by what the market can bear. That meant that western shippers, with few competitive options, typically paid higher freight rates on commodities like lumber and minerals than their eastern counterparts did on manufactured goods, which could move by either truck or rail.

A Royal Commission was appointed in 1948 to look into the question of how Canada's national transportation policy should deal with the competing interests of shippers and railways. There were rhetorical concessions to the company's need for an adequate return on capital. However, the results of the Commission's work, as implemented by the Board of Transport Commissioners (the body that regulated rail rates), was a formula for calculating a fair return that, from CPR's perspective, left much to be desired. CPR felt that it needed a return of 6 percent or more in order to justify the ongoing reinvestment in plant and equipment that would keep the railroad alive; actual returns in the period 1953–1955 were between 2 and 3 percent.

The compression between wages that rose with each new round of negotiations, and freight rates that could never be increased enough to offset inflation, led the railway to focus on productivity. Crump's modernization replaced labor with capital: diesels could haul more tonnage with less maintenance than steam engines; Centralized Traffic Control that allowed the elimination of train order operators at remote stations; computer systems that mechanized the work formerly done by rooms full of clerks; and track machinery that reduced the labor involved in right-of-way maintenance. The result was a

From the photographer's notes: "The CPR local at Teeswater, Ontario, at the end of a wandering branch in southern Ontario, on the last day of mixed train passenger service." This photo was taken on August 2, 1957. The 83-mile (134-kilometer) line branched off the Toronto–Owen Sound line at Orangeville, which is where this mixed train originated. *Jim Shaughnessy*

At Vallée Junction, Quebec, in May 1959, the baggageman on the Quebec Central local from Lac Frontier unloads shipments for transfer to a Quebec City–bound train. *Jim Shaughnessy*

dramatic decline in the railway's labor force from its peak of 83,848 workers in 1952 to 57,778 in 1962. It would see further declines in the years ahead.

One particular issue addressed during Crump's tenure was the question of firemen on diesel locomotives. At its simplest level, the dispute centered on the railway's assertion that firemen were not necessary to the safe operation of diesels. The union representing these employees, the Brotherhood of Locomotive Firemen and Enginemen, said that they were. Following strikes in 1956 and 1958, and the appointment of a Royal Commission (under Justice R. L. Kellock), CPR ultimately implemented a policy of eliminating firemen's positions through attrition.

Even though it had substantially cut its labor force, CPR complained to regulators that it was not earning an adequate return on capital. In 1959, Regina lawyer M. A. McPherson was appointed to chair another Royal Commission charged with investigating the economic situation of the railways. In a series of findings, the Commission said, first, that the railways should be relieved of the burden imposed by the low level of grain rates under the Crow's Nest Pass Agreement. Second, the Commission said that the government's economic regulation of the railways should be relaxed, though not eliminated. It would be a long time before this recommendation would have any tangible effect, but it was a start.

The National Transportation Act of 1967 took several important steps toward relaxing the rigid regulatory framework under which Canadian railways operated. One step toward greater market freedom was the ability to publish multicar rates, which encouraged the development of unit trains. The first such train in Canada was a 1967 movement of sulfuric acid from Copper Cliff, Ontario, on CPR, to Sarnia, Ontario, on CN. Three years later, coal began to move in trainload quantities

In February 1966, CPR Train 951 digs in while leaving the yard at Smiths Falls, Ontario, with a tonnage westbound train on a very cold morning in February 1966. The train is en route to Winnipeg, Manitoba. Leading this train is CP 4050, an MLW FA-2, delivered in 1951. It was scrapped in 1977. *Bill Linley*

from mines in southeastern British Columbia to the Roberts Bank terminal near Vancouver for export to Japan. The movement of coal soon became a major source of revenue for CPR.

Still, even with some market freedoms, the Crow Rates on grain were a significant constraint. By CPR's reckoning, these rates were below cost. Given the poor economics of moving grain, both CPR and CN cut back on their investments in the business. Even while U.S. railroads were converting to 100-ton covered hoppers, Canadian grain moved in 40-foot boxcars with a capacity of 70 tons or less. In the early 1970s, the Canadian government stepped in to provide 6,000 modern covered hopper cars, assigning some to each major railway. But this was not a complete solution.

Diversification Picks up Steam

One reality of the postwar years was that trucking became an important factor in the movement of freight. Canadian Pacific took steps to add trucking to its portfolio of services, through the formation of Canadian Pacific Transport Limited in 1947. The services offered by CP Transport were largely an adjunct to the company's rail service, providing off-line customers with a way of moving their goods to and from rail-served stations.

Piggyback (trailer-on-flatcar, or TOFC) service was initiated in December 1952, meaning that goods once placed in a trailer by the shipper did not have to be transloaded into boxcars in order to take advantage of the economies of line-haul rail service. They could stay in the trailer from origin to destination, with over-the-road service provided by truckers at both ends of the movement. In 1958, CPR acquired Smith Transport Limited, at the time Canada's largest trucker, and it soon became commonplace to see Smith trailers moving across Canada by rail.

Diversification took another significant step forward with the formation in 1962 of Canadian Pacific Investments Limited, which became the company's vehicle for ownership and management of non-transportation ventures. It started with Canadian Pacific's existing

In July 1966, MLW C-424 CP 4242 leads Train 903 just west of Smiths Falls, Ontario, on the Belleville Subdivision. *Bill Linley*

Photographer Bill Linley's notes state that "commuter train 250 with 1600-horsepower MLW RS-10 8472 awaits the highball at 9:45 A.M. on Wednesday June 1, 1965. Six more station stops will be made by the time the 9.5-mile (15.3-kilometer) run is completed at Montreal's Windsor Station. CPR rostered 66 of these versatile locomotives, which were a Canada-only model that superseded the RS-3. Forty-six RS-10 units such as the 8472 were boiler-equipped for dual service, as signified by the nose-mounted beaver shield, and they powered many eastern passenger runs throughout the 1960s." *Bill Linley*

oil and gas subsidiary, plus a timber operation. It soon added Consolidated Mining and Smelting Company (later shortened to Cominco), the company's hotels, and a real estate unit, Marathon Realty.

By branching out into non-transportation businesses, Canadian Pacific followed a popular trend among North American railways, but it had an advantage: most of these operating units did not require acquisition or new investment, but simply a reorganization and a redefinition of their relationship to the parent company. They were no longer ancillary to the railway, but succeeded or failed on their own ability to compete in their respective markets.

Over time, CP Investments extended its reach beyond the original holdings. The oil and gas and timber units both added to their original properties. Hotels were built in new locations, including some overseas cities, and new operating units were added, including Great Lakes Paper, a part interest in forest products and paper producer MacMillan Bloedel, and a controlling interest in Algoma Steel.

When unit coal train service began from southern British Columbia to Roberts Bank, near Vancouver, the cars supplied by CPR were painted red, as shown in this August 1970 photo of an 803 train on the Windermere Subdivision, led by MLW M-630 4552. The cars soon turned black from coal dust, and by 1972 the railway conceded defeat. All new coal cars from that time forward were delivered in black paint. *Stan Smaill*

A coal train is loaded on the loop track at the Kaiser Balmer loadout at Elkview, British Columbia, in August 1975. *Phil Mason*

Most diesel locomotives are actually diesel-electrics, but CP 23, shown here at Vallée Junction, Quebec, in August 1964, was a rare exception: a diesel-hydraulic, or more specifically, a diesel-torque-convertor locomotive. CPR had a handful of these small units, and CP 23 was in fact part of the last group of locomotives built for a Canadian railway by Canadian Locomotive Company of Kingston, Ontario: five 44-ton D-T-C units, delivered in 1960. Here, it switches a local that has just arrived from Lac Frontier. *Jim Shaughnessy*

CP Investments also became involved in the coal business in the early 1970s through a venture known as Fording Coal. The company had owned land in southeastern British Columbia with known coal deposits since 1909, but they were not considered economical to develop. In the 1960s, nearby deposits were acquired by Kaiser Resources Limited, which sold the coal to Japanese steel mills, moving it in unit trains through the port of Vancouver. This encouraged Canadian Pacific to take a closer look at its own coal interest in the region. The result was Fording.

Reflecting the reduced role of the railway in generating earnings for the company's shareholders, in 1971 the corporate name was formally changed to Canadian Pacific Limited. This was hard for some longtime employees and other stakeholders to accept, but it was symbolic of the fact that the company had been foresighted enough to spread its bets around. If the company had been forced to stand or fall on the financial results of the railway alone, it is doubtful that it would have weathered the economic pressures of the postwar years as well as it did.

Canadian Pacific Enters the Airline Business

CPR had been given an opportunity to become a part-owner of Trans-Canada Airlines (later Air Canada) during the 1930s. It declined because of the limited control it would have over the airline, but it remained interested in adding air services to its portfolio. Canadian Pacific Air Lines came into existence in 1942. Its assets included the employees, aircraft, and facilities of ten small airlines that the company had acquired during 1941. The war gave the nascent airline an opportunity to participate in ferrying aircraft across the Atlantic and from Canada to Alaska, and in the training of pilots for military service. It was restricted from competing with Trans-

CPR had 21 Fairbanks-Morse-designed Train Masters (Model H24-66): former demonstrator 8900, built in 1955 by F-M at Beloit, Wisconsin, and 20 units delivered in 1956, all built to F-M's design by CLC. Although they were used at various locations during their careers, by the 1970s they were concentrated in two places: Montreal and Tadanac Yard near Trail, British Columbia. Here, CP 8917 rides high on the St. Lawrence River Bridge as it sets off cars in the yard at LaSalle, Quebec. *Stan Smaill*

Canada, but Canadian Pacific Air Lines found a niche in regional services, primarily in the West but also in eastern Canada.

In 1948, the government authorized Canadian Pacific to begin air service across the Pacific. The company intended to serve China, Japan, and Australia. Service began in 1949 using Canadair Four aircraft, a Canadian version of the Douglas DC-4. China was

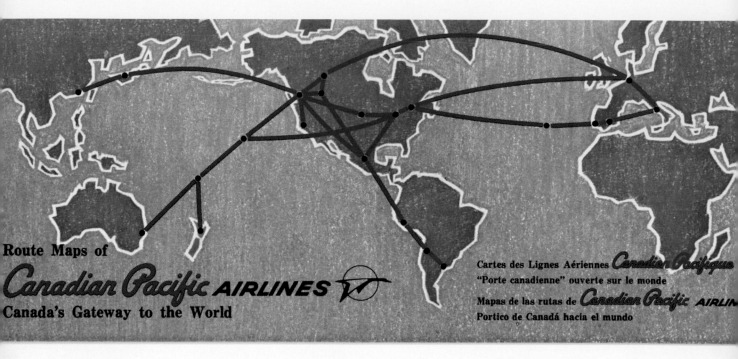

Route Maps of

Canadian Pacific AIRLINES

Canada's Gateway to the World

Cartes des Lignes Aériennes *Canadian Pacifique*
"Porte canadienne" ouverte sur le monde

Mapas de las rutas de *Canadian Pacific* AIRLIN

Portico de Canadá hacia el mundo

A 1960s map of
Canadian Pacific
Airlines' domestic and
international routes.
Author collection

quickly dropped as a destination when the Communists came to power. However, the company's Tokyo service proved to be a great success.

In the early 1950s, the fleet was updated with Convair planes for domestic routes and Douglas DC-6s for international routes. Vancouver became the operational hub of the growing airline, which started service to Mexico and Peru in 1953. Two years later, service to Amsterdam via the polar route began, and soon after a Toronto–Mexico City route was inaugurated.

Although the airline struggled financially in the late 1950s and early 1960s, Crump was confident enough about its long-term prospects to support the acquisition of DC-8 jet aircraft in 1961. With faster, more comfortable aircraft, the airline was able to cultivate the international travel market and go from red ink to black by the mid-1960s.

It expanded its jet fleet with stretched DC-8s and Boeing 737s in the late 1960s, and in 1973 it invested in 747s to serve its long-distance routes. By the mid-1970s the airline served Japan, China, Australia, Hawaii, Mexico, Peru, Chile, Argentina, the

Netherlands, Portugal, Spain, Italy, Greece, and Israel. It continued to serve destinations in western Canada, and although required by the government to play second fiddle to Air Canada, it had a modest presence in cross-Canada markets.

The Last Stand of the Passenger Liners

Steamship services were restored slowly after the war, in part because the government was slow to release the remaining vessels from the company's prewar fleet. Like the railway, the ship line found itself in a new environment after the war, and eventually Canadian Pacific decided that it would restore passenger service only on the Atlantic, since airline service seemed likely to siphon off business from its Pacific routes. By the summer of 1950, three *Empress* vessels were serving the transatlantic trade (and doing cruise duty in the off-season). In 1956, the company began to order ships to reequip this service.

Between 1955 and 1961, the company acquired three new vessels for the summer transatlantic trade and the winter cruise business: a new *Empress of Britain*, followed soon

For a world of service . . .
travel Canadian Pacific

Across Canada...from the picturesque East Coast...to the inspiring Canadian Rockies and the evergreen playground on the Pacific Coast ...Canadian Pacific trains carry you smoothly, comfortably.

Enjoy the finest in travel comfort...modern equipment...friendly service...superb meals ...all these are yours when you travel The Canadian Pacific Way.

Sea to Sea...on Canada's West Coast in Victoria, B.C., visit the gracious Empress Hotel, or any of Canadian Pacific's 18 other hotels and lodges from sea to sea. The Canadian Pacific is your host in many of Canada's great cities... in the magnificent Canadian Rockies... beside the mighty St. Lawrence...on the colorful East Coast.

As you travel across Canada you are never more than 24 hours from a Canadian Pacific hotel.

Across the Pacific...fly Canadian Pacific style to Australia and the Far East.

Enjoy the same high standard of Canadian Pacific service in the air as on land or sea when you fly pressurized "EMPRESS" aircraft from Vancouver via Honolulu and Fiji to Australia.

From Vancouver via Alaska to Tokyo and Hong Kong you will fly the shortest and fastest air route to the Orient.

Canadian Pacific

SPANS THE WORLD
RAILWAYS • STEAMSHIPS
AIR LINES • HOTELS
COMMUNICATIONS • EXPRESS

by the *Empress of England* and, in 1961, the largest of the three, the *Empress of Canada*. Beginning in the mid-1960s, however, the company yielded to the reality that airlines had replaced steamships as the preferred method of travel between Canada and Britain. By the 1971 summer season, only the *Empress of Canada* remained, and by the end of the year it, too, had made its last voyage under the Canadian Pacific flag.

The company remained actively involved in cargo shipping and successfully made the transition from break-bulk methods of handling freight to the new and far more efficient style of international shipping: containerization. Not only did containers reduce port labor and improve vessel utilization, but inland transportation for shippers located significant

On the back cover of its October 1949 timetable, Canadian Pacific advertises both its airline and its hotels, in addition to its rail passenger service. *Author collection*

12 vacation treats
White Empress style to Europe
go Canadian Pacific for service!

1: Europe awaits you! Sail there in luxurious White Empress Cruise style. **2:** The only sheltered Trans-Atlantic route—⅓ the way down the St. Lawrence River—with 1000 miles of sight-seeing.

3: Six or seven days to relax and have shipboard fun between Montreal and Liverpool. **4:** An ocean vacation with the satisfaction of real thrift. First-class Empress luxury from $230. Tourist comfort from $152, depending on ship and season.

5: Make new friends among the discriminating people who sail Empress style. **6:** Active fun: deck sports, swimming. **7:** Social games. **8:** The comfort of attended children's rooms.

9: Airy staterooms for perfect rest! **10:** The Captain's dinner, grand climax of Empress hospitality. **11:** Gourmet meals, dancing every night, movies. **12:** And 'round the clock, the blessing of Canadian Pacific's skilled, courteous service.

Ask your travel agent about a world of Canadian Pacific service. Canadian Pacific trains across Canada. Your choice of 19 hotels and resorts. Cruises to Alaska. Airliners to the Far East, New Zealand and Australia.

Canadian Pacific

See your local agent or Canadian Pacific in principal cities in U. S. and Canada.

The *Empress of Scotland* is depicted in an advertisement from the mid-1950s. Originally the *Empress of Japan*, the vessel was used in transpacific service from 1930 to 1939, and then as a troop ship from late 1939 until 1948. It entered transatlantic and cruise service in 1950, and remained in service for Canadian Pacific through the 1957 transatlantic season, at the end of which it was sold to the Hamburg-Atlantic line. *Author collection*

In May 1971, the eastbound *Canadian* pauses at the former Fort William station in Thunder Bay, Ontario. The passenger standing near the door of the sleeping car is en route to Montreal, where she will board Canadian Pacific's *Empress of Canada* to sail to England; this would be the last season for the company's transatlantic passenger services. Grain is delivered by rail to the massive Saskatchewan Wheat Pool elevator, and then shipped out on Great Lakes vessels. *Tom Murray*

distances from ports was typically by rail. In 1970 and 1971, three new ships were delivered, all of them designed specifically to handle containers. In Canada, they served the port of Quebec (through the Wolfe's Cove terminal) and in Europe they called weekly at Rotterdam, London, and LeHavre.

Through a separate subsidiary, Canadian Pacific (Bermuda) Limited, the company entered another steamship market, this one involving the transportation of petroleum and other bulk commodities. Throughout the late 1960s and into the 1970s, this unit built up a fleet of tankers and other vessels that far outranked the container fleet in terms of sheer tonnage. In addition, the company continued to provide coastal passenger services through vessels based at Vancouver, as well as a Bay of Fundy service between Saint John, New Brunswick, and Digby, Nova Scotia.

The dome seating of the observation car *Algonquin Park* on the westbound *Canadian* appears quite full, as a rainbow appears on the south side of the train, at Field, British Columbia, in June 1975. *Steve Patterson*

CHAPTER FIVE

CPR's Passenger Trains

Today, Canadian Pacific Railway is freight only, except where it hosts

passenger trains operated by VIA Rail Canada, Amtrak, private com-

panies (such as Rocky Mountaineer Vacations), and government-spon-

sored commuter authorities. The railway does operate a limited

cruise-type service, the Royal Canadian Pacific, based in Calgary, and,

on an irregular basis, special trains designed to enhance the company's

community relations efforts. Such services are, no doubt, important to

their users, but they are not part of the railway's core business.

Canadian Pacific has always taken pride in its history. In 2000, it inaugurated a luxury train service, the Royal Canadian Pacific, using restored heavyweight cars and locomotives in the historic CPR grey and Tuscan red livery. Although the train's normal route takes it on a loop from Calgary west to Golden, British Columbia, then south through the Crowsnest Pass, and back to Calgary, it occasionally ventures to other points on the CPR system. Here, it departs Revelstoke, British Columbia, westbound in August 2000. On the rear is the dining car *Mount Stephen*, originally built as a venue for meetings of the Canadian Pacific board of directors. *Phil Mason*

However, for the first 80-plus years of Canadian Pacific's existence, passenger service was an integral part of its daily operations. CPR did not just operate passenger trains: it provided a totality of passenger services unmatched by any other North American railway, including lake, coastal, and transoceanic steamers, and hotels that set high standards in both architecture and amenities. Management did not consider passenger service an afterthought, but a central part of what the company did.

Transcontinental Service

The most visible part of CPR's passenger train network was its transcontinental service. In the company's early years, this service focused on two things: scenery and settlement. Any railway across western Canada would have found itself traversing the Rocky Mountains and the river canyons of British Columbia, but the decision of CPR's founders to push through Kicking Horse Pass and over the Selkirk Mountains gave this railway a spectacular array of natural attractions to lure passengers onto its trains. One of

William Van Horne's most oft-repeated quotations was, "If we can't export the scenery, we will import the tourists."

Van Horne, in fact, was the driving force behind CPR's investment in resort hotels. The CPR dining halls at Laggan (Lake Louise), Field, and Glacier soon added lodging. Van Horne, always eager to exploit new business opportunities, saw that by turning these accommodations into destinations, Canadian Pacific could build a clientele of relatively well-to-do urban dwellers who wanted to be pampered while taking in the natural beauty of British Columbia and western Alberta. That's exactly what Canadian Pacific did at its western resorts, the most famous of which became Château Lake Louise and Banff Springs Hotel.

CPR had another market to serve with its long-distance trains, one that would prove just as important to the company's long-term health. That market was the settler, the immigrant, the farmer relocating to western Canada. "Colonization" was the term used to describe this process, and the railway devoted considerable energy to recruiting people who

Right: Two adjacent panels from a November 1919 CPR timetable cover are aimed at the principal markets for the company's transcontinental passenger services: immigrants interested in settling in the West and those who could afford to indulge themselves at the company's hotels, such as the Empress in Victoria. *Author collection* **Below:** An August 1899 advertisement for CPR's new transcontinental train, the *Imperial Limited. Author collection*

would gamble on starting a new life in a territory they had never seen. Some of the settlers came from the European continent, some from Ireland, and some from within North America.

The first cross-country trains inaugurated by CPR in 1886 were dubbed, fittingly, the *Pacific Express* (westbound) and *Atlantic Express* (eastbound). In his book *More Classic Trains*, Arthur Dubin describes their equipment: "The new cars were built with exteriors of varnished solid mahogany; interiors were satinwood, inlaid with brass and mother-of-pearl in Japanese designs. Parisian marble lavatories contained fittings of beaten bronze. Clerestory window ventilators were of colored Venetian glass; upholstery was sea-green plush; floors were covered with Turkey carpets." Total running time was almost 139 hours, for an average speed of less than 21 mph (34 kmh) on the 2,906-mile (4,688-kilometer) journey.

In 1899, CPR launched a new transcontinental train, the *Imperial Limited*, using cars whose appointments were, the railway said, "near perfection." The name, Lamb says,

Soo Line SEASON 1935

"Notes by the Way" was Soo Line's guide to the route from Chicago to Vancouver and included extensive descriptions of CPR's resort properties in the Rockies. The cover depicts Banff Springs Hotel. *Author collection*

10:00 p.m.; the train's schedule denied westbound passengers the opportunity to see the Rockies and Selkirks in daylight. However, after a noon departure from Kamloops, four days after leaving Montreal, travelers were able to enjoy the scenic Thompson and Fraser river canyons before a 10:00 p.m. arrival in Vancouver.

Equipment on the *Imperial Limited* consisted of first-class coaches, standard sleepers, tourist sleepers, and colonist cars. The tourist sleepers were for the budget-minded traveler and were less luxuriously appointed than standard sleeping cars.

The colonist cars were a very Spartan type of conveyance aimed at the settler market. They were, quite literally, a hard class of service, lacking both upholstery and bedding (which the passenger was expected to supply). Dubin notes that "thousands of immigrants from Europe who arrived in Canada at the turn of the century spent their first nights in Canada aboard Colonist cars."

One variation from standard North American practice, introduced by Van Horne, was that CPR's sleepers and diners were operated by the railway itself, and not by the Pullman Company. This gave CPR control over the quality of service, which was paramount in its approach to the passenger business. Van Horne's former employer, the Milwaukee Road, followed a similar practice. Many CPR passenger cars were constructed at the company's Angus Shops in Montreal.

CPR recognized that if it wanted to fully exploit the potential of its western resorts, it had to serve not just Canada, but the U.S. market as well. Soo Line, with its route from Chicago to the West, was ideally

reflected "the conception of the Canadian Pacific as an all-Imperial British route to the Orient." This seasonal train initially operated on a schedule of just over 100 hours between Montreal and Vancouver, increasing the average speed to 29 mph (47 kmh), although in subsequent years its schedule was lengthened somewhat.

A June 1909 timetable shows Train 1, the *Imperial Limited*, departing Montreal at 10:10 a.m. The next day, the traveler arrived at Fort William at 8:30 p.m., having traveled the north shore of Lake Superior for much of the day. Arrival at Winnipeg was the next morning at 9:45 a.m. That afternoon and most of the next day were spent crossing the prairies, with arrival at Calgary at 5:20 p.m. The Great Divide between Alberta and British Columbia was reached just before

suited for this purpose, and in June 1900 a section of the *Imperial Limited* began operating via Moose Jaw, Saskatchewan, and the Soo–CPR interchange at Portal, North Dakota, with cars running through between Chicago and Vancouver.

The Soo Line also represented the eastern leg of a through service that CPR established between St. Paul and Portland, Oregon. From east to west, the complete route was:

- Soo Line from St. Paul to Portal, North Dakota;
- CPR from Portal, via Moose Jaw and Crowsnest Pass, to Kingsgate, British Columbia/Eastport, Idaho;
- CPR's Spokane International subsidiary from Eastport to Spokane; and
- Union Pacific affiliate Oregon Railway & Navigation from Spokane to Portland.

The *Imperial Limited* was eclipsed as CPR's premier passenger train by the *Trans-Canada Limited* in June 1919. That name had been used on summer-season trains as early as 1907, but the train introduced in 1919 represented a higher standard than any of its forebears. It carried only standard (i.e., first-class) sleepers, including a seven-compartment, one–drawing room car, and a three-compartment, one–drawing room observation car, plus a dining car between Montreal and Vancouver. A Toronto section connected at Sudbury.

Initially the train operated on a schedule of 93 hours and 30 minutes from Montreal to Vancouver, and 92 hours and 15 minutes in the opposite direction. By June 1925, an additional four hours had been cut out of the train's schedule, and the CPR timetable alerted passengers to "the convenient hours of arrival and departure at all major cities and resorts." In both directions, the spectacular

CPR train No. 8, the eastbound *Dominion*, is powered by Class T1a Selkirk 5906 as its passes Yoho, British Columbia, just out of the Lower Spiral Tunnel, in August 1938. *Photo by Otto Perry, Courtesy of Denver Public Library, Western History Collection/OP-20506*

The motor car was a low-cost solution to the need for passenger service on lightly used branch lines, and was a precursor of the Budd Rail Diesel Car. Here, CPR 9004 pauses at Guelph Junction, Ontario, in August 1957, while express is loaded. *Jim Shaughnessy*

segment between Banff and Revelstoke was traversed in daylight.

CPR's transcontinental service reached a new peak in 1931, with four passenger trains in each direction wending their way through the tunnels and mountain passes of western Canada:

- The all–sleeping car *Trans-Canada Limited*, between Montreal and Vancouver, with a connecting section to Toronto;
- The *Mountaineer*, an all-sleeper train between Chicago and Vancouver, operating via Soo Line east of Portal;
- The Montreal–Vancouver *Imperial*, carrying coaches and sleepers, including cars that connected at Moose Jaw with the *Soo-Pacific Express* to and from Chicago; and
- *The Dominion*, a Toronto–Vancouver coach and sleeper train that also handled a number of shorter-distance cars, including sleepers between Toronto and Winnipeg, Fort William and Winnipeg, Winnipeg and Calgary, Medicine Hat, Alberta, and Calgary, and Calgary and Vancouver.

The Dominion was the only one of these named trains to survive World War II, although the remnants of the *Imperial* lived on as unnamed Trains 1 and 2 between Montreal and Vancouver. There were, in fact, two *Dominions*: one between Vancouver and Montreal (Trains 7 and 8), the other serving Toronto (Trains 3 and 4). The latter had a U.S. connection at Moose Jaw, the *Soo-Dominion*, which operated via Soo Line between Portal and St. Paul, and Chicago & North Western between St. Paul and Chicago.

Passenger Service Reaches a Peak

The year 1944 represented an all-time peak in passengers carried by CPR: 18,461,000. For comparative purposes, passengers carried in other selected years were:

- 1886: 1,791,000 (the first year following completion of the transcontinental line)
- 1910: 11,173,000 (the first year that passenger volume exceeded 10 million)
- 1920: 16,925,000 (a record that held until 1944)
- 1933: 7,174,000 (the low point between the World Wars)

- 1940: 7,781,000 (less than half the volume that the railway would carry only four years later)

In any year, most passengers who rode CPR did so in coach. But by looking at those trains that carried first-class equipment (sleeping cars for overnight travel and parlor cars for day trips) during the peak year of 1944, it's possible to gain an appreciation for the changes that occurred over the next three decades, when all but a handful of the first-class services would be eliminated. All of the trains described below carried coaches as well.

In the East, CPR's November 1944 timetable shows two trains daily in each direction between Montreal and Saint John, New Brunswick: Trains 40 and 42 eastbound and 39 and 41 westbound, all of which carried sleepers. Trains 39 and 40 also had a buffet parlor car between Montreal and Megantic, Quebec (the point where the route crossed into Maine). Some cars on these trains operated through to Halifax via Canadian National (CPR's own route to Halifax required a ferry crossing, but the ferry did not carry railcars).

Another important overnight train serving Saint John was the *Gull*, which originated on CN in Halifax. CPR took the *Gull* from Saint John as far as the McAdam, New Brunswick/Vanceboro, Maine, border crossing, and it then ran on Maine Central to Portland and Boston & Maine to Boston.

CPR's Nova Scotia subsidiary, the Dominion Atlantic Railway, had its own first-class service in the form of a parlor car (as well as a diner) that ran between Halifax and Yarmouth, Nova Scotia, on Trains 95 and 98.

Between Montreal and Boston, on trains operated jointly by CPR and Boston & Maine (via their connection at Wells River, Vermont), travelers had a choice between the daytime *Alouette* (with a buffet parlor observation car) and the overnight *Red Wing*, which ran with a three-compartment, one–drawing

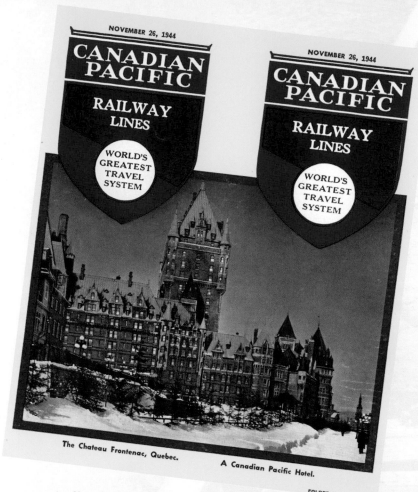

The Chateau Frontenac, Quebec.

A Canadian Pacific Hotel.

FOLDER A

The November 1944 CPR timetable portrays the company's landmark Château Frontenac hotel at Quebec City. The contents of the timetable provide information on a cornucopia of rail passenger services. *Author collection*

room buffet observation car, as well as a twelve-section, two–double bedroom sleeper.

In the Quebec–Montreal–Ottawa–Toronto–Windsor corridor, where CPR and CN had pooled their passenger services since the early 1930s, there were a number of coach-only services, but also several trains that offered first-class service.

Trains 357 and 358 between Quebec and Montreal departed each day just before midnight, each with a sleeping car and coaches. Thanks to a slow schedule on the 178-mile (286-kilometer) route, they arrived at their destinations after 6:00 a.m., but sleeping car passengers could remain on board until 7:45 a.m. (Montreal) or 8:00 a.m. (Quebec City).

Four trains in each direction operated each day between Montreal and Toronto, two via CPR and two via CN. There were, in fact, two 11:00 p.m. departures from Montreal, one via each route. Both of these evening trains carried a heavy complement of sleeping cars on the

route, which was just over 330 miles (531 kilometers) via either railway. The CPR edition, Train 21 (the *Chicago Express*) had sleepers for Toronto, Hamilton, London, and Detroit. They returned eastbound on Train 22, the *Overseas*, arriving each morning at 7:45 a.m. at CPR's Windsor Station, Montreal.

The other named trains on this route were the *Canadian* and the *Royal York*. There was some irony here, because the Royal York was CPR's huge hotel in Toronto, yet the train of this name operated westbound from CN's Montreal station and eastbound into CPR's. The *Canadian* ran westbound from the CPR

A Montreal-bound commuter train makes its way through an early-spring snowstorm, at Westmount, Quebec, in April 1975. *Phil Mason*

station, and eastbound into CN's. That name would be used, starting in 1955, by CPR's transcontinental train.

Sleepers also ran in this corridor between Ottawa and Toronto, Toronto and Detroit, and Toronto and Chicago (via New York Central's affiliate, Michigan Central, west of Detroit).

Toronto was also the endpoint for sleeper operations to several destinations in the northeastern United States: Boston, New York, Pittsburgh, and Cleveland. Trains carrying these cars operated via CPR between Toronto and Hamilton, and then via the Toronto, Hamilton & Buffalo Railway, which served as CPR's link to several U.S. railroads at Buffalo, but primarily the New York Central system. TH&B was later absorbed by CPR.

Toronto, Hamilton & Buffalo was controlled by New York Central System and its affiliates, Michigan Central Railroad and Canada Southern Railway, which together owned 73 percent of its stock. CPR owned the remainder. In 1977, Canadian Pacific bought the former NYC-controlled shares from Penn Central, and subsequently integrated the TH&B into the CPR system. *Author collection*

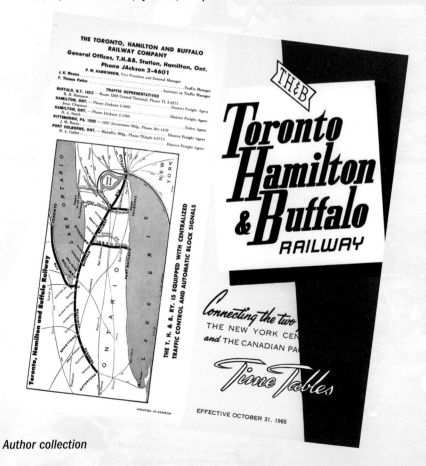

Train 11, the *Kootenay Express*, seen here in May 1951, ran from Medicine Hat, Alberta, to Vancouver. The sleeper *Shaunavon* was a twelve-section, one–drawing room car, part of a group built in 1930 and 1931. Photographer Philip Hastings did not record the location of this photo, but it is believed to be on the Boundary Subdivision in southern British Columbia. *Photo by Philip Hastings, courtesy of California State Railroad Museum/negative no. 212*

Another train that carried sleepers (as well as a café parlor car) was unnamed 27 and 28, between Toronto, Sudbury, and Sault Ste. Marie.

In the West, to reach St. Paul from Winnipeg, one could ride a sleeping car on the *Winnipeger*, which operated via the Soo Line south of the border at Emerson, Manitoba/Noyes, Minnesota. Soo Line also operated sleepers on its own routes between Chicago and both Duluth-Superior and Minneapolis–St. Paul.

Sleepers operated between Calgary and Edmonton, Alberta; Regina and Prince Albert, Saskatchewan; and Regina and Saskatoon, Saskatchewan.

Between Calgary and Vancouver the traveler who wanted to experience something different could enjoy a sleeper operating via Lethbridge, Alberta, and the Crowsnest Pass route, on trains 542/11 and 12/537. Train 11

Photographer Jim Shaughnessy's notes for this January 1955 photo read, "A -10° Fahrenheit breeze from the west blows steam around F9A 1416 as it waits to depart CPR's Montreal Windsor Station for Toronto." To the left is the dome of St. James Cathedral, renamed Mary Queen of the World Cathedral in 1955. At right is CPR's headquarters tower, part of Windsor Station. *Jim Shaughnessy*

(the *Kootenay Express*) covered the 962 miles (1,548 kilometers) between Medicine Hat, Alberta, and Vancouver, in approximately 41 hours, for an average speed of 23 mph (37 kmh). Its eastbound counterpart, Train 12 (the *Kettle Valley Express*) consumed just over 48 hours for the trip, with the longer time attributable to a layover of six hours at Nelson, British Columbia. These trains carried sleepers between Vancouver and both Penticton, British Columbia, and Lethbridge, as well as the Vancouver–Calgary sleeper. A café parlor car also operated between Penticton and Calgary.

Aside from these first-class services, CPR's November 1944 timetable showed coach-only trains on thousands of miles of trackage, both main and branch line. In addition, the timetable provided information about Canadian Pacific hotels and lodges; "express motor vehicle" routes in British Columbia; British Columbia coast steamship services; Canadian Pacific Air Lines schedules; and both transatlantic and transpacific steamship services. It was hard to refute CPR's claim to being the "World's Greatest Travel System."

Postwar Changes

Life changed for the railroads after World War II. The war effort had given a boost to the young airline industry, promoting technological improvements that were adapted in commercial aircraft and giving many Canadians their first taste of air travel (even if it was in an uncomfortable military transport plane). Automobile ownership increased and the trend toward suburban living made rail travel less practical.

CPR was not willing to concede the passenger travel market to other modes without a fight. It staked its claim to a share of that market on April 24, 1955, with the launching of the streamlined *Canadian*.

CPR's Web site (www.cpr.ca) describes the train as follows: "Two dome cars, a handsome dining car with excellent food, and a variety of sleeping arrangements: roomettes, double bedrooms, drawing rooms, berths and more. . . . The last car of each train . . . had a rounded-end observation lounge, a beverage room with the dome level above it, and first class sleeping space made up of a large drawing room and two bedrooms." The 173 cars, which had stainless-steel exteriors and were built by the Budd Company of Philadelphia, represented an investment of $40 million.

An advertisement by the Budd Company of Philadelphia, builder of the equipment for *The Canadian*, which made its debut in 1955. *Author collection*

When CPR launched *The Canadian* in 1955 there was enough equipment available to put some stainless-steel cars, including dome observations, on the now-secondary *Dominion*. Here, one of the Park-series cars prepares to depart Montreal on *The Dominion*, train No. 7. *Jim Shaughnessy*

The new train operated on a tighter schedule than any of its predecessors: 71 hours and 10 minutes from Montreal to Vancouver, and 50 minutes less eastbound. "Crump was hopeful," writes Lamb, "that with new equipment of the highest standard the transcontinental service could be both a prestige operation and a paying proposition for many years to come." According to those who knew him, Norris Crump would later consider his support for the new service to be one of the biggest blunders of his career, since it prolonged the railway's participation in a money-losing business.

But in the summer of 1955, the optimism of the time was reflected in the robust schedules of the railway's transcontinental service, which featured five distinct schedules west of Moose Jaw. Aside from *The Canadian*, they included *The Dominion*, the CPR-Soo *Mountaineer*, and two unnamed transcontinental trains in each direction.

Despite CPR's heavy investment in passenger equipment in the mid-1950s, financial losses mounted during the 1960s. Part of the reason can be seen in the company's declining passenger volumes:

9,529,000 in 1954; 7,059,000 in 1960; and 5,306,000 in 1970.

By 1966, all transcontinental trains except *The Canadian* had been discontinued (although *The Dominion* was briefly revived in 1967 in connection with Expo 67 in Montreal), and many other passenger trains had come to their end as well. In 1970, CPR announced that it wished to discontinue transcontinental passenger service completely. Predictably, the traveling public's reaction was negative, but even the Canadian Transportation Commission acknowledged that CPR was losing upwards of $15 million per year on the service.

This occurred at a time when the U.S. government's answer to money-losing rail passenger services, Amtrak, was in its formative stages. Canada would follow suit with its equiv-

It's July 1968, and *The Canadian*, CPR Train 1, sails west at track speed through Alfred, Ontario, en route to Ottawa on the M&O Subdivision, on the first leg of its transcontinental voyage from Montreal to Vancouver. *Bill Linley*

In early April 1970, a snow squall greets the passengers on westbound Train 1, *The Canadian*, at Medicine Hat, Alberta. On the right, Budd Rail Diesel Car 9022 waits to depart on Train 307 to Lethbridge, Alberta. The RDC, or "Dayliner" on CPR, was found in services throughout Canada, from Vancouver Island in the West to Nova Scotia in the East. *Steve Patterson*

CPR Dayliner 9058, operating as Dominion Atlantic Train 2 from Yarmouth to Halifax, crosses the Bear River in May 1975. *Stan Smaill*

In 1979, VIA Rail Canada took over operation of the Montreal–Saint John *Atlantic Limited* from CPR. Here, a holiday-lengthened Train 12, led by a former CN FPA-4, and carrying green flags to indicate a following section, makes a nocturnal stop for its crew change at Brownville Junction, Maine. *George Pitarys*

alent several years later. In the meantime, CPR continued to operate *The Canadian*, the Montreal–Saint John *Atlantic Limited* (which used equipment identical to that of *The Canadian*), and several secondary services, albeit with government subsidies helping to stem the red ink.

CN, at the time still a government-owned corporation with a more extensive (and therefore more draining) investment in passenger service than CPR, took the lead in extricating itself from the passenger service through the formation of a new entity, to be known as VIA. The change was at first more a matter of

The date is Sunday, July 25, 1965. According to photographer Bill Linley, "A gaggle of RDCs was a regular feature of quiet Sunday afternoons in the Ottawa Coach Yard adjacent to the Rideau Canal. These five cars will be filled to capacity by the time they arrive in Montreal from Ottawa this evening, after operating as Lachute Subdivision Train 134." In the background at left is the Château Laurier hotel, built by Grand Trunk Railway. *Bill Linley*

marketing and brand identity than a real solution to the passenger problem, but it soon evolved into a joint effort between both railways. In the fall of 1976, a VIA timetable was distributed listing both companies' passenger services.

With the model of government involvement in the passenger business already well established in the United States, Canada soon followed suit with the 1978 formation of a crown corporation, VIA Rail Canada. It took over operation and financial responsibility for the country's intercity passenger trains.

The Canadian lived on as the name of VIA Rail's transcontinental train, even though it operated over CN trackage. Its splendid stainless-steel Budd equipment was still operating in the twenty-first century, more than 50 years after it was delivered, with a new generation of passengers enjoying the view from its *Park* series observation dome cars.

In August 1969, Budd-built Rail Diesel Car 9111 is ready to depart Megantic, Quebec, en route to Montreal as Train 201. *Bill Linley*

In the mid-1980s, CPR's U.S. affiliate, Soo Line Railroad, negotiated an agreement with CSX that allowed Soo trains to operate via CSX between Chicago and Detroit. This eliminated a circuitous Soo Line–CPR routing via Sault Ste. Marie, Michigan, and Sudbury, Ontario. The main beneficiary of the shorter route was container traffic, as shown on this westbound train at Newtonville, Ontario, in October 1986, en route to Chicago via Windsor and Detroit. In 2005, several of CPR's Chicago–Detroit trains were shifted to a Norfolk Southern routing. The blue containers belong to Cast North America, which was a longtime CPR customer and a CP Ships competitor in the North Atlantic. In 1995, Canadian Pacific purchased Cast and merged it into CP Ships. *Eric Blasko*

CHAPTER SIX

CANADIAN PACIFIC BULKS UP, THEN SLIMS DOWN: *1972–1996*

The company that Norris "Buck" Crump left to his successors in 1972 was far more diverse than it had been when he moved into the president's office 17 years earlier. The railway generated just over 50 percent more in earnings in 1972 than it had in 1955, but the company as a whole was producing more than twice as much net income. The difference? Oil and gas, timberlands, real estate, and other non-rail operations were a more important part of the company in 1972, and were, for the most part, very profitable ventures.

One-of-a-kind RSD17 CP 8921 was built by MLW as a demonstrator in 1957 and saw service on Pacific Great Eastern and Canadian National before it was acquired by CPR in 1959. It spent much of its CPR career based at CPR's Toronto Yard in Agincourt, Ontario, and was known locally as the "Empress of Agincourt." In October 1993, it is on the head end of Montreal–Windsor automotive Train 919, crossing the Mud Lake Bridge west of Perth, Ontario, on the Belleville Subdivision.
John Leopard

But CP Limited was not at the end of its diversification phase; it was actually at the start of it. Over the next several years, the company added a diverse array of companies to the CP Investments portfolio, including Algoma Steel (1974), Great Lakes Forest Products (1974), Baker Commodities (1976), Syracuse China (1978), Maple Leaf Mills (1980), and Canadian International Paper (1981).

Much of this acquisition activity was accomplished through the efforts of Crump's successor (first as president of the company from 1966 to 1972, and then as chairman from 1972 to 1981), Ian D. Sinclair. The diversification of Canadian Pacific had started almost 90 years before, under George Stephen's leadership, when he and William Van Horne set up enterprises connected to the railway—steamships, hotels, communications—and continued as the company made the most of assets it acquired through the operation of the railway. In the 1970s, however, acquisitions were motivated purely by financial goals, not by how well they could produce traffic for the railway.

Sinclair prided himself on being a businessman, not a railwayman. The railway, Sinclair believed, was an inherently cyclical business; it was too dependent, he felt, on commodities like grain, timber, and steel that could be up one year and down the next. His emphasis on diversification was timely—the 1970s were a tough time to make money in the railway business.

But as with many business trends, the cycle soon started going the other way, not just at Canadian Pacific but at other North American railways, which began to adopt a new business mantra: "Stick to your knitting." CP Limited shareholders faced the unwelcome news that not all of their non-rail investments were consistent moneymakers.

In 1981, Sinclair relinquished the positions of chairman and CEO of CP Limited to Fred Burbidge, and the board of directors picked William Stinson to succeed him as president. In 1986, Stinson became CEO and R. W. Campbell succeeded Burbidge as chairman.

David Cruise and Alison Griffiths note that this change "signaled a return to the CP tradition of making the president the real power in the company," as well as a sea change in the company's business portfolio: "In a flurry of activity, matched only by Sinclair's acquisition spree of the seventies, Stinson hacked away at the company. Gone were a host of subsidiaries:

After the CP sold the Dominion Atlantic Railway in Nova Scotia, it transferred the SW1200RS units that had been the mainstay of the DAR for many years to McAdam, New Brunswick. In October 1994 a trio of them is seen in front of McAdam's impressive station. *George Pitarys*

the flight kitchens; Château Insurance; Maple Leaf Mills; Express Airborne (a division of CP Trucks); an office building in London; several assets controlled by AMCA, an equipment-manufacturing firm; and Steep Rock Resources Inc." In 1986, CP Limited's 52.46 percent interest in Cominco was sold to Teck Corporation, and the following year CP Air was sold to Pacific Western Airlines. Syracuse China was sold in 1989.

MLW C424 4222 leads Train 281 past milepost 19 in Maine's very remote Moosehead Subdivision. Only a mile to the west is the site of Maine's worst railway disaster, a head-on collision in December 1919 in which 19 passengers and 4 crewmen lost their lives. This line is today operated by the Montreal, Maine & Atlantic Railway. *George Pitarys*

Maine's largest lake, Moosehead, gave its name to the CPR subdivision between Brownville Junction, Maine, and Megantic, Quebec. Here, it provides a beautiful backdrop from the high rock cut locally known as Bald Bluff, west of Greenville, Maine. In July 1992, a pair of RS18 units snakes Train 281 along the desolate west shore of the lake. *George Pitarys*

However, Stinson was a pragmatist on the subject of diversification, not an ideologue. In 1988, the company sold its 53.8 percent interest in Algoma Steel, but acquired school bus operator and waste management company Laidlaw Transportation Limited. The same year, it bought out CN's interest in CNCP Telecommunications, as well as CN's nine-property hotel chain.

As it entered the 1990s, Canadian Pacific was, by any definition, still a conglomerate, even if it wasn't as diverse as it had been a decade earlier. The company's business portfolio included rail, shipping, and trucking services, petroleum, coal, forest products, hotels, real estate, telecommunications, industrial and construction services, and waste services. Some of these subsidiaries would fall by the wayside in the early 1990s, but CP Limited would remain a diverse enterprise for the next decade.

Grain Transport:
Toward a More Rational System

CPR had agreed in 1897 to reduce its rates on grain from specific prairie origins to Port Arthur and Fort William, in return for a federal subsidy in connection with the line being built through Crows Nest Pass and into the interior of southern British Columbia. Over time, the Crow Rate structure was expanded to apply to Canadian National, as well as CPR; to cover all grain origins, as well as certain types of grain not included in the original agreement; and to include westward shipments of grain to Vancouver. Most

It's minus 11 degrees Fahrenheit as Train 281 races by one of the most dominating features in Quebec's eastern townships, Mount Orford, in February 1993. Mount Orford is 23 miles (37 kilometers) west of Sherbrooke, Quebec, on the line to Montreal. This segment is now part of Montreal, Maine & Atlantic. *George Pitarys*

significantly, in 1925 the Crow Rates were enacted into law and were thereafter considered "statutory rates." There was no escalation mechanism built into them; they remained fixed regardless of inflation.

Although larger cars, longer trains, and other operating efficiencies helped offset increases in wages and other operating expenses, the net effect of more than a half-century of inflation was to eliminate the railways' profit from the transportation of grain and, therefore, their incentive to invest in the grain transportation system. In 1974, a consultant was appointed by the government to analyze the cost of moving grain and determine which parties were bearing that cost. He determined that 38 percent of the cost was being paid by farmers through the rail rates they paid, 24 percent was being borne by the federal government through subsidies, and 38 percent was being absorbed by the railways.

Although a series of investigations in the 1960s and 1970s all reached a similar conclusion—that the Crow rates were too low to support railway investment in the grain net-

Grain is an important contributor to CPR's revenue base. Here, a covered hopper is loaded at Tompkins, Saskatchewan, in October 1989. *Phil Mason*

The Vancouver waterfront has long featured a rich variety of transportation operations. The dining car York is ready to depart as part of the Montreal-bound *Canadian* in September 1971. In the background a CPR switch engine handles freight for some of the waterfront area's many industries. Farther in the background is the *Indian Mail*, a 605-foot (185-meter) cargo liner operated by American Mail Lines. *Photo by Philip Hastings, courtesy of California State Railroad Museum/negative no. 2439CPR*

In this May 1982 view of CPR's waterfront yard in Vancouver, the former CP steamship *Princess Patricia* can be seen on the right. The *Princess Patricia* was launched in 1948 and entered service the following year between Vancouver, Victoria, and Seattle. It later saw service between Vancouver and Alaska before being retired in 1981. *Phil Mason*

Beginning with the advent of unit coal trains in 1970, and continuing with the growth in coal, grain, sulfur, and container traffic, CPR has engaged in one project after another designed to allow it to run more and longer trains west of Calgary. One such project was a grade reduction west of Revelstoke, British Columbia, between mileposts 70 and 80 on the Shuswap Subdivision. This grade, Notch Hill, at 1.8 percent, was the last significant obstacle encountered by westbound tonnage trains destined for Vancouver. In 1978, CPR constructed a new 11-mile (18-kilometer) track between Tappen and Notch Hill, with a 2-mile loop that allowed the ruling grade to be reduced to 1.0 percent. Here, in July 1984, a westbound grain train traverses the loop track. *Phil Mason*

work—only limited measures were taken to address the problem. Primarily, those measures consisted of government subsidies to the railways and government purchase of covered hopper cars for the grain business (by 1981, the federal government had bought 10,000 such cars).

Closely related to the grain rate question was the issue of branch line abandonments, which were difficult for the railways to implement under prevailing regulations. The tide turned following the release of the Hall Commission report in 1977, which recommended that CPR and CN be allowed to abandon 2,165 miles (3,484 kilometers) of prairie branches over a four-year period. This set the stage for eventual abandonment of many light-density lines.

As for rates, relief came for CPR and CN in 1983 with the passage of the Western Grain Transportation Act (WGTA). It provided for a new grain rate structure, effective on January 1, 1984, and subject to annual review. Grain rates would be based on the railways' operating costs, but capped at 10 percent of the world price of grain. Theoretically, at least, the grain business would now be profitable for the railways. Although CPR is never eager to publicize its profit margin on specific lines of business, its words and actions concerning the grain business since 1984 indicate that it does, indeed, view the business as profitable.

Part of the Mount Macdonald project was a 4,032-foot (1,229-meter) viaduct that allowed the eastern approach to be constructed on a 40-degree slope while minimizing environmental impacts. In October 1989, Train 471 comes off the viaduct, which was named after CPR chief engineer John Fox. *Steve Patterson*

An Increasing Focus on the West

By the 1970s, the CPR was increasingly focused on the West. The watershed event was the beginning of unit-train coal movements to Vancouver for export in 1970; other commodities soon became part of that export flow, notably potash and sulfur. With the passage of the Western Grain Transportation Act, unit grain trains moving toward Vancouver also became a welcome sight in the eyes of CPR management.

The growth in western traffic prompted CPR to look at its Calgary–Vancouver main line and ask how it could move more business over the mountainous territory. Largely single-track, it posed several obstacles to be dealt with, three of which were completed between 1977 and 1981:

- The 1.7 percent grade on the Shuswap Subdivision immediately west of Revelstoke to Clanwilliam. A 4.5-mile (7.2-kilometer) westbound track, separate from the original route, was constructed starting in June 1977.
- The 1.8 percent grade over Notch Hill, also on the Shuswap Subdivision. To reduce the grade, an 11-mile (18-kilometer) westbound track was constructed, incorporating a horseshoe-type loop. Construction began in late 1977. Both Shuswap Subdivision projects were completed in December 1979.
- The 1.8 percent grade from Lake Louise to the Continental Divide (known locally as the Great Divide) at Stephen, British

Westbound Train 481, operating as Extra 5912 West, emerges from the Mount Macdonald tunnel at Ross Peak, British Columbia, in October 1989. The tunnel is 9.1 miles (14.6 kilometers) in length and was placed into service on December 12, 1988. It eased the ruling westbound grade from 2.2 percent to 1 percent. The new tunnel passes 298 feet (91 meters) below the 1916 Connaught Tunnel, which remains in service and is used mainly by eastbound trains. *Steve Patterson*

Columbia, on the Laggan Subdivision. A 5.5-mile (8.9-kilometer) westbound track was constructed between September 1978 and May 1981.

At each of these locations, the westbound grade was reduced to approximately 1 percent. The completion of these projects left one major physical barrier to westbound tonnage trains: the long westward climb from Golden to the Connaught Tunnel in Rogers Pass. In 1981, CPR announced it would undertake a grade-reduction project in Rogers Pass by building a new tunnel under Mount Macdonald, at an ele-

vation 298 feet (91 meters) lower than the Connaught Tunnel. It would do so, however, only if a solution could be found to the economic loss that CPR sustained on the movement of export grain. That solution came in the form of the Western Grain Transportation Act.

The same year that the WGTA went into effect, 1984, CPR began work on the Rogers Pass project, CPR's most ambitious engineering project since the completion of the Spiral Tunnels and the Connaught Tunnel before World War I. In December 1988, the first revenue train operated through the new Mount Shaughnessy and Mount Macdonald tunnels.

The increasing volume of western business only served to accentuate the fact that CPR was really two railroads: bulk commodities west of Thunder Bay (formerly Port Arthur and Fort William) and manufactured products east of that point. The contrast was stark enough that CPR began to worry about how, or even whether, it could make money in the East.

A Soo Line SD60 and SD40-2 power eastbound Train 204 at Donehower, Minnesota, in October 1995. This route was once Milwaukee Road's Chicago–Milwaukee–Twin Cities corridor, and at that time was mainly double-track with automatic block signals. Soo Line acquired the assets of the Milwaukee Road in 1985. In the late 1980s, Soo converted the route to single-track operation with centralized traffic control and 2.5-mile (4-kilometer) passing sidings approximately every 10 miles (16 kilometers).
John Leopard

In 1987, CPR divided its rail operations into two business units: one to focus on heavy haul freight and the other to develop intermodal freight systems. "This realignment," the company explained, "allows a more flexible response to market opportunities and competitive pressures resulting from regulatory reforms and changing business patterns in Canada and internationally." The names "heavy haul" and "intermodal" were, in a sense, euphemisms for the western and eastern parts of the CPR network.

Besides bulk business, the other source of growth in the West was international container traffic, largely consisting of imports from Asia destined to North American markets. In the 1980s, double-stack technology changed the economics of this business, but CPR's tunnels had to be modified to handle the higher-dimension loads. In 1993, it completed an 18-month project to enlarge 48 of its tunnels.

As the 1980s drew to a close, CPR became more deeply involved in the United States. The three midwestern roads in which CPR owned stock—Minneapolis, St. Paul & Sault Ste. Marie; Duluth, South Shore & Atlantic; and Wisconsin Central—had merged on January 1, 1961, to form Soo Line Railroad Company. CPR held approximately 56 percent of Soo Line's stock, and the two roads interchanged large volumes of traffic, but they were managed independently of each other. In 1985, Minneapolis-based Soo Line acquired the assets of the bankrupt Milwaukee Road.

In February 1991, units 4101-4302-4200 are on Soo Line's Humboldt transfer on the Mississippi River Bridge at Camden Place, Minneapolis. GP15C 4101 and GP30C 4302 had been recently repowered with Caterpillar diesel prime movers; all of the Caterpillar-powered units were off the roster by 1999. GP9 4200 was a former New York Central unit rebuilt by CPR in Montreal, retaining its EMD engine. Soo Line's candy-apple-red paint scheme was developed in 1989, replacing the railroad's previous livery of red, black, and light grey. *John Leopard*

The next few years were difficult ones for Soo Line as it digested the Milwaukee Road. The company shed much of its legacy trackage, primarily in Wisconsin, and moved its Minneapolis–Chicago traffic to the former Milwaukee Road main line. CPR attempted to sell its interest in Soo Line, but then reversed course and in 1990 acquired full ownership of Soo Line. In 1991, CPR began to eliminate the Soo Line identity, integrating the U.S. operations into its Canadian organization.

CPR took another step toward greater involvement in the U.S. with its 1991 purchase of the Delaware & Hudson Railway. The D&H had once billed itself as "The Bridge Line to New England and Canada"; its routes ran across New York State from west to east, and on a north-south axis from the Canadian border, just south of Montreal, to Albany and, via trackage rights, to the New York metropolitan area (Oak Island, New Jersey), Philadelphia, and all the way to Potomac Yard, Virginia. CPR would spend the next 15 years trying to make D&H profitable.

CPR Cuts Back in the East

In eastern Canada, CPR was ready to either radically remake the rail map or call it quits. Decades of erosion in the volume and profitability of eastern business had taken their toll. In 1988, the company carved out the portion of its network east of Megantic, Quebec, as a separate entity called Canadian Atlantic Railway. Giving the Maine and Maritime operations a separate identity did not, however, change their basic economics.

Early in 1993, the company announced: "Thousands of miles of uneconomic trackage must be shed in Canada. . . . After sustaining losses of $52 million in the last three years, CP Rail System announced it would seek regulatory approval to abandon all operations east of Sherbrooke, Quebec, a total of about 400 miles (645 kilometers) of track. . . . CP Rail System is also involved

in ongoing discussions with CN North America to rationalize railway facilities in Eastern Canada."

The talks with CN would drag on but ultimately lead nowhere. Government opposition to a rail monopoly in eastern Canada killed whatever chance might have existed for the two carriers to combine their systems east of Montreal. Elsewhere, CPR and CN did have more success in sharing facilities, such as between Montreal and North Bay, Ontario, where they agreed to a shared-track arrangement. Over the next decade they would find opportunities throughout Canada and the northeastern United States to cooperate operationally while competing commercially.

Between 1994 and 1996, CPR shed many eastern lines it considered uneconomic. Most were transferred to short-line operators whose more favorable cost structures and more focused local managements gave them an opportunity to compete where CPR had failed. Some of the milestones included:

- In 1994, the former Dominion Atlantic Railway in Nova Scotia began operation as the Windsor & Hantsport Railway.

Train 80, a Farnham, Quebec–Newport, Vermont, turn job, rolls into the small Vermont village of North Troy, 14 miles (22 kilometers) short of its turnaround point, behind RS-18 8775 in February 1981. Like the east–west line across southern Quebec and western Maine, the segment from Farnham to Newport is now operated by Montreal, Maine & Atlantic. *George Pitarys*

Beginning in 1980, and continuing for the rest of the 1980s, CPR rebuilt RS-18s into RS-18us, with emphasis on upgrading the units' wiring, electrical systems, and cabs, as well as cutting down their short hoods for improved visibility. By the end of 1989, 69 of the MLW products had been rebuilt at Angus Shops in Montreal. Three graduates of the program, CP 1800-1842-1804, power the CPR wayfreight from Newport, Vermont, to Farnham, Quebec, as it performs switching at Richford, Vermont, in February 1988. *Jim Shaughnessy*

CPR had a fleet of 44 MLW M-636 locomotives. The units, built in 1969 and 1970, were troublesome, but most of them remained in service until the early 1990s. Here, M-636 4708 leads Train 522 through Bury, Quebec, in April 1981. *Stan Smaill*

Extra 8470 north almost appears to be at sea as it crosses the windswept plains south of St. Pie, Quebec, on the St. Guillaume Subdivision, in February 1976. Mount Yamaska looms in the distance. A large feed mill in Ste. Rosalie is the train's destination. *George Pitarys*

- In 1995, the New Brunswick Southern Railway began operating over former CPR trackage from McAdam to Saint John, New Brunswick.
- In 1996, privately owned Iron Road Railways inaugurated service under the Quebec Southern Railway name on several Quebec lines: Lennoxville–St. Jean; Brookport–Wells River, Vermont; Farnham–Ste. Rosalie Junction; and Farnham–Stanbridge. The same year, short-line RaiLink–Ottawa Valley took over former CPR lines between Cartier and Smiths Falls, Ontario, and between Mattawa and Temiskaming, Quebec.
- In 1997, Huron Central Railway became the operator of the Sault Ste. Marie –Sudbury, Ontario, line. Also in 1997, Quebec Gatineau Railway took over two CPR subdivisions between Quebec City and Hull, Quebec.

Additional short-line conversions followed over the next several years, but by 1998 CPR's operations in eastern Canada had been radically trimmed.

CP 4555, an M-630 produced by MLW in 1970, is southbound on Train 908 at LaSalle, Quebec, in May 1985. Like the M-636, the M-630 had high maintenance costs and a poor reputation for reliability. Nevertheless, CPR kept its fleet of six-axle MLW units in service for more than 20 years, as it was faced with steadily increasing traffic and a shortage of funds to invest in new power. *Stan Smaill*

Eastbound Train 522 passes through Cookshire, Quebec, in February 1982, with a set of three six-axle MLW units for power, led by M-630 4550. *Stan Smaill*

Near Parson, British Columbia, on the Windermere Subdivision, in September 1999, CP 3135 and two other GP38-2 units power the Golden wayfreight. This line is used mainly by coal trains from mines in southeastern British Columbia. *John Leopard*

CHAPTER SEVEN

UNWINDING THIRTY YEARS OF DIVERSIFICATION: *1996–2006*

Early in 1995, Canadian Pacific Limited recorded two executive

changes in the annual report sent to shareholders: "David O'Brien

joined Canadian Pacific Limited as president and chief operating offi-

cer in February 1995 following a highly-successful tenure as chief exec-

utive officer of PanCanadian Petroleum. . . . In March 1995, Rob

Ritchie was appointed chief executive officer of CP Rail System."

A 1996 financial restructuring gave Canadian Pacific Railway a

new legal identity as a wholly owned subsidiary of the parent company,

General Electric AC4400CW 9679 leads eastbound Train 470 at Ernfold, Saskatchewan, in September 1998. Photographer John Leopard notes that, "Nearly 6,000 wood grain elevators stood above the Canadian prairies in the 1930s; now there are fewer than 1,000. Construction of massive concrete grain-handling facilities capable of loading 100-plus car unit trains was responsible for this drop in numbers. For every new facility built, 8 to 15 wooden elevators were demolished." *John Leopard*

rather than as a division. That might seem like a matter of semantics, but it allowed CPR to deal with the capital markets separately from CP Limited. It was also a way of telling CPR management that from this point forward, the railway's survival was up to them. There would be no more cross-subsidies from CPL's more profitable businesses.

William Stinson retired in May 1996 after ten years as chief executive officer of Canadian Pacific. A key decision made during the final months of his tenure was to move the

headquarters of both CP Limited and the railway from Montreal to Calgary.

O'Brien was now chairman, president, and CEO. Over the next five years, he would preside over a dramatic remaking of Canadian Pacific. But first, there was some housekeeping to be done. Prior to O'Brien's arrival, the company had exited the trucking business and shed its remaining interest in Unitel, the successor to CNCP Telecommunications. In late 1996, it sold Marathon Realty. The following year, it sold its 18 percent interest in Laidlaw Inc. Its business portfolio now included CP Rail System, CP Ships, PanCanadian Petroleum (87 percent ownership), Fording Coal, and Canadian Pacific Hotels & Resorts Inc.

O'Brien's moves prompted the investment community to ask, "What is he up to?" In the three decades since Buck Crump and Ian Sinclair led Canadian Pacific down the

CPR Train 268 from Saratoga Springs to Albany, New York, passes the large GE Chemicals plant at Waterford, New York, on the former Delaware & Hudson, in May 1999. *Jim Shaughnessy*

path of diversification, there had been a change in style among large corporations. Conglomerates were no longer in favor. Investment returns from diversified companies had been disappointing and shareholders often blamed their managements for not being focused enough. In addition, conglomerates were not easy to understand, even for financial analysts, who tended to specialize in certain industries. Most of the analysts who followed Canadian Pacific were experts in transportation, so they didn't necessarily know what questions to ask about CPL's petroleum, coal, or hotel businesses.

O'Brien was cagey about his plans. He acknowledged that CPR might be a player in future North American rail mergers. He suggested that CPL might downplay its exposure to the commodity business, which could indicate a possible sale of the Fording Coal unit.

As late as November 2000, he still wasn't showing his hand. In a press briefing, he said, "We're obviously not going to build five global businesses. But we think we can build a couple of global businesses."

Streamlining the Railway

Although CPR's elimination of light-density lines from the network was well underway by the time that the corporate restructuring was announced in 1995, the railway was still not pleased with the performance of its eastern network.

When it announced that it would move its corporate headquarters to Calgary, CPR explained, "Montreal will be home to a new

After absorbing Soo Line in 1990, and purchasing Delaware & Hudson in 1991, CPR changed its identity from CP Rail to CP Rail System. It also began using an international logo on its motive power, showing the flags of both Canada and the United States. Wearing the dual-flag scheme, CP SD40-2 5421 leads Train 271 at Central Bridge, New York, in May 2000. *Pat Yough*

eastern operating unit that will be run as a separate operation with a management team dedicated to achieving a regional railway cost structure. Its mandate will be to restore a money-losing operation to profitability. Key challenges include excess capacity and surplus network infrastructure, uncompetitive labour costs, modal competition from trucking, and the achievement of equitable treatment in fuel and property taxation policies." The eastern unit would be responsible "for transforming the railway's operations between Montreal, Toronto, Chicago and the U.S. northeast into the most efficient provider of transportation services in the region." Translation: for the right price, our eastern lines are for sale.

The next year, the eastern operation was given the name St. Lawrence & Hudson Railway Company Limited. Locomotives appeared in a modified paint scheme with the StL&H initials, and maps began to appear showing StL&H as the operator of the Chicago–Detroit–Toronto–Montreal main line, as well as the route to Buffalo and the entire D&H.

The network simplification plan already underway in the East was expanded to include portions of the former Soo Line. By

the end of 1996, the company said it "had negotiated or was in the process of negotiating the sale, lease, discontinuance or shortlining of approximately 2,700 miles (4,350 kilometers) of line in Quebec, Ontario, Vermont and the U.S. midwest. The agreements cover 1,143 (1,840 kilometers) miles of line between Kansas City and Chicago, and in Iowa and Minnesota; 383 miles (616 kilometers) of branch lines in North Dakota; 240 miles (386 kilometers) in Quebec and Vermont; and 342 miles (550 kilometers) in Ontario between Smiths Falls and Coniston."

It didn't take CPR long to consummate a sale of the most attractive part of this package. In 1997, it sold the ex–Soo Line (originally

CPR was granted access to the New York City and Long Island markets as a condition of the Conrail breakup in 1999. This allowed New York City and Long Island shippers an alternative to CSX, which operates this part of the former Conrail system. In July 2002, CPR Train 505 (operating between Fresh Pond Yard in Queens and the former D&H yard in Saratoga Springs, New York) rolls north along the Harlem River on the Oak Point Link, built for freight trains to bypass the busy Mott Haven Junction, with SD40-2s 5698–5677. The lead unit wears the CPR logo introduced in 1997, which, in the company's words, "returns the beaver to its lofty position atop a shield with maple leaf motif, encircled by a band that incorporates the Canadian Pacific Railway name and the year 1881." *Pat Yough*

Two GP38-2 units, CP 3118 and 3039, power the westbound Assiniboia Tramp on the Wood Mountain Subdivision in September 1997. This Saskatchewan line was built at a time when the Canadian rail system was in expansion mode in order to open up new areas for agriculture. It was built in 1929 and reached as far west as Mankota. The summer of 1998 saw the last train service by CPR. Efforts to revive the 64-mile (103-kilometer) line as a short line failed, and in October 1999, the rail was removed. *John Leopard*

Milwaukee Road) route between Kansas City and Chicago, as well as the ex-Milwaukee "Corn Lines" in northern Iowa and southern Minnesota, for $380 million. The new operator was I&M Rail Link, an affiliate of Montana Rail Link, owned by Montana entrepreneur and construction magnate Dennis Washington. Within a few years, however, Washington's financial empire came under pressure; in 2002 the operation was sold to Iowa, Chicago

& Eastern Railroad, an affiliate of the Dakota, Minnesota & Eastern Railroad.

If CPR's commitment to retaining its Montreal–Toronto–Detroit–Chicago route seemed questionable when that line was thrown into StL&H, the company aimed to reverse that impression in 1997 when it announced that it would "likely retain [the line] as an integral part of its network." It was by no means an ironclad guarantee, but it meant that the "for sale" sign implied by the formation of StL&H now referred largely to the former D&H.

In 1997, CPR made a symbolic return to its roots when it adopted the name "Canadian Pacific Railway" for public use (in lieu of CP Rail System). In 1997, it restored the beaver and shield to its corporate logo.

That same year, CPR began to revitalize its motive power fleet with AC-traction

Following CPR's acquisition of Delaware & Hudson in 1991, and particularly following the breakup of Conrail in 1999, CPR developed a close working relationship with Norfolk Southern, which utilized the former D&H routes to reach New England and eastern Canada. Symbolizing the transition, locomotives of each of the three roads line up at Kenwood Yard in Albany, New York, in June 1998. *Jim Shaughnessy*

locomotives. AC locomotives are widely thought to be better suited for heavy-duty and mountain operations than conventional DC units. In early 1998, CPR reported that in addition to 90 AC locomotives acquired the previous year, it would buy 91 such units in 1998 and another 81 in 1999, for a total of 262. By mid-2005, CPR's ownership of AC locomotives stood at 503.

By the end of 1998, the company had sold or abandoned 3,850 route miles (6,196 kilometers) over a three-year period, or about 70 percent of the 5,500 miles (8,850 kilometers)

identified as "non-core." As CPR shed unprofitable lines and worked to improve the efficiency of its core network, its operating ratio began to fall, reaching 79.2 in 1998, an improvement of more than 10 percentage points since 1994 when the operating ratio had stood at 89.4.

With the route map stabilized and with new assets in place to support more efficient operations, CPR implemented a new operating plan in 1999 aimed at "making the assets sweat," as Rob Ritchie often said. Key elements of the new plan included longer, heavier trains, as long as 9,000 feet (2,740 meters) in some corridors, up from a previous maximum of 7,200 feet (2,190 meters); fewer intermediate handlings at yard and terminals; and reductions in handling times at yards.

By the end of 2000, CPR had shaved another couple of points off its operating ratio

In October 1997, CP SD40-2 5798 leads an eastbound train past a Manitoba Pool elevator and a CPR water tank at Binscarth, Manitoba, on the Bredenbury Subdivision. This segment is part of the secondary main line between Portage la Prairie, Manitoba, and Wetaskiwin, Alberta (between Calgary and Edmonton), via Saskatoon, Saskatchewan. The line was completed in 1908 as a through route to improve CPR's competitive position versus Canadian Northern and Grand Trunk Pacific. *John Leopard*

since 1998 for an average of 76.9 on the year. Its system route mileage stood at 13,959 (22,465 kilometers), down from 18,100 (29,130 kilometers) in 1994. The railway generated 110 billion revenue ton-miles in 2000, up from 102 billion in 1994. And its workforce had shrunk, from 23,600 in 1994 to 17,519 in 2000.

2001: The Spinoff

Although O'Brien had promised for years to "narrow the focus" of the company, and said as recently as January 2001 that the conglomerate discount on CP's share price "cried for action," the company still took many observers by surprise with its announcement on February 13, 2001, that it planned to separate into five independent, publicly traded companies:

- Canadian Pacific Railway;

- CP Ships, by then the seventh-largest container shipping company in the world;
- PanCanadian Petroleum (86 percent owned by CPL), whose primary business was production and marketing of crude oil and natural gas;
- Fording Coal, Canada's largest coal producer; and
- Canadian Pacific Hotels, which controlled the Fairmont chain of luxury hotels, as well as the Delta chain in Canada.

Legally, the first four companies were spun off from the parent, which retained the hotel business and renamed itself Fairmont Hotels & Resorts Inc.

The spinoff was scheduled for October 1, 2001. Although turbulence in the financial markets following the terrorist attacks of

A westbound freight, led by CP 5773, traverses the steep grades encountered in the valley of the Assiniboine River near Harrowby, Manitoba, on CPR's Bredenbury Subdivision in September 1996. Photographer John Leopard observes, "the Canadian prairies are far from flat: many valleys, lakes, and rivers are remnants of the glacial period that shaped the region's geography." *John Leopard*

September 11 caused some to speculate that the spinoff might be deferred, it was not. Shareholders in CP Limited received shares in the five new operating companies, each of which was now free to chart its own course for the future.

Once Again, a Railway

The early years following CPR's rebirth as a pure rail company were full of challenges. Financially, it started life with a relatively heavy debt load, a parting gift from CP Limited, which had sought to spread its own debt among the operating companies in a way that was "appropriate" for their industries. Early on, there was optimism that the company's debt could be paid down as additional operating efficiencies helped improve its free cash flow, but that optimism didn't take into account the head-

winds that the company would face between 2001 and 2005.

First, there was drought. In 2002, the first full year of its operation as in independent company, CPR was faced with a grain crop that CEO Rob Ritchie described as "one of the smallest ever to come off the Canadian prairies." To compound the revenue shortfall, coal traffic was down, thanks to the ever-shifting dynamics of the world coal market.

Then there was the strong Canadian dollar, which did this Canadian company no

The Crowsnest Pass line west of Lethbridge, Alberta, had steep grades and many curves. In 1904, surveys began on a new line that, it was found, could be constructed with a ruling grade of 0.4 percent and eliminate 37 curves. The main obstruction was the Belly (later Oldman) River, which CPR bridged with a mile-long, 300-foot-high (91-meter) bridge. The bridge was completed in June 1909 and opened to traffic four months later. This is a loaded grain train en route to the Union Pacific interchange at Kingsgate in September 1998. *John Leopard*

favors. As U.S. revenues were translated into Canadian currency, the fluctuation in exchange rates meant lower revenues for CPR.

Third among the challenges of this period was the rise in the price of diesel fuel. In 2003, CPR spent $393 million on fuel. The next year, fuel expenses increased to $440 million. Further increases were to come: in the second quarter of 2005, the company was paying 47 percent more per gallon of diesel fuel than it had a year earlier. Fortunately for

its bottom line, CPR (like most other North American railroads) was able to pass a substantial percentage of the cost increase to its customers.

If there were headwinds, there were also factors that worked in favor of CPR, primarily the strength of its overall business. In 2001, the company generated 211 billion gross ton-miles of freight. By 2004, that figure had grown to 236 billion. Its employees worked hard to handle this growing business more efficiently. Average tons per train increased from 5,533 in 2001 to 5,719 in 2004. Revenue per employee increased from $206,000 in 2001 to $232,000 in 2004.

As it entered the fifth year of independence, CPR kept its focus on the future. Recognizing that its western business would continue to grow, in early 2005 it announced a $160 million capital investment program in

CP SD90MAC/43 units 9127 and 9120 are at the head end of westbound Train 493 (a Toronto–Vancouver double-stack) at Kicking Horse Pass on the Laggan Subdivision in September 1999. Photographer John Leopard notes that, "this photo was taken on the 'new' second main line built on the eastern slope of Kicking Horse Pass. The new track is 5.5 miles (8.9 kilometers) long, was built between Lake Louise and Stephen (on the Continental Divide) at a cost of $14 million, and was completed in May 1981. This track became the westward main track with a ruling grade of 1.0 percent, bypassing the original main's gradient of up to 1.8 percent. The original line became the eastward track." *John Leopard*

At 9,138 feet (2,785 meters) Crowsnest Mountain towers above this westbound train as it skirts the shore of Crowsnest Lake west of Coleman, Alberta, in September 1999. *John Leopard*

western Canada, including 22 projects to extend sidings and install sections of double-track between Vancouver, Calgary, and Moose Jaw. The improvements, CPR said, would give it 12 percent more line capacity between Calgary and Vancouver, which would be used to accommodate increases in intermodal, coal, potash, and other bulk commodity traffic.

CPR's Place on the North American Rail Map

Looking ahead, there is every reason to believe that CPR can continue as a self-sustaining, independent company, able to continue financing the improvements it will need to handle future traffic growth.

The only uncertainty hanging over the company involves factors outside its control, specifically, the structure of the North American rail-freight industry. From time to time,

talk surfaces about future mergers among the six largest railways (four U.S. and two Canadian). Unlike any of the other six, CPR has not participated in a major merger or consolidation in recent history; today it is the smallest of the "big six." With an east–west orientation in an increasingly north-south economy, can CP determine its own fate or will its limited geographic reach in the United States make it an acquiree, rather than an acquirer?

CPR's management and employees would, no doubt, vote to maintain the company's legacy as the railway that created Canada. At the 125th anniversary of its incorporation, CPR is a strong, independent, and growing company. That fact is a testament to the hard work of its people, who deserve to be as proud of their accomplishments as earlier generations—those who built, expanded, and strengthened the company—were of theirs.

SOURCES

Books

Berton, Pierre. *The Impossible Railway: The Building of the Canadian Pacific.* New York: Alfred A. Knopf, 1972.

——.*The Last Spike: The Great Railway, 1881–1885.* Toronto: McClelland and Stewart, 1971.

——.*The National Dream: The Great Railway, 1871–1881.* Toronto: McClelland and Stewart, 1970.

Buck, George. *From Summit to Sea: An Illustrated History of Railroads in British Columbia and Alberta.* Calgary: Fifth House Ltd., 1997.

Burrows, Roger G. *Railway Mileposts: British Columbia, Volume I: The CPR Mainline Route From the Rockies to the Pacific Including the Okanagan Route and CN's Canyon Route.* North Vancouver, B.C.: Railway Milepost Books, 1981.

——.*Railway Mileposts: British Columbia, Volume II: The Southern Routes from the Crowsnest to the Coquihalla.* North Vancouver, B.C.: Railway Milepost Books, 1984.

Cruise, David, and Alison Griffiths. *Lords of the Line: The Men Who Built the CPR.* Markham, Ont.: Viking, 1988.

Dean, Murray W., and David B. Hanna. *Canadian Pacific Diesel Locomotives.* Toronto: Railfare Enterprises Limited, 1981.

Dubin, Arthur D. *More Classic Trains.* Milwaukee, Wis.: Kalmbach Publishing Co., 1974.

Garden, J. F. *The Crow and the Kettle: The CPR in Southern British Columbia and Alberta 1950–1989.* Cowley, Alta.: Footprint Publishing Co. Ltd., 2004.

——.*Nicholas Morant's Canadian Pacific.* Revelstoke, B.C.: Footprint Publishing, 1991.

The Historical Guide to North American Railroads. Waukesha, Wis.: Kalmbach Books, 2000.

Hyde, Frederick W. *Soo Line 1993 Review.* Denver: Hyrail Productions, 1993.

Lamb, W. Kaye. *History of the Canadian Pacific Railway.* New York: MacMillan Publishing, 1977.

Lavallée, Omer. *Canadian Pacific Steam Locomotives.* Toronto: Railfare Enterprises Limited, 1985.

——.*Van Horne's Road: An Illustrated Account of the Construction and First Years of Operation of the Canadian Pacific Transcontinental Railway.* Montreal: Railfare Enterprises Limited, 1974.

Linley, Bill. *Canadian Pacific in Color, Vol. 1: Eastern Lines.* Scotch Plains, N.J.: Morning Sun Books, 2003.

McDonnell, Greg. *Canadian Pacific: Stand Fast, Craigellachie!* Erin, Ont.: Boston Mills Press, 2003.

——.*The History of Canadian Railroads.* London: New Burlington Books, 1985.

McDougall, J. Lorne. *Canadian Pacific: A Brief History.* Montreal: McGill University Press, 1968.

McKee, Bill, and Georgeen Klassen. *Trail of Iron: The CPR and the Birth of the West.* Vancouver: Douglas & McIntyre Ltd., 1983.

Pole, Graeme. *The Spiral Tunnels and the Big Hill: A Canadian Railway Adventure.* Canmore, Alta.: Altitude Publishing Canada Ltd., 1995.

Sanford, Barrie. *The Pictorial History of Railroading in British Columbia.* Vancouver: Whitecap Books Ltd., 1981.

Turner, Robert D. *Sternwheelers and Steam Tugs: An Illustrated History of the Canadian Pacific Railway's British Columbia Lake and River Service.* Victoria, B.C.: Sono Nis Press, 1998.

——.*Vancouver Island Railroads.* San Marino, Calif.: Golden West Books, 1973.

——.*West of the Great Divide: An Illustrated History of the Canadian Pacific Railway in British Columbia 1880–1986.* Winlaw, B.C.: Sono Nis Press, 2003.

Zuters, Gary. *CP Rail 1993 Review.* Ferndale, Wash.: Hyrail Productions, 1994.

Other Publications

Lavallée, Omer, and Robert R. Brown. "Locomotives of the Canadian Pacific Railway Company." *Railroad History,* Issue 83, July 1981.

Moody's Investors Service, *Manual of Investments: Railroad Securities,* various editions.

——.*Transportation Manual,* various editions.

The Official Guide of the Railways, various issues. New York: National Railway Publication Company.

Canadian Pacific Railway and Canadian Pacific Limited Materials

Annual reports, various years.

Canadian Pacific Facts and Figures. Montreal: Canadian Pacific Foundation Library, 1946.

Investor fact books, 2000–2004.

Maps and travel brochures.

Public and employee timetables.

Other Resources

Canadian Pacific Line (steamships) Web site, http://www.theshipslist.com/ships/lines/cp.html

Canadian Pacific Railway Web site, http://www.cpr.ca

Canadian Pacific Railway Archives Web site, http://www.cprheritage.com

Canadian Railway Hall of Fame Web site, http://railfame.ca

Ehrlich, Leslie, and Bob Russell, "Employment Security and Job Loss: Lessons from Canada's National Railways, 1956–1995," *Labour/Le Travail,* Spring 2003, http://www.historycooperative.org/journals/llt/51/ehrlich.html

Old Time Trains Web site (R. L. Kennedy), http://www.trainweb.org/oldtimetrains

Rothstein, Tracey, "A History of Western Canadian Grain Rates 1897–1984," *Manitoba History,* Number 18, Autumn 1989, http://www.mhs.mb.ca/docs/mb_history/18/grainrates.shtml

CANADIAN NATIONAL
RAILWAY

TOM MURRAY

MBI

ACKNOWLEDGMENTS

In undertaking this book, my first task was to become familiar with what had already been written about Canadian National. While there are many books and publications listed as sources at the end of this book, the works of two authors in particular have been invaluable throughout this process: Donald MacKay and G. R. Stevens. Their books are required reading for anyone wanting to learn more about Canadian National and its predecessor companies.

This book would not have been possible without the assistance of more than a dozen people. As this is a volume in MBI's Railroad Color History series, it was clear from the start that photography would be a major element in this project. The people who have allowed their photographs to appear here have been instrumental in bringing this book into existence, and I am grateful to each of them: George Carpenter, Steve Glischinski, Phil Mason, Steve Patterson, George Pitarys, Jim Shaughnessy, Stan Smaill, Brian Solomon, and Richard Jay Solomon. I only regret that I was not able to use more of the slides and prints that they shared with me. A book twice this size would have been possible without compromising the overall caliber of the photos.

In addition to contemporary pictures, archival material was a key part of telling the Canadian National story. For their willingness to help me explore their collections, and for their interest in the success of this project, I offer thanks to Antony Pacey of the Canada Science and Technology Museum, Josée Vallerand of the Canadian Railroad Historical Association, and the staff of the National Archives of Canada and the National Library of Canada.

To help keep this story accurate, and to make sure that it focused on the significant rather than the trivial, I enlisted the help of several railway veterans, each of whom read all or part of the text in draft form. They were all generous with their time and constructive in their comments. I express my deep appreciation to Charles F. Armstrong, Bill Cole, George Fowler, Frederic H. Howard, Wes Kelley, Jack McBain, and Lorne Perry. Any errors that may remain are my responsibility, not theirs.

These railway staff people provided assistance when it was needed: Mark Hallman, Graham Dallas, Nadeem Velani, and Izabelle Racine of CN, and Alan Dever of BC Rail. However, this project was not sponsored or overseen by CN.

Finally, but in no way least, I thank my wife, Marcia, who has been unfailingly supportive and encouraging throughout the development of this book.

For several decades, CN provided medical, dental, and educational services in railway towns located far from any highways. Teacher Fred Sloman worked on CN's School on Wheels car from 1926 to 1965, bringing education to children and adults in remote communities of northern Ontario. He is shown in the school car at Kukatush, Ontario, on the Capreol-Foleyet line in 1943. It would spend a five-day "term" there every six weeks. *Canada Science and Technology Museum, CSTM/CN collection neg. no. X17308*

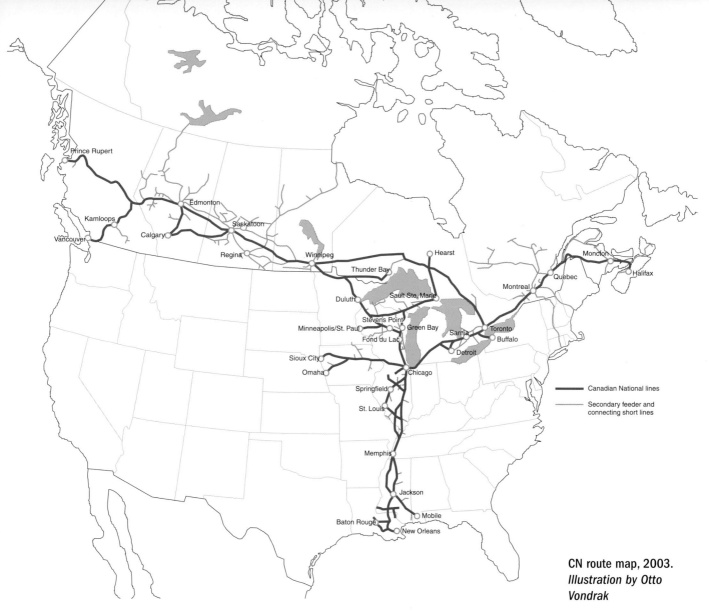

CN route map, 2003.
*Illustration by Otto
Vondrak*

INTRODUCTION

Canadian National Railway has mirrored the history of Canada for more than eight decades. The company's roots lie in the turmoil and disillusionment that accompanied World War I. In the 1920s and 1930s CN's fortunes reflected the peaks and valleys of the Canadian economy. During World War II CN, like Canadians themselves, met challenges that could not have been predicted even a few years earlier. In the decades after the war, Canada became a supplier of resources to the world—lumber, grain, sulfur, potash, petroleum products—and CN carried them. In the 1990s, when the North American economy became more integrated, CN followed suit, as it expanded its U.S. presence and took on a north-south orientation.

Because CN was, for more than 70 years, a government-owned railroad, it had a social role in the life of the country as well as an economic one. This role was exemplified by narrow-gauge freight and passenger service across Newfoundland; by mixed trains on light-density branch-lines; and by passenger cars used for schooling and medical services in remote parts of Ontario and Quebec.

To an observer from the United States, like me, who first became acquainted with CN in the early 1970s, the company was an appealing mix of the traditional and the innovative. In the traditional category were the sleeping cars with open sections, which had virtually disappeared from the United States by the time I rode one from Montreal to Jasper, Alberta; boxcab electrics hauling commuter trains into Central Station, Montreal; and white flags on extra trains. In the innovative category were the Turbo train between Montreal and Toronto, in which the passenger lucky enough to get a seat in the forward dome could look over the engineer's shoulder; the advanced "comfort cab" design that CN pioneered, which first appeared on production diesels in 1973; and a corporate logo that looks as modern today as it did when introduced in 1961.

The purpose of this book is to give an overview of CN's history, beginning with its formation in the second decade of the twentieth century, and to show how that history affected and was influenced by the regions it served. Given the company's geographic reach and the variety of freight, passenger, and non-rail operations conducted under the CN banner, a much larger volume would be required to do justice to the company, its employees and managers, and the communities it has served. Nevertheless, my hope for this book is that it will take the reader to places both familiar and not so familiar, and show how the events of years past have influenced today's CN.

A note on nomenclature: The plural "Canadian National Railways" was used on equipment and company publications for many years, and the company was commonly referred to as "CNR" by both employees and the general public. By the 1970s, the simpler "Canadian National" (*Canadien National* in French) began to appear, reflecting two corporate trends: diversification and bilingualism. Today the company is formally known as Canadian National Railway Company. It uses "CN" as its corporate identity, which is how we will refer to the company in this book.

In the 1970s CN was a blend of old and new. CN 6717, built for the Montreal Harbour Commission Terminal Railway in 1924, epitomizes that blend: rivets and spoked wheels, together with an Automatic Car Identification label and the modernistic CN logo. The boxcab electric is at EJ Tower, north of Montreal, en route to Central Station with a commuter train in September 1971.
Tom Murray

CN crews chat before departing from Brockville, Ontario, in August 1958.
The locomotive, CN 6258, is a 4-8-4 Northern built by Montreal Locomotive
Works in 1944. *Jim Shaughnessy*

Canadian Northern was 30 years behind Canadian Pacific in building through the Thompson and Fraser River canyons of British Columbia. The Thompson River flows into the Fraser at Lytton, British Columbia. Here, westbound train No. 201 crosses the Fraser at Cisco, British Columbia, 9 miles (15 kilometers) south of Lytton in May 1985. The lead locomotive is above the CP mainline. *Phil Mason*

CHAPTER ONE

THE BIRTH OF CANADIAN NATIONAL

The formation of Canadian National did not take place in a single day, or even in a single year. In fact, it consumed almost eight years, beginning in May 1915, when the Canadian Government Railways, which had been operating the Intercolonial and Prince Edward Island Railways for more than four decades, took on the additional task of running the National Transcontinental Railway.

A Grand Trunk train prepares to depart from Toronto in April 1915. *John Boyd/National Archives of Canada/ PA-061436*

In 1917 the government added one more railway, the Canadian Northern, to its portfolio, and in December 1918, the name Canadian National Railways was first authorized for use by the government railway system. The following March, Canada's minister of railways was appointed receiver of the Grand Trunk Pacific, which also became part of the government's rail network.

Three months later, in June 1919, Canadian National Railway Company was incorporated as a holding company for its various operating companies, which were known collectively as Canadian National Railways. This is often used as CN's official date of birth. However, its formative period did not end until January 1923, when the holding company acquired control of the Grand Trunk Railway.

The immediate reason that Canadian National came into existence was that the plans of early–twentieth century railroad builders and politicians had failed; their visions of prosperity and growth had been thwarted by war, recession, and their own extravagance. However, the roots of Canadian National and the reason for its existence go back much earlier. In the nineteenth century building a railway was a source of civic pride and, for many builders, a profitable enterprise. The Canadian government believed that it had a responsibility to unite the country, to foster economic development, and to promote immigration from overseas as well as westward migration by its citizens. For these reasons it generously subsidized the construction of railways.

By 1900, however, Canada already had too much trackage. In some cases, a railroad, once built, would justify its existence by generating revenues greater than its expenses. In other cases, an economic return wasn't even part of the business plan.

To understand how CN came into being, it is important to look at its predecessors, each of which made a distinct contribution to the network of rail lines that, by 1923, was being operated under the Canadian National banner.

CN's Predecessors
Intercolonial Railway
Canada's first venture into public ownership and operation of a railway began with Confederation in 1867, when Ontario, Quebec, New Brunswick, and Nova Scotia joined to form the Dominion of Canada.

One of the conditions set by the two maritime provinces was that the government would agree to build and operate a railway from a connection with Grand Trunk Railway at Rivière-du-Loup, Quebec, to Truro, Nova Scotia, where it would connect with a pre-existing rail line to Halifax. Collectively, these lines were designated the Intercolonial Railway.

After Prince Edward Island became part of Canada in 1873, the Intercolonial was

Intercolonial Railway and Prince Edward Island Railway timetable, October 1909. *Author collection*

This view depicts an arch culvert under construction on the Intercolonial Railway at Black River, Nova Scotia, in August 1871. *National Archives of Canada/PA-021995*

Intercolonial Railway locomotive 249 at Rivière-du-Loup, Quebec, in 1906. *National Archives of Canada/PA-143283*

given the job of completing the island's railway, which had been started in 1871. Both the Rivière-du-Loup–Truro mainline and the Prince Edward Island Railway were completed in 1875.

The Intercolonial, like the Grand Trunk, had originally been built to a gauge of 5 feet, 6 inches. Proponents of the wide gauge believed that it helped keep shippers loyal to one railway, but the benefits of interchangeable equipment soon won the day; following completion in 1875, the Intercolonial converted to standard gauge, 4 feet, 8½ inches. The following year, through service between Halifax and Quebec began, and in 1879 the Intercolonial purchased the Grand Trunk line from Rivière-du-Loup to Lévis, across the St. Lawrence River from Quebec City. Ten years later, the Intercolonial acquired running rights from Lévis to Montreal.

The Intercolonial was not conceived or built as a for-profit venture, and it showed, both in the route it followed and in the company's

financial results. Theoretically, the route was selected on the basis of providing service to important centers of commerce; in reality, it was selected according to which local politician had the most pull. Between Moncton, New Brunswick, and Quebec City, the Intercolonial's route went farther north than it needed to, away from the border with Maine, in part because politicians in Canada and Great Britain feared that the United States might try to push the international border northward into New Brunswick. But the Intercolonial did what its founders intended it to do: It promoted the development of the region it served and helped to unify the maritime provinces with the rest of Canada.

Canadian Northern Railway

By the 1890s Canadian Pacific's (CP) monopoly in the prairie provinces was doing what monopolies often do—inspiring competitors. Combined with the government's desire to promote the settlement of the northern prairies, CP's monopoly gave William Mackenzie and Donald Mann the incentive to build the Canadian Northern Railway (CNoR).

The Mackenzie and Mann partnership started in 1895 with the construction of the Winnipeg Great Northern Railway, a 123-mile (197-kilometer) line between Gladstone and Winnipegosis, Manitoba. By 1899 the CNoR had been chartered, and it was building

at Mair station

No. 9.

Foote

Shovels were (and are) an indispensable part of winter railroading on the prairies, as shown in this undated photo of CNoR 2036 at Mair, Saskatchewan. The Canadian Northern-style numberplate shown on this locomotive was later adopted by Canadian National. *National Archives of Canada/ C-034313*

toward Prince Albert and Saskatoon, in the area of the Northwest Territories that would become the province of Saskatchewan in 1905. The company also had in its employ David Blythe Hanna, who 20 years later would become the first president of Canadian National.

Once they had a foothold in the prairies, the next step for Mackenzie and Mann was to expand toward Lake Superior. By 1902 they had built a line southeast from Winnipeg. After crossing into Minnesota and running along the southern shore of Lake of the Woods, it entered Ontario at Rainy River and terminated at Port Arthur (which many years later would combine with the adjacent Fort William to form Thunder Bay).

Determined to break the CP's dominance in Manitoba, in the early 1900s Mackenzie and Mann leased 313 miles (504 kilometers) of track that had been built by

Northern Pacific between the U.S. border, Winnipeg, and Brandon. According to CN historian G. R. Stevens, they also built 18 branchlines totaling 614 miles (989 kilometers) in the province, making CNoR the largest railway in Manitoba.

Mackenzie and Mann continued to push west, adding trackage to their system and stimulating development on the prairies. The CNoR mainline reached Edmonton, Alberta, in 1905. By 1906, Stevens notes, 132 prairie towns and villages had been built along new Canadian Northern lines. That year CNoR bought a CP-operated line between Regina and Prince Albert, Saskatchewan, which "provided an invaluable north-south spine for branchline construction . . . . In its first year it provided its new owners with 6,000,000 bushels of grain for delivery at lakehead."

By this time Mackenzie and Mann had also turned their sights on eastern Canada. In

The former Canadian Northern line between Winnipeg, Manitoba, and Port Arthur, Ontario (today's Thunder Bay), crosses approximately 40 miles (64 kilometers) of northern Minnesota forest. A grain train passes through Roosevelt, Minnesota, en route to Thunder Bay in February 1974. *Tom Murray*

1903 they bought the Great Northern Railway of Canada, a 400-mile (644-kilometer) line in Ontario and Quebec that included a branchline into Montreal from the north. Although it took them several years to acquire the necessary land, they also built a 3.2-mile (5.2-kilometer) tunnel through Mount Royal to the center of the city, which opened in 1918. In 1906 Mackenzie and Mann opened the first segment of the Canadian Northern Ontario Railway, which eventually extended from Toronto to Capreol, with various branches, including one to Sudbury.

Mackenzie and Mann's first venture in the Maritimes (aside from working on the

One of Canadian Northern's goals was to reach downtown Montreal, and in 1913 it began construction on a 3.2-mile (5.2-kilometer) tunnel under Mt. Royal. CNoR 602 (photographed in 1914, four years before the completion of the project) was one of six electric locomotives acquired from Canadian General Electric for this service. *National Archives of Canada/PA-164733*

Canadian Northern got its start as a farmers' railway on the prairies of Manitoba, but by 1916, when this photo of a CNoR club car was taken, it was a transcontinental enterprise. *National Archives of Canada/ C-034305*

construction of Canadian Pacific's line across Maine to Saint John, New Brunswick) was a 60-mile (97-kilometer) coal line on Cape Breton, Nova Scotia, in 1901. CNoR subsequently acquired a 99-mile (159-kilometer) package of short lines (built and unbuilt), and by 1907 it had constructed 246 additional miles (396 kilometers) of connecting trackage, all in Nova Scotia. The CNoR's main subsidiary in Nova Scotia was the Halifax & South Western Railway, which ran from Halifax to Yarmouth.

Mackenzie and Mann became determined to stitch together their eastern and western lines into a transcontinental system, and in 1911 they started construction from Montreal to Port Arthur, a distance of 1,050 miles (1,690 kilometers). Soon after, they began working their way west from Edmonton to Vancouver. The route west of Edmonton to Jasper, Alberta, and Yellowhead Pass duplicated the Grand Trunk Pacific line to Prince Rupert, British Columbia, and for many miles the two routes ran side by side.

Mackenzie and Mann, unlike some of their contemporary rail builders, had generally used economical construction standards, a practice they abandoned on the 250 miles

(402 kilometers) from Kamloops, British Columbia, to tidewater, where Stevens writes they "elected to build to an even higher specification than CP." When the Pacific route was completed in 1915, CNoR was truly a transcontinental railroad.

Mackenzie and Mann, shrewd businessmen though they were, soon found themselves overextended financially. The earning power of their new lines could not support the debt they had taken on. The outbreak of war in Europe dried up the available capital, and in 1917 CNoR was taken over by its largest creditor, the Canadian government.

Grand Trunk Railway

Although the Grand Trunk Railway (GTR) was the last company to become part of CN during the formative years of 1915 to 1923, it was the linchpin of the system, providing both the geographic reach and the density of traffic necessary to make the system economically viable.

GTR came into existence as a company in 1852 through the sponsorship of railway promoter Francis Hincks. Eventually, however,

Grand Trunk Railway/Grand Trunk Pacific timetable, July 1912. *Author collection*

The morning train from Sherbrooke, Quebec, to Montreal roars through Bromptonville, Quebec, behind CN 4-6-2 No. 5288 in February 1957. The temperature is -24 degrees Fahrenheit (-31 degrees Celsius). Bromptonville is on the former GTR line between Montreal and Portland, Maine. *Jim Shaughnessy*

it acquired railways with even earlier beginnings, including Canada's first railway, a 14-mile (23-kilometer) line between St. John and La Prairie, Quebec, 8 miles (13 kilometers) upstream from Montreal, that opened in 1836. The line was later extended 20 additional miles (32 kilometers) to Rouses Point, New York.

Hincks' vision involved connecting Canada with the United States, or more specifically, connecting U.S. cities through Canada. He planned a railroad that would extend from Portland, Maine, to Chicago, via Quebec and Ontario. When completed, the Portland–Chicago route would be 1,150 miles (1,851 kilometers) in length, 659 miles (1,061 kilometers) of it in Canada. Hincks' plan was beneficial to some constituencies in each country. Portland benefited because the Canadian route was shorter than any all-U.S. rail route to the west. Montreal liked the plan, because Portland was the nearest all-weather port. The losers were Nova Scotia and New Brunswick, both of which had all-weather ports of their own.

Clearing the Grand Trunk line at Chaudière, Quebec, 9 miles (15 kilometers) southwest of Lévis, in February 1869. *Alexander Henderson/ National Archives of Canada/PA-149764*

Hincks proved to be a better promoter than businessman, and GTR ran into financial trouble early on. When the dust settled, company control was in the hands of British financiers, and would remain there until CN took control of the company after World War I. For the balance of the nineteenth century, however, the company's management was to be based in London, England.

Despite financial challenges, GTR opened for business in 1856 on a route from Montreal to Sarnia, Ontario, via Toronto, Hamilton, and London. In December 1859 the Victoria Bridge, 1.7 miles (2.8 kilometers) in length, spanning the St. Lawrence River at Montreal, was placed into service, completing the all-rail route to eastern Quebec and Maine.

The company did not reach Chicago until 1879, when its president, Sir Henry Tyler, outmaneuvered William Vanderbilt by purchasing several small railroads in Michigan and Indiana. In combination with trackage purchased earlier in Chicago itself, these gave GTR the western terminus it had long coveted. G. R. Stevens notes that this extension transformed the company's traffic base and finances: "Within four months of entry into Chicago, almost half the Grand Trunk's traffic originated in that city." Initially, rail traffic was ferried between Sarnia and Port Huron, Michigan, but in 1891 the St. Clair Tunnel opened to create an all-rail route to Chicago.

In the meantime GTR's role as a bridge route between U.S. connections was cemented

Grand Trunk completed the double-tracking of its line between Montreal and Toronto in 1892, and it remains one of the busiest rail segments in Canada. This train is passing through Kingston, Ontario, in August 1991. *Phil Mason*

Railway grading as it was practiced circa 1910. This scene is on the route of the National Transcontinental, east of Nipigon Lake, Ontario. *National Archives of Canada/C-025623*

in 1882 with the acquisition of the Great Western Railway, whose mainline ran from Niagara Falls to Windsor, a route it had opened in 1854. The Great Western's line to Sarnia was better than GTR's own line, and would eventually become a key segment in GTR's (and CN's) mainline. GTR became the seventh-largest North American railroad, measured by mileage.

Fueled by the profits from its Chicago traffic, GTR continued to expand. In 1883, it raised its profile in New England by buying a 50 percent interest in the Central Vermont, which helped it win traffic to Boston (via the Boston & Maine) and to New York City (via steamer from New London, Connecticut). GTR acquired full control of Central Vermont in 1898.

GTR also extended its presence north and northwest of Toronto toward Lake Huron and Lake Nipissing, and it completed the double-tracking of its Montreal–Toronto mainline in 1892. By 1893 GTR lines extended throughout southwestern Ontario; north to North Bay; west across Michigan to Grand Rapids, Grand Haven, and Muskegon (including a ferry service to Milwaukee), as well as Chicago; and east to Rivière-du-Loup, Quebec, and Portland Maine.

As well positioned as it was, GTR's power to control its own destiny was constrained by geographic limitations and competitive realities. Canadian Pacific completed its transcontinental mainline in 1885. By then CP was already looking to the industrial heartland of Canada—southern Ontario—for expansion opportunities. Its first acquisition (but not its last) in GTR's backyard was the Credit Valley Railway between Toronto and Woodstock. CP would not make it easy for GTR to move traffic to and from the west—CP wanted 100 percent of the haul.

Grand Trunk had been offered the opportunity to build the transcontinental railway, but had turned it down. As the nineteenth century turned into the twentieth, GTR's management began to reconsider that decision. It wanted to be in the West.

Grand Trunk Pacific Railway and National Transcontinental Railway

The Grand Trunk Pacific (GTP) and the National Transcontinental were separate railways, legally and financially, but they were conceived as a single continuous line of railroad from Moncton, New Brunswick, to Prince Rupert, British Columbia, and their histories are interwoven.

The life span of the two railways consumed only a little more than a decade from start to finish. Their roots are in a 1903 proposal by GTR's president, Charles Melville Hays, for a second transcontinental railway, running from North Bay, Ontario, to a port along the northern coast of British Columbia (ultimately, Prince Rupert). Although the Dominion government favored the proposal in general, GTR's U.S. orientation gave the government pause. It feared that if the railway were built as proposed, Canadian grain would move via Grand Trunk to Portland, Maine, for export, rather than via Canadian ports.

The government's counterproposal, which GTR accepted to its ultimate regret, was to split the project into two pieces. The

company's plan would be followed west of Winnipeg, where, with government financial aid, it would build and operate a 1,743-mile (2,805-kilometer) railway to be known as Grand Trunk Pacific.

East of Winnipeg, a new 2,019-mile (3,251-kilometer) line, the National Transcontinental, was to be built to a connection with the Intercolonial at Moncton. This line would be financed by the federal government and upon completion leased to the Grand Trunk Pacific.

The GTP line to Prince Rupert via Yellowhead Pass, located in the Rocky Mountains between Alberta and British Columbia, was completed on April 9, 1914.

In addition to its mainline and several branches west of Winnipeg, GTP built one line in the East that connected the National Transcontinental mainline at Sioux Lookout, Ontario, with Fort William, giving GTP a route to move grain from the prairies to Lake Superior.

The National Transcontinental traversed northern Ontario and Quebec through areas that were devoid of population and therefore lacking any means of access, other than the railroad itself. Yet the railway's builders insisted on the highest standards. Steel bridges were built, for example, where wooden ones would have been adequate. In combination

Grand Trunk Pacific was a latecomer to the Canadian prairies, but its mainline became part of the CN transcontinental route. This scene is at St. Lazare, Manitoba, 204.5 miles (329.1 kilometers) west of Winnipeg. GTP 67 was a 1908 product of Montreal Locomotive Works. *National Archives of Canada/ C-010723*

G.T.P. Rolling Stock
Prince Rupert B.C.

Grand Trunk Pacific built through British Columbia from both east and west. Crews on the western end began at Prince Rupert, where these locomotives are being offloaded from barges in 1910. *National Archives of Canada/PA-123743*

A Grand Trunk Pacific train departs Prince Rupert, destined to Winnipeg, in 1915. GTP locomotive No. 614 remained in service for CN until 1954, after being renumbered CN 1437. *Horatio Nelson Tapley/National Archives of Canada/PA-011231*

with inflation in the cost of both labor and materials, this led to an ultimate construction cost of $169 million, more than double the estimated cost—all for a railroad whose traffic outlook was dim at best.

When the National Transcontinental was completed in 1915, GTR refused to follow through on its agreement to lease the property, and the government took over the Winnipeg–Moncton line. It later took over GTP's line between Sioux Lookout and Fort William as well, which gave the government railway a continuous route between Lake Superior and Winnipeg.

Even without having to take financial responsibility for the National Transcontinental, by 1915 GTR was caught between the high interest charges from the debt it took on to build the GTP, and the fact that refinancing was impossible because of the war in Europe. GTR attempted to convince the government to take over the GTP, but was turned down. It was the beginning of the end for Grand Trunk.

Above left: The National Transcontinental line between Quebec City and Moncton, New Brunswick, had several high steel bridges, including this one at Cap Rouge, Quebec, photographed in 1916. *National Archives of Canada/PA-110907.* **Above:** A track-layer at work 117 miles (188 kilometers) east of Winnipeg on the National Transcontinental Railway, circa 1906. CN historian G. R. Stevens, discussing the challenges that faced the builders of the NTR, refers to "the great stony extrusions that barricaded the passage between Lake Superior and Hudson Bay." This segment of the NTR is now part of the CN mainline between Winnipeg and eastern Canada. *National Archives of Canada/C-046485*

Nationalization and Consolidation

CN historian Donald MacKay has said that in Canada "governments and railways had been so entangled, and so much tax money had been spent, that nationalization was logical if not inevitable." There were certainly missed opportunities and decisions of colossal shortsightedness that, had they gone the other way, might have postponed or even prevented nationalization.

Suppose, for example, that Mackenzie and Mann had been willing to sell the

In April 2000 CN train No. 308 crosses the Salmon River Bridge in New Denmark, New Brunswick. This is the second-longest railway bridge in Canada, and one of four large trestles the former National Transcontinental route crosses in a 30-mile (48-kilometer) stretch of track east of Grand Falls. *George Pitarys*

Canadian Northern to Grand Trunk. This would have given GTR the western access it wanted while avoiding the building of duplicate trackage in the West. The National Transcontinental was poorly conceived, and its decision to build parallel to the Intercolonial between Quebec and Moncton also represented a costly redundancy. Further, the excesses of optimism that led to the building of these railways collided with the realities of World War I, which diverted resources and capital away from domestic industries and toward the war effort.

As MacKay suggests, the undoing of the privately owned Canadian Northern and Grand Trunk systems was based largely on their dependence on public funds for construction of the western rail lines. When they got into financial trouble, the government

was able to dictate the terms of takeover. In 1917, CNoR became the first private company to become part of the expanding government rail system. The government took over responsibility for the company's debt and, after some negotiation, made a modest settlement with the company's shareholders.

The acquisition of GTR took much longer. Most of its shareholders were British, and after years of hearings, reports, and legal wrangling, they got nothing, prompting a long-lasting mistrust in the United Kingdom of the Canadian government and financial system.

With the absorption of CNoR, the government rail system had more than 14,000 miles (22,500 kilometers) of trackage. Two-thirds of the total was from CNoR, and that company's president, D. B. Hanna, was

appointed to the same position in the new organization. Hanna was determined that CN would operate free of political interference, and for a time he succeeded. However, in 1922 William Lyon Mackenzie King became prime minister. Hanna had been appointed president by the Conservative party, and King was a Liberal. Hanna submitted his resignation. To replace him, King selected Sir Henry Thornton, an American by birth who had been running the Great Eastern Railway in England, and who had been knighted for his service during the war.

By the time Thornton became president of CN in December 1922, the company had been treating GTR as part of the system for more than two years, a relationship that became official in January 1923. The company now had more than 22,000 route miles (35,000 kilometers) and almost 100,000 employees, making it the largest railway in the world. Financially, however, CN was barely covering its operating expenses. Thornton had a big job ahead of him.

Following the retirement of CN 6218, Mountain type 6060, which had been on display at Jasper, Alberta, was restored to service in 1972. Here it crosses the Richelieu River on an excursion in September 1973. *Jim Shaughnessy*

CHAPTER TWO

THE FIRST QUARTER CENTURY:
Surviving Depression and War

By the time Sir Henry Thornton took the helm of Canadian National Railways, the new company was showing signs of a turnaround from the financial distress that followed World War I. That distress was triggered by two factors: postwar inflation in expenses and a drop-off in business. CN's operating ratio (expenses as a percentage of revenues) peaked at 114.5 percent in 1920. Efficient, well-run railways tend to have operating ratios of about 75 percent,

187

The two most recognizable groups of steam locomotives on the CN roster were the five streamlined 6400 series Northerns delivered in 1936 and the 20 Mountains numbered 6060 through 6079 and delivered in 1944. The latter were CN's last new steam locomotives. CN 6079 and 6404 pose at Toronto. *Jim Shaughnessy*

and preferably lower. By 1922 CN's operating ratio was down to 98.7 percent, but this was still far too high.

One key to making CN more efficient was to integrate the lines of its predecessor companies. A notable example was the 30.7-mile (49.4-kilometer) Long Lake cutoff between the former Canadian Northern line at Longlac, Ontario, and the National Transcontinental route at Nakina, opened in September 1924. This permitted trains between Montreal and Toronto in the east and Winnipeg in the west to be operated on a more direct route, bypassing Port Arthur and the CNoR line through northern Minnesota.

CN advertisements trumpeted the company's size and geographic scope. A 1928 ad asked, "Do you know . . . the largest railway system in America is *NOT* in the United States? It is in Canada—the 22,681 miles of Canadian National Railways which span Canada from coast to coast."

CN was deriving roughly 75 percent of its revenue from freight service, but the company offered a diverse array of transportation services. A 1925 tourist brochure listed its non-rail operations: five steamers along the coast of British Columbia, four lake steamers, 11 car ferries, 102,000 miles (164,000 kilometers) of telegraph lines, 10 hotels, and an

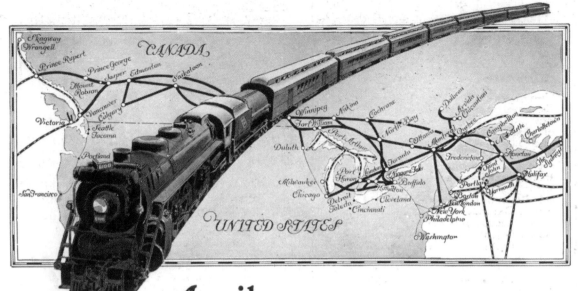

A railway system that spans a continent and links two great nations

NEW YORK and Montreal; Chicago and Toronto; Duluth and Winnipeg lie south and north of the International Line. But they are not foreign ground to the citizens of either the United States or Canada. Language, race and customs and the luxurious trains of Canadian National Railways link them together and make them neighbors.

Wherever you wish to go in Canada—whether to the playgrounds of the Maritime Provinces, Historic Quebec, the lake and forest regions of Ontario, the great prairie provinces, the mighty Canadian Rockies, to the Pacific Coast and Alaska—Canadian National will take you, speedily, comfortably and over a route replete with magnificent scenery.

But Canadian National is more than a railroad. It operates year 'round hotels and summer resorts. It provides freight, express and telegraph service with connections to all parts of the world. Canadian National Steamships carry Canada's ensign over the seven seas. Eleven Canadian National radio stations broadcast from coast to coast.

For information on Canada's natural resources and business opportunities, for tickets and accommodations, call at, write or telephone the nearest Canadian National office.

In Ottawa, Ont., the capital of the Dominion, is the Chateau Laurier, one of the distinctive hotels owned and operated by Canadian National Railways.

OFFICES

BOSTON
333 Washington St.
BUFFALO
420 Main St.
CHICAGO
108 W. Adams St.
CINCINNATI
49 E. Fourth St.
CLEVELAND
925 Euclid Ave.
DETROIT
1259 Griswold St.
DULUTH
430 W. Superior St.
KANSAS CITY
705 Walnut St.
LOS ANGELES
607 So. Grand Ave.
MINNEAPOLIS
518 Second Ave. So.
NEW YORK
505 Fifth Ave.
PHILADELPHIA
1420-22 Chestnut St.
PITTSBURGH
355 Fifth Ave.
PORTLAND, ME.
Grand Trunk Ry. Sta.
PORTLAND, ORE.
302 Yamhill St.
ST. LOUIS
314 No. Broadway
ST. PAUL
83 East Fifth Street
SAN FRANCISCO
689 Market St.
SEATTLE
1329 Fourth Avenue
WASHINGTON, D. C.
901—15th St., N. W.

CANADIAN NATIONAL
The Largest Railway System in America

OPERATING RAILWAYS · STEAMSHIPS · HOTELS · TELEGRAPH AND EXPRESS SERVICE · RADIO STATIONS

Much of CN's early advertising was devoted to promoting awareness in the United States of the company's size and scope. This 1929 ad appeared in *National Geographic. Author collection*

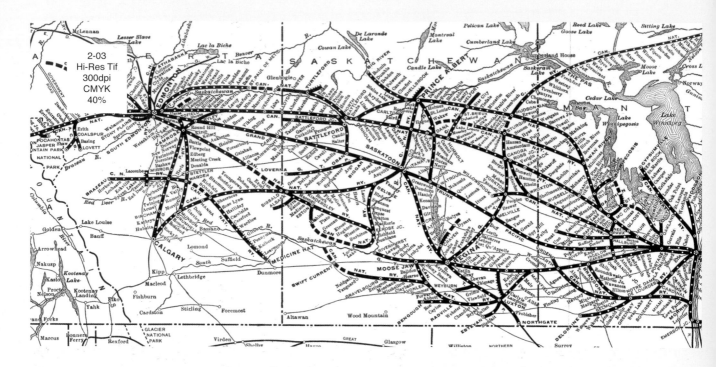

This detail of the prairie provinces is from a CN-GTR-GTP map dated March 24, 1921, during CN's formative period. It shows the heritage of CN's prairie branchlines: Those marked "Can. Nat. Ry." are former Canadian Northern routes, while GTP lines are labeled as such. *Author collection*

Opposite: CN 3496 at Fort Erie, Ontario, in August 1957. This engine was built in 1913 for Grand Trunk Railway and was retired in 1960, the same year that CN ceased regular steam operations. *Jim Shaughnessy*

express company. CN also managed Canada's merchant marine, consisting of 57 vessels operating in worldwide service.

Although rail passenger service generated only 15 percent of CN's revenues, CN did its best to improve the returns from this business. In 1923 a radio service was started to provide entertainment and news for passengers on CN trains. This gave CN a unique selling point that it could use to win riders away from competitor Canadian Pacific. Within a few years CN ads would boast that "eleven Canadian National radio stations broadcast from coast to coast." Eventually, this service was transformed into the Canadian Broadcasting Corporation.

In 1927 three new trains were inaugurated. The *Confederation* between Toronto and Vancouver supplemented the *Continental Limited,* which ran between Montreal and Vancouver. The *Confederation* featured a radio-equipped compartment-observation-library buffet car, as well as sleepers, coaches, and a dining car. The Chicago–Toronto–Montreal *Maple Leaf* augmented the existing *International Limited* on the same route, giving travelers a choice of morning or evening

departures from Chicago. Between Montreal and Halifax, where the *Ocean Limited* had been operating since 1904, a second summer-only train, the *Acadian,* began service in June 1927. It offered a radio-equipped compartment-observation-sleeping car.

Too Much Railway, Too Little Traffic

Thornton was an optimist by nature. He inherited a system that was overbuilt for the population and economy it served, but he believed that through aggressive efforts on CN's part to support government immigration policies, the population of the prairie provinces could be increased. With more farmers, there would be more traffic for the railway to carry. According to Donald MacKay, in the mid-1920s CN had 400 field agents whose job was to look for settlement locations and assist immigrants in moving to the prairies. As a result of their efforts, CN settled 4,200 families between 1926 and 1930. Spartan sleeping cars known as "colonist cars" were operated on transcontinental trains to provide settlers with an affordable means of reaching their new homes.

Given the overbuilding of the rail network that had taken place before World War I, and

Engineer L. L. Wood in the cab of Northern No. 6154 in January 1943. *Nicholas Morant/National Film Board of Canada. Photothèque/National Archives of Canada/PA-153050*

the role this played in the financial disintegration of CN's predecessors, one might have expected railway executives of the 1920s to avoid any further construction of rail lines. However, there was still territory that was not served by the rail network. Spurred by its rivalry with Canadian Pacific, CN built 1,895 miles (3,051 kilometers) of new branchlines in the 1920s. According to MacKay, some of these lines "were of questionable value even then in the days before trucking." Between them, he writes, CN and CP "increased Canadian railway mileage by almost one-third in a decade."

Despite the building of new branchlines of marginal economic worth, CN's financial results were improving. In 1929, the company had an operating ratio of 82.5 percent, meaning that roughly 17.5 cents of every dollar that came in from customers was available to cover the cost of CN's debt. Unfortunately, because of the massive financial obligations that the railway had inherited from its predecessors, and the additional debt taken on to fund CN's capital improvements since 1923, this was not enough. The government had to make up the difference. Still, Thornton had brought the operating ratio down significantly in the prior six years. Also, thanks in part to the significant investments in new equipment CN made during the 1920s, the public perception of the government railway had changed dramatically for the better.

John W. Barriger, then president of the Monon Railroad, said in 1944 that during the period from 1920 to 1929, Thornton "was backed by a generous, friendly, and cooperative Government. Parliament approved all of the drafts upon the Dominion treasury for capital expenditures, of every description, which the Canadian National's President recommended were required for the improvement and extension of this railroad."

It did not take long for the collapse of the stock market in October 1929, and the ensuing depression, to undo most of the financial progress CN had made since its formation. By the end of 1930, MacKay notes, "freight traffic had sunk to the lowest level in a decade and passenger travel was the lightest in twenty years." Grain prices fell "to the lowest level in memory. Two hundred thousand Canadians had lost their jobs" by the time of the 1930 general election. CN's operating ratio increased to 88.1 for the year 1930.

The Niagara, St. Catharines & Toronto Railway became a CN subsidiary, along with four other electric lines, in 1923, but kept its own identity until 1958. Car 620, shown here in 1959, was built by Ottawa Car in 1930 and had been operated by another CN electric line, Montreal & Southern Counties, before being transferred to NStC&T in 1956. *Richard Jay Solomon*

The election brought the Conservative party into power. Thornton had done a respectable job of walking the line between the demands of a business and those of a government agency, but some of the excesses that had occurred on his watch made him an easy target for political sniping. The competition with CP had gone to irrational lengths, including the building of unnecessary hotels and ships. CP used its status as a privately owned company, free from political interference, as a platform from which it called for the two railways to be unified.

In November 1931 the Conservative prime minister, R. B. Bennett, appointed a Royal Commission on Railways and Transportation. When it issued its report 10 months later, it took both railways to task for wasteful competition. By then Thornton had resigned effective August 1, 1932. His vice president of operations, maintenance, and construction, Samuel J. Hungerford, was appointed to succeed him. Hungerford had begun his railway career with CP as an apprentice machinist and had joined Canadian Northern in 1910.

The general economic situation was aggravated by drought in both Canada and the United States. Canadian grain production fell by more than two-thirds between 1929 and 1932, and the price of grain dropped even more.

Belt-tightening at CN had already begun before Hungerford was named president. In 1931 two of the passenger trains announced with much fanfare only four years earlier, the *Confederation* and the *Acadian,* were discontinued. Wages were cut and service was curtailed.

In 1933 CN was reorganized, with the semi-independent board of directors replaced by three government-appointed trustees. Job cuts began at the top and extended throughout the company. G. R. Stevens notes that 11 of the top officers appointed by Thornton resigned. Over three years the total payroll at CN was reduced from 111,389 employees to 70,525.

Although the Royal Commission had rejected a merger of CN and CP, political leverage was used to force cooperation between the two. In the 1920s the only two significant examples of cooperation between the two rivals were in Toronto, where they opened a new Union Station in 1927, and in Alberta, where they took over four provincially owned railways in 1929, renaming them Northern Alberta Railways.

One of the few cooperative efforts to emerge in the early 1930s was a 1933 agreement to pool the two railways' passenger services between Toronto, Ottawa, Montreal, and Quebec City. They also worked together as owners of a fledgling airline, Canadian Airways, which had been built up from a small, privately operated firm. CP's role in the airline was eventually eliminated through parliamentary action, and CN became sole owner of the renamed Trans-Canada Air Lines. Later, the airline would become known as Air Canada.

In 1935 the Liberal party and William Lyon Mackenzie King returned to power. Stevens writes that for CN, "by 1935, the times were on the mend, and the hard climb back to normalcy had begun." Under the King administration, CN management, which had been pleading for years to have the debt on the company's books reduced, got a receptive hearing. The government decided to write off the $1.174 billion in government debt on the company's balance sheet. This left it with $1.185 billion in private debt that the company had inherited from its predecessors. In 1936 another CN responsibility was eliminated when the last nine ships in Canada's merchant marine fleet were sold.

CN Goes to War

In December 1939 CN got an early taste of what would be expected of it during World War II. The Canadian 1st Division was

ordered to embark for Europe through the port of Halifax. According to Donald MacKay, 25 CN trains were used for the movement in a period of 48 hours.

Another early movement through Halifax was in the other direction, and it involved the transfer of $7.5 billion in gold and securities from the Bank of England to more secure facilities in Ottawa and Montreal. MacKay notes that CN trains carrying these valuables were timed to arrive in the early-morning hours so that transfer to Canadian vaults could be accomplished under cover of darkness.

As CN geared up for the war effort, it made a change in the executive ranks. In July 1941 Hungerford retired and R. C. Vaughan became president. He had previously served as CN's vice president of purchasing and stores.

The war put a strain on several of CN's critical routes, most notably Halifax–Moncton. It took as many as 700 boxcars to

CN enginehouse employees wipe down an engine at Edmonton in January 1943. During World War II women were hired for jobs that had traditionally been closed to them, although the "running trades" (engineer, conductor, and brakeman) remained male-only for many years after the war. *Nicholas Morant/National Film Board of Canada. Photothèque/National Archives of Canada/C-079524*

fill up a ship being loaded at Halifax, and the port city lacked the yard capacity to allow for an orderly flow of cars prior to each ship. Moncton became a key staging point for this traffic, and on the route between there and Halifax, Centralized Traffic Control (CTC) was installed starting in 1941 to increase line capacity and ensure safe operations.

With an abundance of wartime traffic, and with every employee being worked to his or her maximum, CN's operating efficiency reached new levels. In 1943 its operating ratio was 73.6 percent, a level it would not see again for more than 50 years. By the time 1944 came to an end, 20,165 CN employees had entered military or merchant marine service, and 582 had lost their lives in the war. Several hundred women were employed in jobs that had previously been restricted to men (although the ranks of

CN 6207, shown here at Brockville, Ontario, in August 1958, was built by Montreal Locomotive Works and delivered in July 1942. *Jim Shaughnessy*

CN 4207 at Bridge Station, Quebec, near the former National Transcontinental Bridge crossing the St. Lawrence River in November 1955. This engine was one of a group of ten 2-10-2 Santa Fe-type locomotives that CN acquired from the Boston & Albany Railroad in 1928. *Jim Shaughnessy*

engineers, conductors, and trainmen were still male only).

During the war some projects that had been in the works for years finally came to fruition. Two of these were in Montreal. In 1943 a new Central Station that had been in development since 1929 opened at the south end of the tunnel under Mount Royal. The former GTR Bonaventure station, which had served as CN's main passenger terminal in Montreal, was restricted to Lakeshore commuter trains and troop movements for the balance of the war and then converted to a CN Express freight terminal.

Another long-planned improvement was a connection between CN's yards east and west of downtown Montreal. The former GTR yard at Turcot was CN's main freight terminal in the city, but there was no direct connection to rail-served industries at the eastern end of the island. Freight between the two zones required a 108-mile (174-kilometer) detour via Joliette and Fresnière Junction, Quebec. To solve this, a 14.3-mile (23.0-kilometer) cutoff was opened in 1945.

When World War II ended, CN had posted an enviable record of service. In both 1943 and 1944 the railway generated more than 36 billion revenue ton-miles (RTMs)— i.e., one ton moved one mile, compared with 17 billion RTMs in 1939. The increase in passenger traffic was even more dramatic: CN recorded 3.6 billion passenger miles in 1943, and slightly more in 1944, versus 875 million in 1939.

But as with World War I, the return to peacetime was a mixed blessing. Cost inflation began to put a squeeze on the company's financial results, and both freight and passenger revenues were drained away by the highway system.

CN's Steam Locomotives

Following the absorption of GTR, CN's roster included 3,265 locomotives, 3,363 passenger cars, and 124,648 freight cars. Some new equipment had already arrived to replace the worn-out cars and locomotives of CN's predecessor railroads. Under the management of D. B. Hanna, the government railway had received 163 new locomotives, 200 passenger cars, and 8,450 freight cars. But this made only a small improvement in the quality of the new railway's fleet, given its vast size.

Over the next several years the average age of CN's fleet dropped as old equipment was scrapped and replaced. In 1923 58 engines were retired, and 420 additional loco-

In 1929 Montreal Locomotive Works delivered 20 Northerns to CN, numbered 6140 through 6159. Here, one of these locomotives is shown under construction. *National Archives of Canada/PA-041340*

motives met the same fate over the next four
years. CN replaced obsolete engines with 2-8-2
Mikados, 4-8-2 Mountains, 4-8-4 Northerns
(also known as Confederations to mark the
sixtieth anniversary of Canada's unification),
and 2-10-2 Santa Fe types.

By the time Henry Thornton came on
board in 1922, the company already had 225
relatively new Mikados, all delivered since
1916. In 1923 and 1924 an additional 75 of
the 2-8-2 type arrived. The final group of five
arrived in 1936.

Another early locomotive order was for 16
of the Mountain types, numbered 6000
through 6015 and delivered in 1923. By 1930
an additional 38 Mountains had been delivered. These 4-8-2s featured automatic stokers,
superheaters, and all-weather cabs. A final
group of 20 semi-streamlined Mountains,
numbered 6060 through 6079 and easily
identified by their conical noses, was delivered
in 1944.

During the Thornton years the Northern
represented another key steam locomotive
development for CN. The 4-8-4 Northern
was as close to a universal locomotive as any-
thing on the CN roster. Deliveries started in
1927, and by 1929 CN had 60 of the
engines, numbered 6100 through 6159.
Grand Trunk Western (GTW), CN's U.S.
subsidiary serving Michigan, Indiana, and
Illinois, owned an additional 12, numbered
6300 through 6311. Northerns and
Mountains were used in both freight and passenger service, and they were equally at home
on the mainline and on secondary routes.

From 1924 through 1930 CN added 48
Santa Fe types (for freight service), five 4-6-4
Hudson locomotives (for fast passenger trains
between Montreal and Toronto), and a number of smaller locomotives (notably 0-8-0
yard engines and 2-8-0 Consolidations) to its
roster. Locomotive deliveries dried up in the
early 1930s, but in 1936 CN added a few

CN's dual-service 4-8-2 Mountains and 4-8-4 Northerns combined pulling power with the ability to negotiate light rail on branchlines. CN 6007 was among the first group of Mountains delivered to CN in 1923. It is shown here at Stratford, Ontario, in February 1959. *Jim Shaughnessy*

more engines to its roster, including 10 Northerns. Five of them, numbered 6400 through 6404, were streamlined, built to a joint design of the railway and the National Research Council. The intent was to keep smoke away from the cab. While they were not successful in meeting that objective, these five photogenic engines were much in demand for special trains.

CN added another 25 Northerns in 1940, 35 more in 1943, and the final group of 30 in 1944. By the end of 1944, CN had

CN 6218 crosses the Richelieu River, approximately 20 miles (32 kilometers) east of Montreal on the St. Hyacinthe Subdivision, in February 1970. The 6218 was used on dozens of excursions following the end of regular CN steam locomotive operation in 1960. It continued in service until 1971. *Jim Shaughnessy*

203 Northerns (more than any other road) and 78 Mountains. The best-known CN Northern, No. 6218, which operated on dozens of fan trips after regular steam operations had ceased, was a member of the class of 1943. Following its retirement, CN 6218 was replaced in excursion service by Mountain 6060.

Early Experiments with the Diesel

One irony of diesel-electric locomotive development in North America is that CN was a pioneer in experimenting with diesel propulsion, yet lagged behind virtually every major U.S. railroad in adopting the new form of motive power for regular operations.

However, even before it acquired its first diesel, CN experimented with other forms of internal combustion, most notably self-propelled passenger cars, which permitted cost savings on branchline runs. One such car could replace a steam locomotive, baggage car, and coach. The operating unions also permitted smaller crews on these cars than on regular trains.

CN historian J. Norman Lowe notes that "the first record of a self-propelled car operating on a CN predecessor line dates back to 1912" on CNoR. By 1926, he says, "CN had 36 self-propelled cars for passenger service. These comprised two steam cars, 10 storage battery units, three gas-electric cars, seven

CN 15709 was a diesel-electric self-propelled car built in 1930, rebuilt at Montreal's Point St. Charles shops in 1951, and converted in 1964 for use in maintaining the suburban electrification north of Montreal. At the time of this photo Suburban electrification was the task of the CN 15709 and trailer No. 15708. The car was replaced by a truck in 1970 and scrapped in 1972. *Jim Shaughnessy*

The twin units of pioneer diesel-electric locomotive No. 9000 were built at the Canadian Locomotive Company shop in Kingston, Ontario, in 1929. Here, one of the units has its 1,330-horsepower, Scottish-built Beardmore engine installed. The units were subsequently separated and operated as CN 9000 and 9001.
Canada Science and Technology Museum, CSTM/CN collection neg. no. 30664

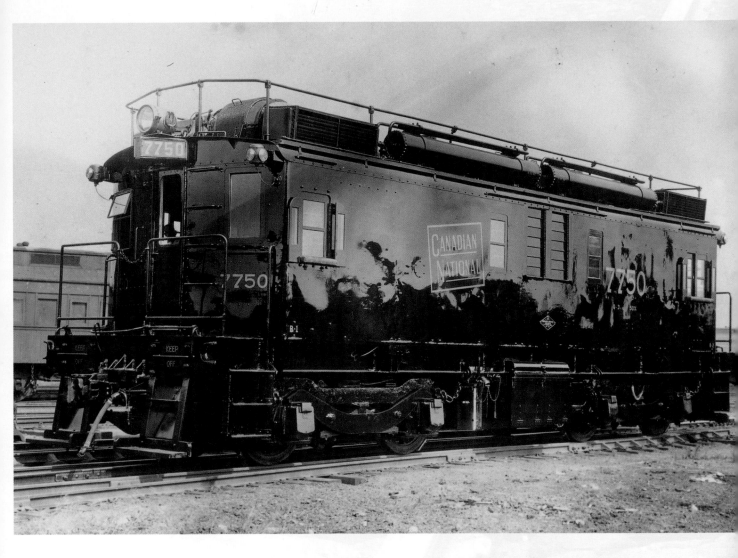

oil-electric cars with four-cylinder engines, two oil-electric articulated units with eight-cylinder engines, 10 gasoline units and two multiple-unit electrics." Clearly, this was a time of experimentation.

In 1929 a two-unit diesel, built at Canadian Locomotive Company's (CLC) Kingston, Ontario, shop, began its career on CN. CN No. 9000 (which became two separate units, 9000 and 9001, in 1931) had a 12-cylinder, 1,330-horsepower Beardmore diesel engine in each unit. CN 9000 was the brainchild of CN's chief of motive power, C. E. (Ned) Brooks. After a series of test runs, including one to Vancouver, this pioneer diesel was put into revenue service on passenger trains between Toronto and Montreal.

The twin units, 9000 and 9001, were withdrawn from revenue service in 1939, but number 9000 had a second life during World War II as part of an armored train designed to protect the Prince Rupert line. It saw revenue service between Moncton and Quebec City in 1945, but both units were scrapped in 1946.

CN also fielded two other early diesels, CN No. 7700 (later CN 77), built in 1929 at CLC, and Grand Trunk Western No. 7730 (later GTW 73), a Brill product built in 1926. However, with the premature death of Ned Brooks in 1933 at age 46, the diesel locomotive lost its most ardent sponsor at CN. It would be 1948 before CN bought another diesel locomotive for road service.

CN 7750 was one of the company's pioneer diesel-electric locomotives. Constructed in 1932 at the Point St. Charles shops in Montreal, it survived until 1948, when it was heavily damaged in a collision in the Mount Royal Tunnel. *National Archives of Canada/PA-164829*

During its years as a government-owned railway, CN had limited freedom to abandon trackage and so was forced to continue operating many lines that had light traffic and light rail. The RSC13, with its A1A-A1A axle arrangement, was one way that CN dealt with this dilemma. CN 1729, 1701, and 1718 are seen here at Opleman, Prince Edward Island (near O'Leary station) in May 1975. This train consisted of empty potato reefers and supplies for the Canadian Forces base at Summerside, P.E.I. *Phil Mason*

CHAPTER THREE

POSTWAR CN:
Years of Modernization and Growth

World War II left Canadian National in much the same situation as World War I: physically worn out and faced with rampant cost inflation. Between 1944 and 1948 operating expenses increased 28 percent, but revenues rose only 11 percent. As a regulated company CN could not simply raise freight rates to offset its higher costs. If the company was going to survive, it had to become more efficient, so that it could keep more of every dollar it took in.

In August 1962 the morning eastbound train from Summerside pulls into a Hunter River stop en route to Charlottetown. Prince Edward Island was the first region of CN to be dieselized, and Nos. 28 and 25 were among a group of 18 General Electric 70-tonners that CN acquired for this purpose in 1950. *Jim Shaughnessy*

Dieselization

The most obvious route to efficiency was one that was already well under way in the United States: converting from steam locomotives to diesel-electrics. Steam locomotives were high-maintenance machines. Their operating range was limited because they needed frequent watering and fueling. They had to be turned at the end of their runs. Each steam locomotive required an engineer and fireman. In terms of economics, the diesel was clearly superior to steam.

Although it had pioneered the use of diesel locomotives in mainline service, CN had since been surpassed by U.S. railroads. By January 1948 the company (including its U.S. subsidiaries) had 75 diesels in yard service, but no diesel road locomotives.

That year the dieselization process moved ahead in a small way with the purchase of 28 F3 units from General Motors' Electro-Motive Division for mainline service (six for CN and 22 for GTW). CN also acquired several 650-horsepower units built by Whitcomb Locomotive Works (a U.S. manufacturer of mining and industrial locomotives) and CLC for use on Prince Edward Island. Why P.E.I.? First, it was small. Any issues that needed to be addressed would be local ones, and wouldn't affect the rest of the CN system. Second, operating steam engines on the island was expensive because coal had to be brought in by ship from Nova Scotia. The Prince Edward Island pilot project wasn't an immediate success (the Whitcomb units were rejected as mechanically unfit for service and replaced with 18 similar units from General Electric), however, CN was moving in the right direction.

Full-scale dieselization would have to wait for the arrival of a fresh face in CN corporate headquarters. Donald Gordon was a Scotsman by birth and banker by trade who moved to CN from the Bank of Canada in December 1949. At 47 he was the youngest person to hold the title of president at CN, and the first non-railroader. He took over a company that was struggling financially. CN recorded a deficit of $42 million in 1949. It was what would be called in later years a "multi-modal" company, operating a fleet of coastal and ocean-going ships, trucks to serve its express customers, and buses that connected with its passenger trains. It also owned Trans-Canada Air Lines. But the heart of the business was the railway, and it was this part of the business that got most of Gordon's attention.

Even to a non-railroader it was clear that CN's equipment fleet needed to be rejuvenated. Donald MacKay, in his book *The People's Railway*, tells the story of a vice president who asked for authority to buy 1,000 boxcars but was told by Gordon to increase the order to 5,000. He believed that if CN was to be taken seriously by its customers, it had to offer them modern equipment, both freight and passenger.

Three of the GE 70-tonners that dieselized Prince Edward Island team up on the westbound freight from Souris to Charlottetown at Mt. Stewart Junction in May 1975. *Phil Mason*

CN 8702 was among the railroad's earliest road diesel locomotives, having been built in 1952 by Canadian Locomotive Company. Here the unit leads a freight train at Ballantyne, Quebec, outside Montreal, in November 1955. *Jim Shaughnessy*

The extent of the job that lay ahead in the motive power department is indicated in a December 31, 1951, summary of CN's locomotive fleet. On that date CN (excluding its U.S. subsidiaries) had 68 road diesels, 30 road switchers, and 120 diesel yard engines. But these diesels made up only 7 percent of the CN fleet's total tractive power. At the time CN rostered 2,226 steam locomotives, many of them coal-fired. Three out of every four were more than 30 years old. Among the antiquities in this fleet were 198 4-6-0 Ten-Wheelers, 34 2-6-0 Moguls, and 249 0-6-0

switchers. The most powerful steam locomotives in the fleet were 93 2-10-2 Santa Fe types, followed by 179 4-8-4 Northerns.

CN dieselized on a terminal-by-terminal and region-by-region basis, which allowed operating and mechanical personnel on each part of the railway to learn about the new machines. But by mid-1952, aside from P.E.I., only one region had been converted: Quebec's Gaspé Peninsula, where a fleet of 15 1,200-horsepower road switchers built by CLC to a Fairbanks-Morse design had superseded steam. Diesels were also operating on selected long-distance freight trains out of Montreal, but they were working side-by-side with steam. On the passenger side, steam still ruled.

Despite the preponderance of steam engines on CN's roster, diesels were hauling an increasing share of the company's trains. In 1952 diesels generated 23 percent of the railway's gross ton-miles. By the end of that year the company had 58 F7A and 18 F7B units, representing its first significant group of road-freight diesels. These were in addition to the four F3As and two F3Bs for CN, and 22 F3A units for Grand Trunk Western, delivered in 1948. The F3 units, like CN's early General Motors (GM) switchers, were built by GM's Electro-Motive Division (EMD) at its LaGrange, Illinois, plant. In 1950, GM set up a Canadian locomotive assembly plant at London, Ontario which became known as General Motors Diesel Division (GMD). From 1950 to 1988, CN's U.S. subsidiaries received their GM products from EMD, while GM diesels for CN itself were built by GMD at London. In 1988 GM consolidated North American locomotive assembly operations at London.

Some of the notable deliveries over the next few years included:

• 1953 and 1954: 41 RS3 units built by Montreal Locomotive Works (MLW). Over the period 1955 through 1960, these road switchers would be followed by 51 1,600-horsepower RS10 units and 225 1,800-horsepower RS18 units from MLW.

• 1954: 17 GP9 units from EMD for Grand

CN 7603 was built by Canadian Locomotive Company to a Fairbanks-Morse design, with an A1A-A1A axle configuration. Here it makes a station stop at Cross Point, 12.8 miles (20.6 kilometers) east of Matapédia, Quebec, in January 1952. *Canada Science and Technology Museum, CSTM/CN collection neg. no. 47702*

CN had one H24-66 Trainmaster. It was built at Beloit, Wisconsin, by Fairbanks-Morse and delivered to CN in 1955 as CN No. 3000. The following year it was renumbered CN 2900. Here it handles a cut of ore cars at Port Arthur, Ontario, in 1956. *Canada Science and Technology Museum, CSTM/CN collection neg. no. X42527*

Trunk Western (2 for passenger service and 15 for freight). These were the first of what would become the CN family's 434 GP9s (349 on CN, 57 on GTW, and 28 on Central Vermont), the largest fleet of this locomotive model in North America.

• 1954 and 1955: 14 FP9A and 14 F9B units from GMD to power the new *Super Continental,* followed by 29 additional FP9A and 24 more F9B units in 1957 and 1958.

In April 1960 CN retired its last steam locomotive from regular service. By the end of that year it had 2,134 diesel locomotives in service.

Technology: CTC and the Computer

The 1950s were clearly the decade of dieselization on CN, but that was not all that was being done to modernize the railway. Centralized Traffic Control (CTC), which

offered improved safety, higher line capacity, and lower operating costs, was also spreading. It combined elements of Automatic Block Signaling (ABS) which CN already had in place on many of its busiest routes, with remote control of switches and signals by an operator or train dispatcher.

The first CTC installation on CN had been between Halifax and Moncton, 185 miles (298 kilometers), during World War II. In 1949 the second mainline segment of CTC was completed, between West Junction and Ste. Rosalie on the Drummondville Subdivision, giving CN a total of 301 miles (485 kilometers) of CTC.

New CTC installations continued over the next decade, and by the end of 1960 CN had CTC on 2,039 miles (3,283 kilometers) of its mainline. Over the next four years an additional 1,336 miles (2,151 kilometers) of

CTC were installed. Most of the CTC installed in the 1950s and early 1960s was what CN called "modified" CTC, which had a power switch at only one end of each controlled siding, as opposed to conventional CTC, which has a power switch at both ends. This meant that the train approaching the power switch would always take the siding, and then exit through a spring switch at the other end. It was not a perfect solution, but it was a big advance over the timetable-and-train order system that had preceded it. Eventually, CN would upgrade to a full CTC system on its mainlines as traffic growth in the 1970s forced it to extend sidings and take other measures to increase line capacity.

CN was making progress on other fronts as well. In 1960 it opened its first modern classification yard at Moncton, to be followed by other automatically controlled hump yards at Edmonton, Winnipeg, Montreal, and Toronto. It was also beginning to use radio for field operations, first in yards, and then for end-to-end train communication on the road.

The single technological advance of the 1960s and 1970s that most changed the way railroading had been practiced for decades was the computer. Electronic data systems were first used in the rail industry for payroll and other accounting functions, where batch processing could be used to simplify tasks that had once taken rooms full of clerks to perform. What changed starting in the late

Montreal Locomotive Works built diesel locomotives under a partnership with U.S. builder Alco, and many of its models had Alco counterparts. RS18 No. 3115, shown here at Toronto in 1962, is identical, except cosmetically, to the RS11 model produced by Alco in the United States. *Collection of George Carpenter*

Between 1954 and 1958 CN acquired 43 FP9A units and 38 F9B units to power its prestige transcontinental trains. CN 6539 is shown here at North Bay, Ontario. *Richard Jay Solomon*

1960s was an increasing use of computers for "real-time" functions. In 1961 and 1962 CN installed new computers at its Montreal headquarters and at several key points around the system to help handle car tracing, revenue accounting, and equipment control. This involved sending data on a magnetic tape to the master computer in Montreal—clearly not a real-time application.

In 1967 CN began to develop a Traffic Reporting and Control System (TRACS) that allowed for timely reporting of train arrivals and departures, car locations, and other information critical for the operation of the railway. This made CN less dependent on local station and yard personnel for recording car locations and movements. In 1970 CN estab-

lished eight "Servocentres" that were, in essence, centralized freight billing and customer service units. Increasing centralization of clerical functions would continue for the next two decades.

New computer systems did more than reduce the labor intensity and timeliness of data collection, however. Car distribution was an early beneficiary of improvements in information technology. For many years empty cars would be sent to stations on the basis of past loading patterns. Now CN could respond quickly to specific customer requirements. In 1977 CN credited TRACS with a 10 percent improvement in car utilization, which it said was "equivalent to a saving of about $30 million a year."

Growing to Serve the Canadian Economy

CN needed all the help it could get from the diesel locomotive, CTC, computers, and other forms of technology. In 1943, the peak traffic year of World War II, it had generated 36.3 billion revenue ton-miles (RTMs). Despite the falloff in business immediately after the war, by the mid-1950s the railway was setting new traffic records. In 1956 CN achieved a temporary record of 41.9 billion RTMs, but by 1964 that record, too, had been eclipsed. After 1964, traffic grew almost every year. In 1973 CN generated 72.4 billion RTMs, almost double the World War II peak. And it was doing so with about 13 percent fewer employees than it had during the war.

Bulk traffic was growing, and, in response, CN began to operate unit trains that kept cars together from origin to destination and back again, in a continuous cycle that would be interrupted only for car maintenance. In 1968 CN began operating what it called "the first predesigned unit train in Canada," carrying pelletized ore from a mine near Temagami in northern Ontario to Hamilton on a 72-hour cycle. Unit trains reduced costs for the railway and made service more predictable for shippers. Most of them included an empty movement back to origin, but CN came up with one unit train operating plan that shipped potash westbound to Vancouver and a return movement of phosphate rock to fertilizer plants near Edmonton.

CN 1299 was part of a fleet of 187 CN units of model SW1200RS. They were equipped with Flexicoil trucks and large numberboard/headlight assemblies so that they could be used in road service on branchlines. No. 1299 is shown at Turcot Yard, Montreal, in May 1958. *Richard Jay Solomon*

CN extra 5403 west carries export sulfur through Yellowhead Pass, Alberta, in October 1989, en route to the port of Vancouver. The growth of such bulk commodities in the 1980s put a strain on CN's western network, and the company invested millions of dollars in siding extensions, signal system improvements and other capacity enhancements. *Steve Patterson*

Another source of growth was intermodal traffic trailers on flatcars (TOFC, or "piggyback"), and, in the 1960s, containers on flatcars (COFC, mainly for international traffic). CN got into the intermodal business in December 1952 when it began moving trailers on overnight trains between Toronto and Montreal. Over the next several years piggyback service was extended to locations large and small in eastern Canada. In 1959 TOFC facilities opened in Regina, Calgary, Edmonton, and Vancouver. The young intermodal business grew much faster than the rest of CN's traffic. By the early 1960s CN began to invest in modern handling facilities at larger terminals to reduce the cost and improve the timeliness of loading and unloading. In 1964, the company reported that piggyback volumes had grown 30.9 percent over the previous year, with revenues increasing 27.3 percent. In 1967 CN established rates specifically for container movements between East Coast ports (Halifax, Saint John, and Montreal) and interior Canadian points. In 1971 a new container terminal opened at Halifax. That year the company handled more than 90,000 import-export containers. By 1974 that number had grown to 166,000.

In the early days of piggyback service, before volumes justified dedicated intermodal trains, it was common to see a few trailers on the rear of a manifest freight. These trailers are at Cote de Noir, Quebec, en route to Quebec City, in 1962. *Canada Science and Technology Museum, CSTM/CN collection neg. no. 55565.1*

The Economics of a National Railway: People or Profits?

CN was led during these years by Norman MacMillan, a CN veteran who had succeeded Donald Gordon as president in January 1967. The MacMillan years were ones not only of growth for CN, but also of an increasingly commercial business philosophy for the railway. His move to the president's office coincided with the passage of the National Transportation Act, which eased the regulatory environment in Canada a full 13 years before such changes would occur in the United States. This made it easier for Canadian railways to implement services geared to the needs of specific customers and to abandon money-losing operations.

MacMillan, who retired as chief executive officer in 1974, had hoped to see CN turn a profit during his tenure. While it made good progress in that direction, the company continued to run yearly operating deficits until 1976. By that time Robert Bandeen, a 43-year-old Ph.D. economist and a graduate of CN's research-and-development department who had also run its U.S. subsidiaries for a time, had succeeded MacMillan. He reorganized CN into "profit centres" to quantify the financial contribution (or loss) of each CN operating unit. In the words of Donald MacKay, Bandeen "made CN more entrepreneurial . . . . He set out to end the deficits in what was, technologically, one of the best railways in North America."

In 1976 the company recorded its first operating profit in two decades. CN Rail, as the Canadian freight operation was designated, generated income of $157 million, an improvement over the $23 million in income for 1975, and enough to offset money-losing operations in express, passenger, and hotel services. Income at CN's U.S. rail unit, Grand Trunk Corporation (which included Grand Trunk Western Railroad; Central Vermont Railway; and Duluth, Winnipeg & Pacific Railway) went from $3.5 million in

1975 to $13.9 million in 1976. These figures were a bit misleading, because they did not take into account the fact that CN continued to struggle under a huge debt burden, but they did represent a milestone in the evolution of the company from a government agency to a free-enterprise corporation.

In CN's annual report for 1976, management noted that the financial improvement was the result of "stringent cost control, alert marketing, and benefits from past technological advances." The report went on, "while

earning a profit in 1976, CN continued to fulfill its mandate of service to its owners—the people of Canada." But what did its owners really want—a profitable corporation or an organization that would provide social benefits in the form of jobs and services?

Most of the big issues that Robert Bandeen would grapple with over the next few years involved, in one way or another, the question of whether CN could become financially self-sustaining. The issues included the following:

Insulating CN from the continuing cash drain of the passenger business. In 1977 a new CN subsidiary, VIA Rail Canada, was established to take over the operation of both CN and CP passenger trains. The following year the company became a separate government-established corporation (a "crown corporation" in Canadian parlance), thus eliminating this financial drain on CN.

Financial losses in the Atlantic provinces. In 1979 CN formed a subsidiary, TerraTransport, to operate rail, intermodal,

The last surviving Grand Trunk Western F3, No. 9013, was transferred to CN in 1972 for an F7 rebuilding program. It reemerged in 1973 as CN No. 9171, shown here as the trailing unit on a CN locomotive consist at Kitwanga, British Columbia, in October 1978. *Stan Smaill*

CN 1732 after a branchline run in February 1959 at Stratford, Ontario. CN 1732 was one of a group of 35 RSC13 units owned by CN. *Jim Shaughnessy*

bus, and package services in Newfoundland. In itself, this didn't stem the tide of red ink, but it did give CN a set of specific numbers to back up its talk on this issue. One of the cost-saving initiatives was to shift freight out of traditional freight cars and into containers. Rail service in Newfoundland would ultimately be discontinued, but not until 1988. Although financial losses on Prince Edward Island were smaller than those on Newfoundland, CN followed a similar strategy there. Potatoes represented a substantial portion of P.E.I.s outbound rail traffic, and this business was converted from railcars to insulated trailers that could be hauled on ferries. Rail service on P.E.I. ended in 1989.

The fight by both CN and CP to end the government-mandated rate on grain, commonly known as the "Crow rate." The Crow rate went back to a deal that CP made in 1897 for government assistance in building its Crowsnest line into southern British Columbia. The Crow rate was enacted into law and extended to cover CN as well as CP in 1924.

The capital investment required to expand capacity in light of increasing business volumes. In early 1981 CN management forecast that capital expenditures over the next five years would amount to $4.2 billion. It said that it could not generate that much cash internally unless it was allowed to eliminate

losses on Newfoundland operations, Montreal commuter service, the handling of grain at low government-mandated rates, and the Express business that had taken over the railway's former less-than-carload freight.

On one long-time battlefront Bandeen scored a victory. On December 31, 1977, the government reduced CN's debt by $800 million, which put its ratio of debt to capital in the same range as other large North American railroads. The price for the recapitalization was that CN had to secure future borrowing on the private capital markets. Privatization of the company was still several years away, but CN was looking and acting

less like a government agency and more like a business.

Part of Bandeen's strategy to make CN self-sufficient was to diversify it outside the transportation business. His predecessor, Norman MacMillan, had already taken steps to broaden the CN franchise, including the purchase of several trucking companies. During MacMillan's tenure CN formed a consulting unit, CANAC, which leveraged CN's transportation expertise across the globe on behalf of railways, governments, and other clients.

Former CN executive Charles F. Armstrong recalls:

CN purchased the only four RSC24s every built. They were constructed by Montreal Locomotive Works using engines from rebuilt FPA2 units, and their short hoods contained the electrical compartment. CN 1802 is westbound between Ste. Anne de Beaupré and Quebec City in August 1964. *Jim Shaughnessy*

CN 5082 is eastbound at Cisco, British Columbia, in June 1975 with covered hoppers returning from the port of Vancouver. Power for this train is a set of three General Motors Diesel Division SD40 units. *Steve Patterson*

In 1973 CN received 30 M420(W) locomotives, the first with the redesigned "comfort cab" from Montreal Locomotive Works. CN 2551, seen here at Rouses Point, New York, in July 1975, is from a second M420(W) order, delivered the following year. *Tom Murray*

In 1975 CN converted 38 RS18 locomotives, built with a B-B axle arrangement, to an A1A-A1A configuration. During the rebuilding, the units were de-rated from 1,800 to 1,400 horsepower, and when completed they were given model designation RSC14. CN 1753 and 1750, shown here at Hunter Island, Prince Edward Island, in August 1984, were part of that group. *Steve Patterson*

CN was never reluctant to order innovative, unconventional, or unique locomotives. One of its innovations was the "Draper taper." CN wanted a full-width (or "cowl") body for its locomotives to allow for engine compartment access with some protection from the elements. The drawback was that such a design had limited visibility from the cab toward the rear. CN's assistant chief of motive power, William Draper, solved the problem with a slight narrowing of the cowl, a design first used on a 1985 order. Here the headlight of a passing train shows the Draper taper on SD50F No. 5403 at Henry House, Alberta, in October 1989. *Steve Patterson*

"In 1978, there was a major move to segregate rail and non-rail operations. CN Rail assumed responsibility for all continental rail and intermodal operations. CN Holdings [of which Mr. Armstrong became president] assumed responsibility for Trucking, Hotels, CN Tower, Telecommunications, Express, Marine, Newfoundland, Drydocks, and Real Estate with a mandate to promote stand-alone enterprises. An additional venture, Explorations, was subsequently added to exploit corporate gas and oil interests. This proved a well-planned tactic that facilitated the later disposal of non-core assets and the transfer of the real estate portfolio to the Government as part of the [1995] privatization package."

Some of the new business ventures during the Bandeen years made use of existing CN assets, like its oil and gas exploration unit, which was focused on land that CN had inherited from Canadian Northern. Other ventures took CN into businesses that, while related to the railway, were seen by some as distractions from CN's core business. One of these ventures was CN's 1975 investment in the CAST container line. This deal helped put business on the railway, but CN's timing was not good. A North Atlantic rate war hurt CAST's financial performance, and CN ended up writing off its investment in the company in 1982.

Bandeen served as CN's chief executive officer until April 1982. He played a pivotal role not only in modernizing the way the corporation was organized, financed, and operated, but also in framing the conversation with CN's owners—the people of Canada—about what role the company should play in the life of the country.

Opposite: Trains designated as express trains were allowed 5 miles per hour more than ordinary freight trains. No. 212 was so designated. In February 1978 a trio of six-axle Montreal Locomotive Works Century Series locomotives lead that train past the CN depot at St. Hyacinthe, Quebec. During the 1970s these locomotives were the backbone of the mainline fleet east of Montreal. *George Pitarys*

Above: There was a lot of light rail on the prairies, and the A1A-A1A GMD1 from General Motors Diesel was CN's answer to that challenge. It was essentially an SW1200 on a longer frame. GMD built 78 of the six-axle GMD1 units for CN, and five for Northern Alberta Railways. It also built 18 four-axle GMD1 units for CN, which were equipped with steam generators for passenger service. Here No. 1069 is seen at Winnipeg, Manitoba, in May 1976. *Stan Smaill*

Eastbound and westbound *Super Continentals* meet at Lucerne, British Columbia, 4 miles (6 kilometers) west of Yellowhead Pass, in September 1978. *Steve Patterson*

CHAPTER FOUR

CN PASSENGER SERVICE

Canadian National offered a diversity of passenger services and equipment that was arguably as great as that of any North American railroad—a diversity that could often be sampled in the course of a single trip. In 1970, for example, a traveler making his way from Cartierville, Quebec, (in suburban Montreal) to Dewey, British Columbia, (200 miles [322 kilometers] west of Jasper, Alberta) would board a day coach hauled by an electric locomotive. At Central

Station, Montreal, he would step onto Train 1, the *Super Continental*, for a 5:05 p.m. departure. He would dine that evening and for the next two days-plus in a dining car built by Pullman-Standard in 1954 as part of CN's program to re-equip its premier long-distance trains. Overnight, he might be booked into the *Evanston*, a sleeping car consisting of four open sections (upper and lower berths with curtains for privacy), four double bedrooms, and eight duplex roomettes, from the same 1954 car order.

At Edmonton a former Milwaukee Road full-length dome car with lounge facilities (known as a Sceneramic car on CN) would be added for the trip through the mountains of western Alberta and British Columbia. At Jasper, the traveler would transfer to Train 9, the tri-weekly train to Prince Rupert, British Columbia, consisting of coaches, dining car, and sleeping car (and generally hauled by a freight locomotive augmented by a steam generator car) for the next 107 miles (172 kilometers) to McBride, British Columbia, where he would arrive at 1:30 a.m. If it was a Sunday night, he might get a room in the McBride Hotel, and at 6:30 a.m. on Tuesday he would depart on a mixed train, No. 297, for the last 92-mile (148-kilometer) lap to his destination. No. 297 would likely have a GP9 up front, a few boxcars, and, on the rear, a combine with a baggage compartment at one end and seating for passengers and crew at the other. If it was winter, then the crew would have the coal stove in the passenger compartment fired up before leaving McBride.

From Streamliners to Mixed Trains, and Everything in Between

The CN timetable of 1970 contained a variety of other trains:

• In addition to the *Super Continental*, transcontinental travelers could ride an unnamed coach-only train (No. 7) from Montreal to Winnipeg (with a connecting train between Capreol, Ontario, and

Toronto) and, after a daylong layover at Winnipeg, board the *Panorama*, which carried sleeping cars as well as coaches from Winnipeg to Vancouver.

• East of Montreal, three trains operated with coaches, sleeping cars, diners, and lounge cars

similar to those on the *Super Continental*: the *Scotian* and the *Ocean* to Halifax (with a section of the *Ocean* being switched out at Truro, Nova Scotia, to continue to Sydney, Nova Scotia), and the *Chaleur* to Gaspé, Quebec.
• Intercity trains, some with club cars, operated in the Montreal–Quebec, Montreal–Toronto, Montreal–Ottawa, and Ottawa–Toronto corridors. In the heavily traveled region between Windsor, London, and Toronto, *Tempo* trains with dedicated equipment provided five schedules daily, augmented by three Railiner (Budd

Trains on several of CN's secondary passenger routes operated with freight locomotives and steam generator cars. Train 19, photographed at Coxheath, Nova Scotia, in July 1976, is operating from Sydney to Truro, Nova Scotia, where it will connect with train 11, the westbound *Scotian* for Montreal, and with train 12, the eastbound *Scotian* for Halifax. *Tom Murray*

rail diesel car, or RDC) trains and three daily trains between Toronto and Chicago.

• Between Montreal and Toronto, two of the five daily trains were *Rapidos* that made no stops between suburban Montreal and suburban Toronto, and covered the 335 miles (539 kilometers) between center-city stations in 4 hours and 59 minutes—an average speed of 67 miles per hour (108 kilometers per hour), including the two suburban stops. The overnight *Cavalier* between the same cities carried five sleeping cars, one of which continued west of Toronto on the *Maple Leaf* to Port Huron, Michigan.

• Sleeping cars also operated between Ottawa and Toronto on the *Capitol*; between Toronto and Chicago on the *International*; between Montreal and Senneterre, in northern Quebec (on the former National Transcontinental line); between Toronto and Noranda, Quebec, and Kapuskasing, Ontario, on the *Northland,*

which was handled by Ontario Northland Railway between North Bay and Cochrane; and on two trains that ran north out of Winnipeg on alternate days, one to Thompson, Manitoba, and the other all the way to Churchill, on the shore of Hudson Bay.

• A number of Railiner services operated in Nova Scotia, New Brunswick, Quebec, Ontario, Alberta, and Saskatchewan, generally on routes used by local travelers rather than tourists.

• On those routes that couldn't justify a Railiner, an even more spartan service, the mixed train, was provided. One such route was in northern Quebec, where mixed trains augmented train Nos. 74 and 75, making flag stops for sportsmen and locals at locations such as Oskelaneo River, Maniwawa Club, and Club Wigwam. There were also mixed train services in Newfoundland, Ontario, Manitoba, and Saskatchewan.

A CN Budd rail diesel car (RDC), or Railiner, operates as train No. 612 in October 1970 as it passes through Norton, New Brunswick, en route from Saint John to Moncton. *Tom Murray*

In 1967 the arrival and departure board at Toronto Union Station shows trains to and from Montreal, Ottawa, Stratford, Brockville, Sarnia, Port Huron, Chicago, Windsor, London, Niagara Falls, Guelph, Owen Sound, Kapuskasing, North Bay, and Vancouver. Did she miss her train? *Canada Science and Technology Museum, CSTM/CN collection neg. no. 67571-9*

CN train No. 41 operated between Ottawa and Brockville, Ontario, where it connected with train No. 51, the *Lakeshore,* from Montreal to Toronto. It is shown here making a stop at the Canadian Pacific station in Smiths Falls, Ontario, in September 1971. From here to Brockville, No. 41 will operate on CP via trackage rights. *Tom Murray*

Three days a week, train No. 93 left Winnipeg en route to Churchill, Manitoba, a distance of 976.4 miles (1,571.4 kilometers). On this day in February 1974, the train is ready to depart Winnipeg with freight F7s for power and two steam generator cars for heat. *Tom Murray*

Several routes that had once had passenger trains were listed in the CN timetable, but the conveyances were now buses. This category included the mainline in Newfoundland between St. John's and Port aux Basques; Prince Edward Island; London to St. Thomas, Ontario; and Kamloops to Kelowna, British Columbia. Not included in the CN system timetable, but operated by it, were commuter services in Montreal, Toronto, and Detroit.

Serving All Canada

Canadian National had always made passenger service a priority. In part this was because CN was not strictly a for-profit business, but was an organization intended to serve Canada's broader social and economic needs. In its early years the emphasis on passenger service was influenced by its leader, Sir Henry Thornton, who had spent a substantial part of his pre-CN career running passenger operations in the United States (the Long Island Rail Road) and the United Kingdom (the Great Eastern Railway).

Unlike CP, which was able to look at passenger trains as a business segment (within the constraints set by government regulators), CN was expected to provide service for its own sake. A traditional argument for offering a high-class passenger service was that it would send a positive message to shippers, but CN needed to send a positive message to a wider constituency: the taxpayers and voters who were ultimately responsible for funding the company.

One motto that CN used for many years was "To Everywhere in Canada." Because of the extensive nature of its passenger network,

CN 804 and 805 at Brigus Junction, Newfoundland, in July 1984 on the Carbonear mixed train. *Steve Patterson*

In February 1954 the *Inter-City Limited* with Mountain-type CN 6071 has departed Hamilton, Ontario, and is passing through Bayview Junction en route to Toronto. *Jim Shaughnessy*

CN played an important role in the lives of Canadians. CN trains took immigrants to their new homes on the prairies, brought the necessities of life to remote communities, and carried the mail. Whenever a major change in someone's life occurred—going off to college, joining the military, relocating to a new city—CN was likely to be involved.

Yet CN didn't serve Canadians exclusively. It actively promoted its passenger services to those outside Canada. In 1925,

for example, the company published *Scenic Canada,* a book of photographs taken across Canada and even as far afield as Alaska (CN did, after all, operate coastal vessels in the Pacific). The four pages of text that preceded the photos began with flowery prose: "The route of the Canadian National Railways from the Atlantic to the Pacific lies through a part of the North American continent upon which Nature has been particularly beneficent in the bestowal of gifts that excite

Grand Trunk Western No. 4913 passes through Bayview Junction, Ontario, in August 1957 with a Windsor-bound passenger train. Helper No. 3467 waits on the siding to push westbounds up Dundas Hill. *Jim Shaughnessy*

Hotels of Distinction

The Canadian National system maintains, in some of the principal cities of Canada, hotels which are a credit both to a great transcontinental railway and to the cities served. The Chateau Laurier, (upper left),which stands in the Dominion capital, Ottawa, is one of the finest buildings in Canada and is the centre of the city's most brilliant social life. Other dignified buildings in the Canadian National hotel chain are the Fort Garry, at Winnipeg (left), the Macdonald, at Edmonton (right), and the Nova Scotian, at Halifax (upper right), opened in 1930. In addition to these are: the Prince Arthur, at Port Arthur, Ontario, and the Prince Edward, at Brandon, Manitoba.

If CN wanted to fill up its passenger trains, it then had to give passengers some destinations to motivate them to travel. Its hotels, as well as resorts like the Jasper Park Lodge, were part of that strategy, as shown in this excerpt from a 1931 travel brochure. *Author collection*

the admiration and wonder of mankind." By the late 1920s CN had 20 offices in the United States where travelers could book rail, steamship, and hotel reservations, as well as all-inclusive vacation packages.

Jasper Park, with its "sky-piercing mountains, colossal glaciers, torrential rivers, foam-flaked rapids, placid mirror-like lakes, cool deep forests and amid all this a splendid golf course, winding bridle paths and shady nooks," was a centerpiece of CN's advertising. CN owned the Jasper Park Lodge, opened in 1921, and it anchored the Triangle Tour, a staple of CN passenger promotion for decades. The legs of the triangle consisted of rail from Vancouver to Jasper and from Jasper to Prince Rupert, followed by a 600-mile (960-kilometer) cruise from Prince Rupert to Vancouver through the "mountain-guarded Inside Passage of the North Pacific."

CN complemented its passenger trains with hotels at strategic locations across Canada. Between 1912 and 1915 Grand Trunk Railway opened three chateau-style hotels: the Chateau Laurier in Ottawa, the Hotel Fort Garry in Winnipeg, and the Hotel Macdonald in Edmonton. GTR also operated the Minaki Lodge in western Ontario, opened in 1914 and rebuilt by CN following a fire in the 1920s.

From 1928 to 1932 CN opened the Hotel Nova Scotian in Halifax, the Canadian National Hotel (later renamed the Hotel Charlottetown) on Prince Edward Island, and the Bessborough Hotel in Saskatoon. The Hotel Vancouver was started by CN and completed in 1939 in a joint arrangement with CP. The Queen Elizabeth in Montreal, built over Central Station, was opened by CN in 1958. The company's final two hotel ventures were in the Maritimes: the Hotel Beausejour in Moncton, New Brunswick (1972) and a new Hotel Newfoundland in St. John's (1982). In the mid-1980s CN's hotel properties were sold to Canadian Pacific.

The Evolution of CN Passenger Service

Some of the trains operated by CN had long histories. Notable among them were the *International Limited,* which began service in 1900 between Montreal and Chicago on the Grand Trunk, and the *Ocean Limited,* which was inaugurated by the Intercolonial Railway in 1904.

All of CN's predecessors contributed passenger services of their own. Canadian Northern had started a transcontinental service in 1916, using 78 new passenger cars. The trip between Toronto and Vancouver on CNoR's premier train, No. 1 westbound and No. 2 eastbound, took five full days.

Grand Trunk Pacific's prestige train, also numbered 1 and 2, offered "electric lighted standard sleeping cars, containing drawing room, compartment and ten sections, reading lamps in all berths upper and lower," and "meals a la carte," on the three-day journey between Winnipeg and Prince Rupert.

In 1955 CN acquired 12 Fairbanks-Morse-designed, CLC-built passenger units (6 A and 6 B units) in an unusual B-A1A axle configuration. The units spent most of their lives in eastern Canada. Here, CN 6704 prepares to depart from Halifax, Nova Scotia, with the *Ocean Limited* in August 1959. *Jim Shaughnessy*

Following World War II CN found itself with a passenger car fleet badly in need of modernization. It addressed the problem in 1953 when it ordered 218 coaches from Canadian Car & Foundry, and 141 sleeping, dining, and parlor cars from Pullman-Standard. *Author collection*

Opposite: Once it acquired new equipment for the *Super Continental* and its other premier trains, CN improved their operation and promoted them heavily. Inside this 1955 brochure the railway provided photos of sleeping car and coach accommodations and discussed the tightening of the train's schedule by up to 14 hours. *Author collection*

To make your vacation in Canada even more wonderful...

For a between-meal "snack" or moderately priced meal, you'll find that the new and novel dinette cars provide convenient dining service in the modern manner.

Attend the Shakespearean Festival at Stratford, Ont. July-Aug. Visit Canada's romantic Eastern Cities. The walled city of Quebec; Ottawa, Canada's capital; Montreal, "The Paris of North America"; the great city of Toronto.

With three wide, comfortable berths and completely enclosed toilet facilities, Canadian National's modern drawing rooms offer ideal night and day accommodations for family groups.

Canadian National makes RECORD PURCHASE of new passenger equipment!

This record purchase marks the beginning of a new era in Canadian train travel. These modern cars offer a complete choice of accommodations... are designed to provide the utmost in comfort, in convenience, in beauty. Every day more of these cars are joining our fleet of famous "name" trains. By midsummer, they will all be in service, helping to make your Canadian National vacation more wonderful than ever.

Deep in Ontario's lovely Lake-of-the-Woods region is Minaki Lodge, a luxurious log-bungalow resort in a delightful lakeland district. Marvellous fishing... golf on forest-lined fairways... motorboating, canoeing, swimming and tennis. You will have a vacation you'll never forget.

In spacious new C.N.R. coaches you view the changing scenery through wide picture windows... stretch out on your reclining foam rubber seat.

Choose one of Canada's 10 Top Maple Leaf Vacations

1. The Scenic Route Across Canada
2. Alaska Cruise via the Inside Passage
3. The Provinces-by-the-Sea
4. Eastern Cities and the Laurentians
5. Sub-Arctic Hudson Bay Tour
6. Romantic French Canada
7. Minaki (Lake of the Woods)
8. Highlands of Ontario
9. British Columbia "Triangle Tour"
10. Jasper in the Canadian Rockies

CANADIAN NATIONAL RAILWAYS

THE ONLY RAILWAY SERVING ALL 10 PROVINCES OF CANADA

Ask about Canada's Top Maple Leaf Vacations or let CANADIAN NATIONAL RAILWAYS experts package a tour for you to include side trips and stopovers. Canadian National offices in principal U. S. cities. In Canada, Passenger Department, 360 McGill St., Montreal. Or see your Travel Agent.

The National Transcontinental operated a name train, the *National,* in conjunction with GTR and the Temiskaming & Northern Ontario Railway (T&NO, predecessor of Ontario Northland) between Toronto and Winnipeg. "Finest Equipment" and "Splendid Roadbed" proclaimed a 1917 timetable listing for this service.

CN did not take long after its creation to knit together the trackage of its predecessors into a through passenger route. The *Continental Limited* was inaugurated on

Announcing Canadian National's New Train

the **SUPER** **Continental**

FASTER TRANSCONTINENTAL SERVICE

DAILY MONTREAL - OTTAWA - TORONTO - WINNIPEG
SASKATOON - EDMONTON - JASPER - VANCOUVER

COMMENCING APRIL 24th, 1955

✓ convenient inter-city schedules

✓ smart, modern equipment

✓ budget-priced meals

CANADIAN NATIONAL RAILWAYS

DIESELIZED ALL THE WAY!

Train No. 16, the *Chaleur* from Montreal to Gaspé, leaves the mainline at Matapédia, where it will change engine crews, in August 1984. The ex-CN FPA4 locomotive has been repainted to reflect its ownership by VIA Rail Canada. *Steve Patterson*

December 3, 1920 using portions of Grand Trunk, National Transcontinental, Grand Trunk Pacific, and Canadian Northern, as well as the T&NO between North Bay and Cochrane. The route provided a 108-hour schedule from Montreal to Vancouver. Between Kamloops, British Columbia, and Jasper, it carried an open "mountain observation car" that one CN veteran remembers as "an exciting, if somewhat dirty, experience."

The 1920s were a decade of tangible improvements in CN passenger service. A radio service was implemented, and in 1927 new trains were put into service between Toronto and Vancouver (the *Confederation*), Montreal and Chicago (the *Maple Leaf*), and Montreal and Halifax (the *Acadian,* an all-sleeping car train).

The Great Depression brought an end to new service and equipment, and a dramatic reduction in passenger revenues, but throughout the 1930s CN continued to operate a large fleet of passenger trains. A 1936 timetable lists 14 "Important Trains," including the *Continental Limited* between Montreal (and Toronto) and Vancouver; the *International Limited, Maple Leaf,* and *Inter-City Limited* between Montreal, Detroit, and Chicago; the *Washingtonian* and *Montrealer* between Montreal, New York, and Washington; the *Ambassador* and *New Englander* between Montreal, Springfield (Massachusetts), and Boston; the *Ocean Limited* and *Maritime Express* between Montreal and Halifax; the *Toronto* between Toronto and New York City; the *Gull* between Halifax and Boston; the *Owl* between Regina and Saskatoon; and the *Ontario Limited* between London and Toronto. These were in addition to secondary and branchline

CN

System Timetable
April 25, 1976-
October 30, 1976

Indicateur général
25 avril 1976-
30 octobre 1976

VIA—
Heralding the birth of a new era at CN. New name, new colours. Lively. Dynamic. Now on Turbo, VIA will progressively appear on all CN passenger trains.

VIA . . .
signe de la naissance d'un temps nouveau au CN. Nouveau nom, nouvelles couleurs vives, dynamiques, à la nouvelle image du CN. Déjà sur le Turbo, VIA apparaîtra progressivement sur tous les trains du CN.

Canadian National   Canadien National

In 1976 CN debuted the new VIA image on the *Turbo* train, as shown on the cover of this timetable. *Author collection*

The *Turbo* was not the only modernistic rail equipment to get a tryout on CN. The LRC (for lightweight, rapid, comfortable)—produced by a joint venture of Montreal Locomotive Works, Alcan, and Dofasco—was also introduced in the 1970s with somewhat more success than the *Turbo.* An LRC trainset is moved by a CN switcher at Montreal's Central Station in October 1982, while a boxcab electric waits to take a commuter train north through the Mount Royal Tunnel. *Steve Patterson*

trains—in all, enough to fill an 84-page timetable.

CN's passenger equipment was worn out by the end of World War II, but it was not until Donald Gordon started to renew the company's freight car fleet and dieselize its locomotive roster that he turned his attention to the passenger business. In 1953 CN ordered $59 million worth of light-weight, streamlined passenger cars: 218 coaches from Canadian Car & Foundry, and 141 sleeping, dining, and parlor cars from Pullman-Standard—enough to re-equip all the name trains on CN's major passenger routes. Arthur Dubin, in his book *More Classic Trains,* writes "every effort was made to distribute the rolling stock in such a manner that all Canadians benefited from the new trains."

CN promoted the purchase in advertising that described it as the dawn of "a new era in Canadian rail travel." In April 1955 a new transcontinental train, the *Super Continental,* was launched using the lightweight cars, and this equipment was the backbone of CN's passenger fleet for the next two decades. Yet it didn't have the glamour of CP's stainless steel transcontinental, the *Canadian,* which also premiered in 1955. CP's *Canadian* used 173 Budd-built cars, including domes, which CN was prevented from using because of the over-head wires at Central Station, Montreal. But the *Super Continental* was a major step forward for CN's passengers.

The next big change in the marketing and operation of CN's passenger service began in 1963. The essence of the new approach, as described by Donald MacKay, was "better service, cheaper fares and better equipment." It began with running passenger trains as a service, with dedicated management, rather than as an adjunct to everything else the railway did. Employees were trained to deal with passengers in a way that would make the customer want to come back to CN.

Initially, to test whether passengers could be lured back to the rails, CN tinkered with the *Ocean Limited.* An innovative pricing system was set up to achieve maximum revenue on the days where demand was normally greatest and to boost patronage on days when there were normally fewer riders. It was dubbed the "red, white and blue" fare structure. In July, for example, weekends were blue (high fare) and weekdays were white (medium fare); in February, weekends were white (medium fare) and weekdays were red (low fare). The result: a 50 percent increase in passengers.

The new approach was implemented across the railway. There were other changes, too, including the purchase of streamlined equipment from the Reading Company for use on a new Montreal–Quebec train, *Le Champlain*; use of former Milwaukee Road cars, both east and west (observation cars for Maritimes service and full-length domes in the Rockies); and the *Rapido* service between Montreal and Toronto, aimed at regaining business travelers who put a premium on time and convenience.

One experiment did not pan out. The Turbo train, built by United Aircraft, was a complete departure from traditional railroad engineering. It looked more like an aircraft than a train, and was powered by gas turbine engines. CN leased five sets of the equipment and put them into service between Montreal and Toronto in 1968, on a four-hour schedule. Their inaugural run for the press was marred by a collision with a truck at a road crossing near Kingston, Ontario, which left the nose of the lead power unit badly damaged and illustrated the equipment's vulnerability. The Turbos were also fuel-hungry machines, which made them uneconomical in an era of rising oil prices. Furthermore, their reliability was not good, and they were in and out of service throughout their careers, which lasted until the early 1980s.

Despite the success of CN's passenger-service initiatives of the 1960s, the company continued to lose money on passenger operations. In 1976 CN put both a new blue-and-yellow image on its passenger trains (starting with the Turbo) and a new name: VIA. CN hoped that turning the passenger operation into a separate operating unit would help dramatize the extent of its financial losses. VIA quickly evolved into a coordinated marketing effort by CN and CP, and by the fall of 1976 a "VIA" timetable had been issued that contained the passenger train schedules of both companies. Two years later, VIA Rail Canada became a crown corporation, following the business model used by Amtrak in the United States. The government would be financially responsible for rail passenger services and would contract with CN and CP for track access and other services.

CN management was happy to be rid of the financial losses associated with passenger services, but more than five decades of CN passenger trains had left their imprint on the Canadian consciousness.

One of the changes resulting from the operation of passenger trains by VIA Rail Canada was that electrically heated, rebuilt stainless steel cars from Canadian Pacific's *Canadian* started to appear on CN routes. VIA train 5. The *Skeena* from Jasper, Alberta, to Prince Rupert, British Columbia, is seen on CN's Skeena Subdivision in April 1992. This was the first operation of the former CP equipment on this train. *Phil Mason*

The Carbonear mixed train (*sans* freight cars) passes
through Spaniards Bay, Newfoundland, in July 1984.
Steve Patterson

CHAPTER FIVE

FROM SEA TO SEA:
The Regions of CN

Fifty years ago Canadian National extended from St. John's, Newfoundland, in the east, to Churchill, Manitoba, in the north, and Vancouver Island, British Columbia, in the west. Today's CN does not reach any of those locations, but it still extends from the Atlantic to the Pacific and from the Gulf of Alaska (via a railcar barge service between Prince Rupert, British Columbia, and Whittier, Alaska) to the Gulf of Mexico (thanks to the acquisition of Illinois Central in 1999).

CN system map, 1971: Newfoundland, Maritime Provinces, Eastern Quebec, and Grand Trunk and Central Vermont lines in New England. *Author collection*

Operations and traffic patterns have changed, but CN has remained a geographically diverse company as its network has changed to meet the needs of the North American economy. The Latin motto on Canada's coat of arms reads *A Mari Usque Ad Mare,* or "From Sea to Sea." It describes not only Canada but CN as well.

The Maritimes: Railroading at the Water's Edge

CN's lines in the maritime provinces of Nova Scotia and New Brunswick were inherited mainly from the Intercolonial Railway, whose mainline ran from Halifax north to Truro, Nova Scotia, then northwest through Moncton, New Brunswick, to Matapédia, Quebec. From Matapédia, the line turned west and then southwest to run along the St. Lawrence River toward Rivière-du-Loup, Lévis (across the river from Quebec City), and Montreal.

The Intercolonial also had a line from Truro to Sydney, on Cape Breton Island. Rail access to Cape Breton was originally by ferry, but in 1954 the Canso Causeway was completed, allowing uninterrupted rail movements to and from the island. Other

In 1982 *M. V. Abegweit* replaced an older vessel of the same name on the run between Borden, Prince Edward Island, and Cape Tormentine, New Brunswick. The new "Abby" was more than 400 feet (121 meters) in length and was specially designed for handling railcars, as well as motor vehicles and passengers. Here the ship leaves Borden for the mainland in August 1984. *Steve Patterson*

A CN freight with two MLW RS3 units, led by CN 3021, crosses the Canso Causeway en route from Truro to Sydney, Nova Scotia, in September 1960. *Jim Shaughnessy*

Intercolonial lines ran from Moncton to Saint John, New Brunswick, and from Chatham Junction to Fredericton, New Brunswick. The Intercolonial also operated the Prince Edward Island Railway.

The Intercolonial was not the only CN predecessor to serve the Maritimes. The Halifax & South Western Railway, controlled by Canadian Northern, ran from Halifax to Yarmouth, Nova Scotia, with a branch from Bridgewater to Port Wade, on the Bay of Fundy. CNoR also had a 60-mile (97-kilometer) coal line on Cape Breton,

Nova Scotia, which ran from Point Tupper to Inverness. The National Transcontinental Railway contributed one Maritime route to CN, from Moncton to Quebec City via Edmundston, New Brunswick. This line was shorter and ran closer to the border between Canada and Maine than did the Intercolonial's Moncton–Quebec City route.

The economic rationale for most of the rail lines in the maritime provinces had more to do with promoting local development than with generating a return on investment for the lines' various operators and owners. There was freight

to be sure. Both imports and exports moved via rail between Halifax and the rest of Canada. Saint John was also a major port city, although CN's circuitous route put it at a disadvantage versus Canadian Pacific, whose line between Saint John and Montreal ran east-west across Maine. In the area of Sydney, Nova Scotia both coal-mining and steel-making were sources of freight revenue. New Brunswick generated forest products—paper, pulpwood, and lumber— all of which moved by rail.

The conflict between the railways' need for better returns on their Maritime traffic

and the protests of shippers who felt that they were at a disadvantage because rates, in their view, were too high, led to the passage of the Maritime Freight Rate Act in 1927. The act authorized the federal government to pay the railways a 20 percent subsidy on traffic that originated or terminated in the Maritimes.

For many years CN's lines in the Maritimes were best known for the vacation spots they reached. A 1937 CN travel brochure described the region's "smooth, sand-covered beaches over which rolls the surf from the Atlantic; inland vistas of smiling farms,

CN 1775 west at Martins River, Nova Scotia, in July 1984. This scene is 66 miles (106 kilometers) southwest of Halifax on the now-abandoned line to Yarmouth. *Steve Patterson*

CN 1753 west passes a potato warehouse at Albany, Prince Edward Island, in August 1984. *Steve Patterson*

meadows and gently rolling hills, forests and rivers; along the sea coast, picturesque fishing villages and deep-sea fisherman types."

To meet the need of vacationers, CN provided not only passenger trains (most notably the *Ocean Limited* and *Maritime Express* between Montreal and Halifax, both of which carried cars for Sydney), but also two hotels and a resort: the Nova Scotian Hotel in Halifax; the Charlottetown Hotel (originally the Canadian National Hotel) in Charlottetown, Prince Edward Island; and the Pictou Lodge, at Pictou, Nova Scotia.

Tourism remained an important element in the economy of the Maritimes over the decades, but vacationers do not generate freight business. As CN became more profit-oriented, many of its lines in the region were abandoned or, in two cases, turned over to independent operators. Rail operations on Prince Edward Island ended in 1989. The Halifax & South Western line to Yarmouth was abandoned in stages, with the last seg-

ment seeing service in 1993. By 2003, the former Intercolonial routes between Moncton and Campbellton, New Brunswick, and from Truro to Sydney, Nova Scotia, had both been turned over to regional rail operators.

Today, what remains of CN in the Maritimes is the Halifax–Moncton–Edmundston route, which serves as a major corridor for intermodal traffic moving between Halifax and inland points in Canada and the United States, as well as the line between Moncton and Saint John.

The Newfoundland Railway

The final component of CN's system in the Maritimes was the Newfoundland Railway. Newfoundland became Canada's tenth province on April 1, 1949, after more than three centuries as a British colony. One of the conditions of the agreement between Newfoundland and Canada was that the Canadian government would take over the island's railway.

Known as the "mini ore" train, CN train No. 587 operated from Campbellton, New Brunswick, to Brunswick Mines and back. The ore handled from the mine was dropped at the smelter at Belledune, and its weight required two six-axle Century-type locomotives. CN 2021 and 2014, delivered by Montreal Locomotive Works in 1968, are part of a group of 44 C630M units rostered by CN. The train is shown at Dalhousie Junction, New Brunswick, in February 1992 *George Pitarys*

Beginning in 1952 General Motors Diesel Division produced a unique series of locomotives, the six-axle (C-C) NF110 and NF210 models, for Newfoundland service. In this photo they show their family resemblance to the GP and SD models of the same era. This narrow-gauge freight train, en route from Port aux Basques to St. John's, is at Glenwood, Newfoundland, in May 1975. *Phil Mason*

Railway construction in Newfoundland began in 1881 with the building of a line west from the capital, St. John's. By 1884, an 86-mile (138-kilometer) line had been completed to Harbour Grace. To keep construction costs down, it was built to a gauge of 3 feet, 6 inches. Unlike other narrow gauge lines that were later converted to standard gauge, the Newfoundland Railway remained narrow gauge until the end.

In 1890 contractor Robert Gillespie Reid agreed to build an extension of the railway to the west, and in 1893 he signed a contract to operate the railway in return for land grants (5,000 acres per mile of railway). By 1898 a line had been completed to Port aux Basques at the western end of the island, a distance of 547 rail miles (881 kilometers). The Reid

Newfoundland Company became the operator of the railway for the next quarter-century and was also put in charge of Newfoundland's streetcar, telegraph, coastal ferry, and hydro-electric services.

Like other railway builders, Reid saw the railway as a development tool, but the economic pressures caused by World War I, and the downturn that followed the war, left the Reid Newfoundland Company unable to finance needed improvements. The company's contract was terminated in 1923, by which time the construction of various branchlines had given the island more than 900 miles (1,450 kilometers) of railway.

World War II found Newfoundland in a strategically advantageous location. Military bases were built at Argentia, Gander,

Stephenville, and St. John's, and the railway benefited from a doubling of freight traffic. But the end of the war brought a quick end to the traffic surge, and in 1949, when Newfoundlanders voted to join Canada, the federal government agreed to take over the money-losing island railway. CN found itself running not only the rail freight and passenger services, but also the island's telephone service, its ferry services, and the Hotel Newfoundland in St. John's, which CN thoroughly renovated to bring up to the standards of other CN hotels.

Management by CN brought many changes to the railway (which by this time was operating 705 route miles [1,135 kilometers] after several branchline abandonments). Wage levels for the railway's 4,100 employees

were increased, and CN invested in rail, cars, and diesel locomotives.

Newfoundland's economy benefited from confederation with Canada, and more freight started to move over the railway. However, the system for handling freight between CN's railhead at North Sydney, Nova Scotia, and the Newfoundland terminal at Port aux Basques was labor-intensive and time-consuming. Freight moving in either direction was unloaded from railcars, transferred to vessels piece by piece, ferried across the Cabot Strait, and then reloaded onto railcars.

As CN modernized the island's ferry service, a major improvement was the ability to carry standard gauge freight cars across the Cabot Strait. In the shop at Port aux Basques, standard gauge trucks were replaced

Aside from the NF110 and NF210 models, CN also bought from GMD an export-type locomotive, model G8, for Newfoundland service. These A1A-A1A units were lighter by about 50,000 pounds than their C-C cousins. Nos. 800 and 802 are at St. John's in July 1984, with the headquarters building of the Newfoundland rail system in the background. *Steve Patterson*

Despite the gauge difference, cars from CN's regular fleet could carry freight to Newfoundland destinations, as long as they had their wheels changed at Port aux Basques, as seen here in August 1984. Trucks were marked with car numbers so that a car would return to North Sydney, Nova Scotia, with its original equipment. *Steve Patterson*

with narrow gauge. After the car went to its Newfoundland destination, it would return to Port aux Basques, the original trucks would be put back under the car, and it would make the ferry passage back to North Sydney. The narrow gauge could only handle cars of up to 50 tons (at a time when 100-ton cars were becoming a regular sight on many North American rail lines) but it was a big improvement over transloading. In addition to the service across the strait, CN also operated a number of coastal ferry services—a 1961 CN timetable shows nine vessels operating on 12 Newfoundland and Labrador coastal routes.

Newfoundland was not immune to changes in transportation that were occurring throughout North America. The Trans-Canada highway was completed across the island in 1965. *The Caribou* between St. John's and Port aux Basques (unofficially, the *Newfie Bullet*), which made 20 station stops plus 19 flag stops en route and averaged 24 miles per hour (39 kilometers per hour), was replaced by a bus in 1969. Mixed trains on the Argentia, Bonavista, and Carbonear branches survived into the 1970s.

In 1979 CN gave the Newfoundland freight service a new name, TerraTransport, and began a program of putting freight into containers so that it could reach customers without being transloaded between railcars and trucks. Once the traffic was in containers, it could be moved by truck anywhere on the island where there was a road. Rail transport became a costly luxury, and by 1984 all branchlines had been abandoned. Still, financial losses on the Newfoundland rail service persisted despite better equipment, improved operations, and cutbacks in the route map. The last train on the island ran in 1988.

Ontario and Quebec: Factories South, Forests North

The residents of Ontario and Quebec together represent more than 60 percent of Canada's population. They are the most diverse of the Canadian provinces, and CN's operations reflect this. They contain the highest-density segment in the CN network (Toronto–Montreal), as well as some of the lowest-density routes (the lines in northern Quebec). Two of the four major classification yards on the system are located here: Taschereau Yard in Montreal and MacMillan Yard in Toronto.

In southern Ontario and the urban areas of Quebec, smokestack industries—auto plants, steel mills, refineries, and chemical plants—predominate, whereas in the north, most rail traffic is either extracted from below ground or harvested from the coniferous forests that blanket the Canadian Shield. Overlaying the traffic that originates or terminates in these provinces is business (primarily intermodal) moving between Halifax in the east and customers in western Canada and the United States.

The three major contributors to what would become CN's network in these provinces were the Grand Trunk, Canadian Northern, and National Transcontinental railways. In addition, the Intercolonial route from Halifax entered Quebec at Matapédia, extending first to Rivière-du-Loup and

Great Western Railway engine No. 42 ("Diadem") exits the Suspension Bridge at Niagara Falls, Ontario, in 1864. *National Archives of Canada/ PA-138681*

CN system map, 1971: Ontario, Quebec, Grand Trunk Western, and Duluth, Winnipeg & Pacific. *Author collection*

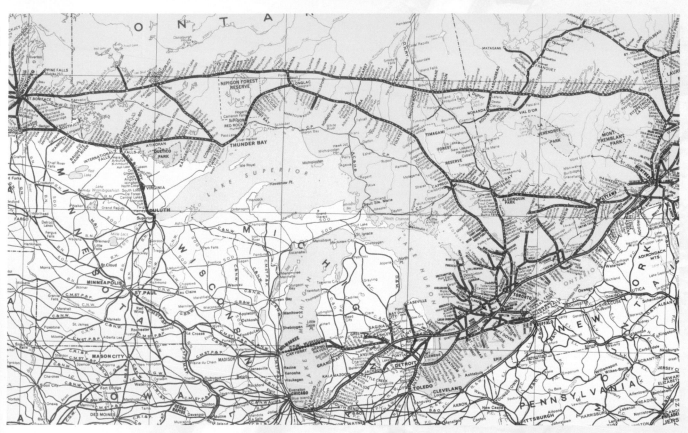

Train No. 416 emerges from miles of running through the northern Quebec wilderness as it passes Hervey Junction in August 1999. Originating in Arvida, the train is laden with finished aluminum blocks from the large Alcan plants in the Lac St. Jean region, as well as a heavy dose of wood and lumber products. *George Pitarys*

In 1929 CN rebuilt the former Grand Trunk shops at Point St. Charles, Montreal. The shop complex, shown here in 1930, covered 30 acres and employed approximately 2,500 people. *National Archives of Canada/ PA-037501*

The St. Lawrence River is never far away in southern Quebec and Ontario. Here CN 6767 pauses at Lévis, Quebec, with the westbound *Scotian* in June 1979. Across the river in Quebec City is Canadian Pacific's landmark hotel, the Chateau Frontenac. *Tom Murray*

The Quebec City-bound *Champlain,* using former Reading *Crusader* equipment, approaches the south end of the Quebec Bridge spanning the St. Lawrence River in August 1964. *Jim Shaughnessy*

Long since rendered obsolete by the discontinuance of passenger service and the installation of CTC signaling that sounded the death knell for train order operation, the well-preserved station at Rivière Bleu, Quebec, is witness to the passage of hot Halifax-to-Toronto intermodal train No. 149 in April 2001. *George Pitarys*

eventually to Lévis and Montreal. On Quebec's Gaspé Peninsula, CN acquired the Atlantic, Quebec & Western Railway and Quebec Oriental Railway in 1929.

The most heavily used lines in southern Quebec and Ontario are of GTR heritage, including the Quebec City–Montreal line, the double-track Montreal–Toronto line, and the route from Toronto to Hamilton, London, Sarnia, and Windsor, Ontario. CN also uses former GTR trackage (originally built by the Great Western Railway) to reach the Niagara gateway and Buffalo, New York.

As railways evolved, crossing the St. Lawrence and other major rivers was a significant engineering challenge. Notable milestones in the crossing of the region's waterways include:

• The Niagara River Suspension Bridge, opened by the Great Western Railway in 1855, which GTR replaced with a steel arch bridge in 1897.

• The Victoria Bridge over the St. Lawrence River at Montreal, opened by GTR in 1859 and rebuilt in place as a double-track steel truss structure in 1897 and 1898.

• The Quebec Bridge, a critical link in the National Transcontinental's mainline, and the world's largest railway cantilever bridge. As construction proceeded in 1907, one section of the bridge collapsed into the river, killing 73 workers. It was redesigned by a new team of engineers, but during the final phase of construction in 1916, the center span collapsed, claiming 13 lives. The bridge was completed in 1917.

From Toronto north, a former Canadian Northern route carries transcontinental traffic toward Winnipeg via Sudbury and Capreol. This was once part of CNoR's route from Toronto to Winnipeg by way of Port Arthur and Fort William, but CN's east-west route uses the Long Lake cutoff between Longlac and Nakina, and the former National Transcontinental line west of Nakina.

Between Winnipeg and Thunder Bay on the former CNoR route, there are two main traffic flows: grain, coal, potash, and other commodities moving to Thunder Bay; and western Canadian resources en route to U.S. markets via the Duluth, Winnipeg & Pacific Railway, which leaves the CNoR route at Fort Frances, Ontario. The ex-CNoR line between Thunder Bay and Longlac carries relatively little traffic today.

North of Montreal and Quebec City, the former National Transcontinental line and various CN-built branchlines carry forest products and minerals. However, the

CN's defining physical characteristic in much of southern Quebec and Ontario is its proximity to the St. Lawrence River, the Great Lakes, and their connecting waterways. The region's first railways were designed to connect rivers rather than to compete with them, and CN still depends on port facilities along the St. Lawrence, particularly at Montreal, for substantial volumes of traffic.

National Transcontinental line is no longer transcontinental, having been abandoned between La Sarre, Quebec, and Cochrane, Ontario, and between Calstock and Nakina, Ontario. The segment between Cochrane and Calstock is now operated by Ontario Northland Railway.

Several former CN lines in Ontario and Quebec have been taken over by short-line and regional rail operators over the past two decades. In Quebec, they include lines from Matapédia to Pabos; Pabos to Gaspé; Limilou to Clermont; Norton, Vermont, to Ste. Rosalie, Quebec; and Mont-Joli, Quebec, to Campbellton, New Brunswick. In Ontario independent operators connecting with CN now provide service from St. Thomas to Delhi; Port Colborne to St. Catharines; Glen Robertson to Hawksbury; Stratford Junction to Goderich; Brantford to Nanticoke; and Pembroke, Ontario, to Coteau, Quebec.

A number of unprofitable and redundant CN lines in the region have been abandoned. However, given the rail-oriented nature of many industries in Ontario and Quebec, and

the critical geographic position these two provinces occupy in terms of North American freight flows, it is safe to say that they will retain their prominent position in the CN route map.

The Prairies: Land of Wheat and Barley

Think of the provinces of Manitoba, Saskatchewan, and Alberta, and the image that comes to mind is a grain elevator against an expanse of broad sky and flat landscape. That image is accurate, but far from complete. In many places, the prairies are not so much flat as they are rolling, with north-south watercourses that railway builders had to contend with as they built from east to west. In addition, all three of these provinces stretch far to the north into mineral-rich areas, some of which took many years for the rail system to penetrate. Besides grain and minerals (notably nickel and copper), the prairie provinces are the source of substantial potash production (in southern Saskatchewan) and petroleum products (in Alberta). Alberta is also home to the eastern slopes of the Canadian Rockies and their large coal deposits.

Two of CN's predecessor lines were responsible for most of the trackage that CN inherited in these provinces: Canadian Northern, which got its start in Manitoba, and eventually reached west toward Vancouver, and Grand Trunk Pacific, which built its own route from Winnipeg to Prince Rupert, British Columbia. The National Transcontinental also reached Winnipeg, but only 75 miles (121 kilometers) of its route was within Manitoba.

In its timetables Canadian Northern called itself the "Saskatchewan Valley Route: The Homeseekers' Way to Western Canada Through Winnipeg." Its lines criss-crossed the prairies, with three principal east-west routes and a variety of other lines serving the region. The CNoR mainline ran from Winnipeg west through Portage la Prairie, Gladstone, and Dauphin, Manitoba; Canora, Warman, and North Battleford, Saskatchewan; and Lloydminster, Edmonton, and Jasper, Alberta. Just west of Jasper, the line entered British Columbia. A secondary CNoR route took a more southerly route, passing through Brandon, Manitoba, and Regina, Saskatchewan, before reaching Saskatoon, while a connecting line reached

CN system map, 1971: Prairie Provinces. *Author collection*

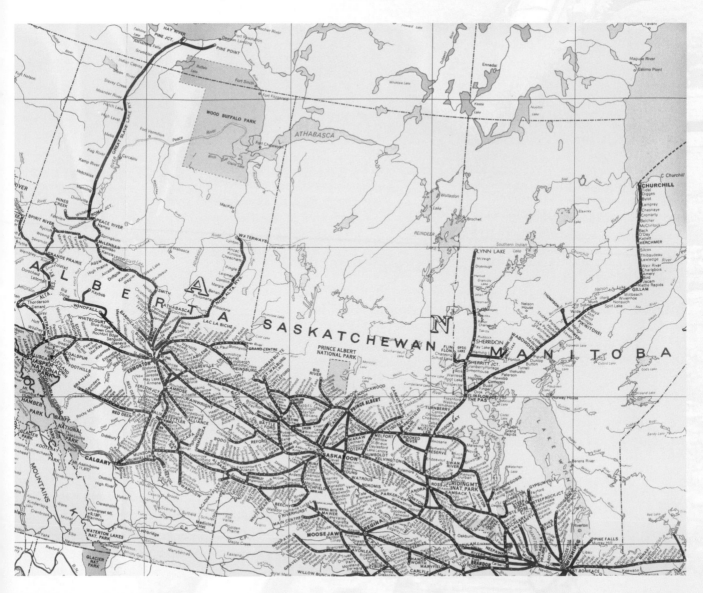

The rolling nature of the terrain in parts of the prairie provinces can create opportunities for snow to accumulate in cuts, particularly those with steep slopes. According to the notes that accompanied this 1947 photo in the CN archives, CN No. 2814 and two other steam engines and plow were being dug out of a drift near Victoria Plains, Saskatchewan, "as work continued to open blockade. Took five days to open drift. Drift was almost a mile long and completely covered pole line in places." *Canada Science and Technology Museum, CSTM/CN collection neg. no. X24091*

west from Saskatoon to Drumheller and Calgary, Alberta. A more northerly east-west route branched off the mainline near Dauphin, Manitoba, and served Melfort and Prince Albert, Saskatchewan, before rejoining the mainline at North Battleford.

As a latecomer, following both the Canadian Pacific and CNoR across the prairies, GTP had a less extensive network than its rivals. Its mainline west of Winnipeg was north of the CP and south of the CNoR. It passed through Portage la Prairie and Rivers, Manitoba, (with a short branch south to Brandon); Melville, Saskatoon, and Biggar, Saskatchewan; and Wainwright, Edmonton, Edson, and Jasper, Alberta, before entering British Columbia to continue toward Prince

Rupert. The GTP line is now CN's mainline across the region. In its short life GTP did construct some prairie branchlines, including Melville to Regina, Saskatchewan; Regina to a connection with the Great Northern Railway at Northgate, Alberta; Regina to Moose Jaw and Riverhurst, Saskatchewan; Melville to Canora, Saskatchewan; Watrous to Prince Albert, Saskatchewan; Biggar to Loverna, Saskatchewan; and the Alberta Coal Branch, running south from Edson.

Together with fertilizers, grain accounts for more than 20 percent of CN's revenues in a good crop year. Wheat is the grain most often associated with the Canadian prairies, but they are a source of barley, oats, rye, flax, and other crops as well. In the past 30 years

A set of three GMD1 units led by CN 1032 are seen at Kindersley, Saskatchewan, on a ballast train in June 1976. *Stan Smaill*

CN GP38-2 7528 works as part of a hump set shoving cars over the crest and into the classification tracks at Symington Yard in Winnipeg in October 1992. A Beltpack console is remotely controlling the locomotive. CN was the first major railway to use this technology, which has since been implemented by other rail carriers in yards and terminals throughout North America. *Phil Mason*

CN SD40 5233 and a GP9 pass the Pioneer elevator at Biggar, Saskatchewan, in May 1976 with an eastbound train carrying forest products. Biggar, population 2,351, is a crew change point between Saskatoon and Edmonton. A sign on the outskirts of town reads, "New York is Big But This is Biggar." *Phil Mason*

the system of gathering and transporting grain on the prairies has been modernized. One of the biggest changes has been the conversion from railway-supplied boxcars with grain doors (which would often leak grain on the ground) to 100-ton covered hopper cars financed by the government. There are fewer elevators today than 30 years ago, with more grain now moving through large facilities where unit trains can be loaded. In 2003 CN reported that it had 75 high-throughput elevators located on its lines, capable of loading 50- to 100-car trains.

Some of the lowest-density grain branchlines, where GMD1 locomotives once tiptoed along light rail, are now gone, and others have been taken over by short-line and regional railroads. In fact, while Canada was late in arriving at a system for transferring low-density lines from large railroads to independent short-line operators, the first significant step in that direction came in the prairies with the creation of Alberta's Central Western Railway in 1986. Aside from the Central Western, which operates a former CN line north of Dinosaur Junction, Alberta, several other prairie lines, now controlled by independent operators, gather grain traffic and interchange it to CN for the line haul. In Manitoba, these include lines from Winnipeg to Pine Falls; Winnipeg to Carman; and Morris to Elgin; and in Saskatchewan, the routes from Saskatoon to Prince Albert, from Denholm to Meadow Lake, and from Moose Jaw to Parry.

Although there is some truck transportation of grain on the prairies, for these crops to reach export and most domestic markets, rail transportation is the only practical way to go. Because of its route structure, CN will continue to be a key player in the grain transportation system regardless of how that system may change in the future.

Reaching Northward

Beginning in 1912 three privately built railways extended rail service into the sparsely populated country north and northwest of Edmonton. By 1920 the government of Alberta had leased two of the lines and contracted out their operation to Canadian Pacific; the government operated the third line. In 1926 the government terminated the CP contract, and CN began operating the lines, which by then included a fourth route built by the government.

Examples of cooperation between CP and CN in the 1920s were rare, but the two companies did join forces in 1929 to operate these lines under the banner of Northern Alberta Railways (NAR). The joint arrangement lasted until 1981, when CP bowed out and the NAR routes became part of CN.

From Edmonton one NAR line ran northeast to Lac La Biche and Fort McMurray. Most of the railway's mileage was northwest of Edmonton, however. NAR ran through Slave Lake to McClennan, where one line continued

There is no question about what drives the local economy at Rosebud, Alberta, as CN 9169 rolls through in June 1983 on train No. 316. Rosebud is 60 miles (97 kilometers) northeast of Calgary, on the former Canadian Northern line to Saskatoon. When this photo was taken, the line had 85-pound rail, and motive power on through freights was typically a mix of F7 and GP9 units. The line was subsequently rebuilt to handle heavier locomotives. *Phil Mason*

During construction of the Great Slave Lake Railway between 1966 and 1969, an automatic train operation system developed by Westinghouse was installed in four GP9 locomotives. The system provided automatic speed control on the mainline, and a remote-control system for switching. The latter was a precursor to the Beltpack system developed in the 1980s by the CN Technical Research Centre (now part of CN's consulting affiliate, CANAC). Here, a GSL employee uses the remote-control system in 1968. *Canada Science and Technology Museum, CSTM/CN collection neg. no. 68533–20*

northwest to Peace River and Hines Creek, while another ran west to Spirit River, then south to Grande Prairie, before turning northwest toward Dawson Creek, British Columbia. NAR's total mileage was approximately 920 miles (1,481 kilometers).

Much of NAR's traffic consisted of grain. However, when the Great Slave Lake Railroad (GSL, a CN-operated line that connected with NAR at Roma Junction, just west of Peace River) opened in 1968, lead and zinc ore taken from a Cominco zinc- and copper-mining operation at Pine Point, Alberta, and destined for the Cominco smelter at Trail in southern British Columbia, began to move over the line.

The 430-mile (692-kilometer) GSL was built and operated by CN for the federal government. It was the first and only rail line to extend into Canada's Northwest Territories. CN historian Donald MacKay observes that the GSL (and NAR) "hauled out grain and lumber and became the main supply line for Arctic oil exploration. By linking the Northern Alberta Railways to Hay River, the staging point for the Mackenzie River barge system, CN lowered the cost of shipments not only to Yellowknife but the Mackenzie delta and the Arctic coast."

The 230-mile (370-kilometer) Alberta Resources Railway (ARR), financed by the

province of Alberta and operated by CN, opened in 1969 from Swan Landing (on the mainline between Jasper and Hinton) to Grande Cache and Grande Prairie, where it connected with NAR. This line was built to serve a coal mine in the Smoky River region and to open up markets for grain and lumber producers in northern Alberta.

Today, independent short-line and regional carriers operate most of the former NAR and the entire GSL and ARR lines.

Another line that pushed toward Canada's sub-Arctic was the Hudson Bay line. According to G. R. Stevens, the idea of such a line was first proposed in 1885 in response to grain producers' desire to have an alternative to the CP monopoly on the prairies. In

1905 William Mackenzie and Donald Mann of the CNoR got involved and mapped out a 538-mile (866-kilometer) route from Prairie River, Saskatchewan, to Port Nelson, Manitoba. In 1924 the terminus was changed to Churchill, Manitoba, and a new route was surveyed, but it was not until 1931 that the line finally opened.

Despite the theoretical appeal of the Hudson Bay route for grain destined to Europe, the reality is that the Port of Churchill is closed roughly eight months out of the year. Less than 3 percent of Canada's grain exports move through the port annually. Nevertheless, the line gained notoriety during its years under CN as the "polar bear route," due to the bears that are a common sight around Churchill. But the line was a drain on CN from the time it was completed. In 1997 its operation was taken over by Denver-based short-line operator OmniTRAX, which operates it as the Hudson Bay Railway.

Other northern extensions included:
• A 144-mile (232-kilometer) line to Lynn Lake, Manitoba, completed in November 1953 and built to tap into the region's nickel, copper, and cobalt deposits.
• A 161-mile (259-kilometer) line from Beattyville to Chibougamau, Quebec (in another mineral rich-area), opened in 1957. This was followed by the construction of a 133-mile (214-kilometer) connecting line from Cache Lake to St. Felicien, Quebec, which opened in 1959.

Northern Alberta Railways Nos. 404-202 are at Carbondale, Alberta, 20 miles (32 kilometers) north of Edmonton, in June 1976. Following the merger of NAR into CN in 1981, this segment was abandoned in favor of the CN line between Dunvegan Yard, Edmonton, and Morinville, Alberta. *Phil Mason*

• A 52-mile (84-kilometer) line from Optic Lake to Chisel Lake, Manitoba, built to serve the Hudson Bay Mining and Smelting Company, which opened in 1960.

CN in the West: Toward the Pacific Rim

At its peak in the 1970s, CN's network west of Edmonton consisted of:

• The Grand Trunk Pacific line from Edmonton to Jasper, Alberta, and Red Pass Junction, British Columbia. (Most of CNoR's parallel line was removed during World War I to provide rail for the war effort.)

• The Alberta Coal Branch south of Edson, built by GTP.

• The Alberta Resources Railway north of Swan Landing.

• The CNoR route from Red Pass Junction to Vancouver via Blue River, Kamloops, and Boston Bar, British Columbia.

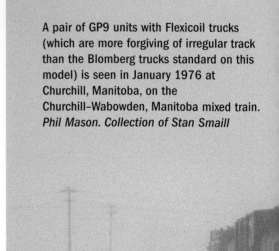

A pair of GP9 units with Flexicoil trucks (which are more forgiving of irregular track than the Blomberg trucks standard on this model) is seen in January 1976 at Churchill, Manitoba, on the Churchill–Wabowden, Manitoba mixed train. *Phil Mason. Collection of Stan Smaill*

CN No. 1147 is shown on VIA No. 291, the Lynn Lake mixed train, at The Pas, Manitoba, in October 1988. *Phil Mason*

Crews arriving on VIA train 93 at Churchill in October 1991 did not have to go far for their lodging—they stayed on the second floor of the depot. *Steve Patterson*

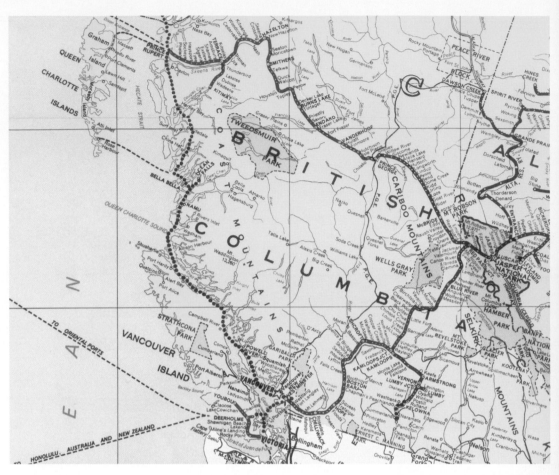

• The Okanagan route from Kamloops to Kelowna, British Columbia, completed by CN in 1925.
• CNoR lines on Vancouver Island.
• The GTP line from Red Pass Junction to Prince Rupert, British Columbia.
• The Kitimat Subdivision, south of Terrace, British Columbia, opened by CN in 1955 to serve a smelter run by the Aluminum Company of Canada.

Grand Trunk Pacific and Canadian Northern were latecomers to western Canada. CP had completed its transcontinental line in 1885. It chose a southern route over the Rockies via Kicking Horse Pass with grades as steep as 4.5 percent. CP subsequently rebuilt the line with a pair of spiral tunnels that reduced the ruling grade to 2.2 percent.

CP's choice of the southern route left a much easier grade via Yellowhead Pass available for both GTP and CNoR. GTP got there first, reaching the continental divide in November 1911. Its ruling grade was 0.5 percent westbound and 0.4 percent eastbound, except for a 19-mile (31-kilometer) segment approaching Yellowhead Pass, where the eastbound grade was 1.0 percent (later eased by CN's construction of a new connection between the former GTP and CNoR lines).

CNoR also used the Yellowhead crossing on its route to Vancouver, reaching the pass in 1913. G. R. Stevens describes this as "perhaps the most foolish trackage ever to be built in Canada." Since both GTP and CNoR received government assistance for their western extensions, "the taxpayer was therefore building two-lines across well-nigh trafficless territory within a stone's throw of each other," Stevens writes. However, the duplication did not last long; in 1916 work began on removing sections of the CNoR line so that

Soldiers of a construction battalion remove rail from the Canadian Northern line between Edmonton and Yellowhead Pass, circa 1917. The rail was shipped to Europe for use in constructing rail lines to support the military effort during World War I. *National Archives of Canada/ C-068790*

CN 5340 west at Henry House, Alberta, a few miles east of Jasper, in October 1989. *Steve Patterson*

In 1924 CN constructed a wharf at Cowichan Bay on Vancouver Island, where lumber from the island's forests could be transferred from railcar to vessel.
Canada Science and Technology Museum, CSTM/CN collection neg. no. 250

the rail could be shipped to Europe for use in the war. The former CNoR grade, as well as remains of bridge foundations, can still be seen in some locations today.

From Kamloops west, CNoR found that being 30 years behind the CP put it at a disadvantage. Through the Thompson and Fraser River canyons, CP had chosen the easier side of the river for its route; CNoR, by default, took the more difficult side. Between Kamloops and Boston Bar, a distance of 125 miles (201 kilometers), the line crosses the Thompson River eight times and the Fraser twice, and originally had 17 tunnels.

Although Vancouver was CNoR's western objective, CP and Great Northern (GN) were already there. GN was willing to provide CNoR with access to Vancouver through the sale of one track segment and trackage rights over another segment. The western end of CNoR construction was at a location it designated Port Mann, about 15 miles (24 kilometers) east of Vancouver, where it built a yard and other servicing facilities.

Today the CN line to Vancouver carries grain, potash, sulfur, and other bulk commodities for export, as well as a large volume of international container traffic. Tunnels were enlarged in the early 1990s to accommodate double-stack equipment. Traffic density on the Vancouver–Edmonton line in 2002 was more than 50 million gross ton-miles, or only about 15 percent less than the volume carried by CN's Montreal–Toronto mainline. The latter, however, is double-track, reverse-signaled, high-capacity railway with long stretches of tangent track; the Vancouver line through the river canyons of British Columbia is single-track with many speed restrictions due to curves.

In 1999 CN and CP began a paired-track arrangement for 155 miles (249 kilometers) in the Thompson and Fraser canyon area. Both CN and CP trains now use CN's line westbound and CP's eastbound. The arrangement increases capacity by eliminating the delays inherent in having trains meet each other in single-track territory.

One price that CNoR paid for financial assistance from the British Columbia provincial government was a requirement to construct a

At Cisco, British Columbia, CN and Canadian Pacific exchange sides of the Fraser River. In this August 1981 photo, a westbound CN freight behind SD40 5154 crosses from the west side of the river to the east, while an eastbound CP freight simultaneously crosses the bridge in the foreground. *Steve Patterson*

Near Seddall, British Columbia, in April 1996 a westbound train navigates tunnels that serve as reminders of the challenges faced by the Canadian Northern Railway in building a route through this portion of the Thompson River Canyon. *Phil Mason*

rail line on Vancouver Island. Work began in 1911, but because of war-related delays the first segment was not opened until 1917. Canadian National completed the Vancouver Island lines in the 1920s, in the process penetrating some of the best logging territory in Canada. However, a typical CN haul for lumber moving to the ferry slip at Cowichan Bay was only 30 miles (48 kilometers), so the economics of this operation were never good. By 1991 CN had ceased operating on Vancouver Island.

Another piece of unfinished business left by CNoR was in the Okanagan territory of southern British Columbia. CNoR had planned a route for the line, but did not begin construction before being absorbed by CN. The 119-mile (192-kilometer) line from Kamloops to Kelowna, which used parts of two CP subdivisions to reach its southern terminus, was completed in 1925. It operates as an independent short line today.

The GTP line to Prince Rupert, commonly known on CN as the B. C. North line,

was built on the theory that Prince Rupert's relative proximity to Asia would give it an advantage over Vancouver in capturing trans-Pacific trade. Yet the rail route from Jasper to Vancouver is 529 miles (852 kilometers), versus 722 miles (1,162 kilometers) to Prince Rupert—a difference of 193 miles (311 kilometers). Other things being equal, freight will generally seek a route that minimizes land mileage even if the route increases in water mileage. And conditions have never been equal between the two ports—Vancouver was a well-established port city before the first train from the east ever reached Prince Rupert.

Following World War I Prince Rupert's freight business was in the doldrums, but it did enjoy a substantial volume of passenger traffic, both as a gateway to Alaska and as part of the Triangle Tour (Vancouver–Jasper–Prince Rupert) promoted heavily by CN's passenger department. World War II brought the port into a prominent role for its strategic location, and the CN line was upgraded to

An eastbound train passes through the Cape Horn rock sheds, east of Lasha, British Columbia, in the White Canyon of the Thompson River Canyon, in April 1996. *Phil Mason*

handle the resulting volume of traffic. CN's original road diesel locomotive, No. 9000, was equipped with armor plate to power a train with four gun-equipped flatcars that protected the CN line between Prince Rupert and Terrace. Gun emplacements were also constructed along the track near Prince Rupert.

In the 1980s a new grain terminal was constructed on Ridley Island, south of the city of Prince Rupert, and today an average of

Kitwanga, British Columbia, is located 154 miles (248 kilometers) east of Prince Rupert. In October 1978, CN 9173, a rebuilt F7, leads a westbound freight. *Stan Smaill*

275

five trains per week arrive there with export grain. Prince Rupert also enjoyed a healthy volume of export coal traffic from the Tumbler Ridge area of British Columbia (originated by BC Rail) from 1983 to 2003, when the mines closed. As of early 2004 the coal facilities at Ridley Island were being used for iron ore moving from Minnesota to China. The Aquatrain service, which moves freight on the world's largest railcar barge (with a capacity of 50 cars) to a connection with the Alaska Railroad at Whittier, Alaska, also puts traffic on the Prince Rupert line. The barge makes 32 trips per year.

East of Prince George, where CN interchanges with BC Rail (the former Pacific Great Eastern Railway), traffic volumes are somewhat higher. CN receives about 300 cars of lumber per week from BC Rail origins for movement eastward. That volume is likely to increase following CN's planned acquisition of the provincially owned BC Rail franchise in 2004. As part of the deal with British Columbia, CN has offered to improve clearances on the Prince Rupert line to allow for the movement of double-stack intermodal trains to a proposed container port. Given capacity constraints on the rail lines to Vancouver, it is possible that Prince Rupert may finally achieve the level of business hoped for by Grand Trunk president Charles Melville Hays, who envisioned this "port at the end of the rainbow."

CN mixed train No. 297 is in the siding at Aleza Lake, British Columbia (between McBride and Prince George), so that freight train 1st 720, with F7 CN 9132 leading, can roll by on the main. *Tom Murray*

VIA train No. 10, eastbound from Prince Rupert to Jasper, approaches Red Pass Junction (west of Jasper) in July 1981. *Steve Patterson*

CN 5414 and BC Rail 4616 lead a freight next to the Thompson River at Martel, British Columbia, in June 1991. *CN*

GTW No. 5802 is eastbound at Griffith, Indiana, 30 miles (48 kilometers) east of Chicago, and headed for Battle Creek, Michigan, in May 1973. It is about to cross two railroads: the Erie Lackawanna and the Elgin, Joliet & Eastern. *Tom Murray*

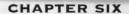

CHAPTER SIX

CN'S U.S. AFFILIATES

Canadian National has always been more than a

Canadian company. One of its predecessors, Grand Trunk

Railway, was easily the most international railway in North

America. It served New England in the east, Quebec and

Ontario in the center of its network, and the heartland

states of Michigan, Indiana, and Illinois in the west.

Another CN predecessor, Canadian Northern, reached as

far south as Duluth, Minnesota.

In 1971 Grand Trunk Western, which had used CN colors on its diesels for more than 20 years, started to differentiate itself by using blue instead of black on an order of 12 GP38AC units, numbered 5800 through 5811. Several of these units were subsequently transferred to Central Vermont. In October 1993, CV No. 5807 and 5811 handle a cut of cars next to the Conrail Boston & Albany line at Palmer, Massachusetts. *Brian Solomon*

Over time, the functions and strategic importance of CN's U.S. routes have changed. CN eventually left New England, but its Midwestern U.S. lines have become critical links in the railway's evolving route structure.

Central Vermont Railway

The Central Vermont (CV) had its roots in two early Vermont railway ventures: Vermont Central, which began operations in 1848 between White River Junction and Bethel, and Vermont & Canada, which opened in 1850 from Essex Junction to St. Albans. Eventually the two railroads connected with each other and came under common control. In 1873 Central Vermont Railroad was incorporated as a holding company for both of these ventures.

The other important component of the Central Vermont was the New London Northern, a predecessor of which opened in 1848. The New London Northern ultimately ran north from its namesake city in Connecticut, through Massachusetts, to Brattleboro, Vermont. Between Brattleboro and Windsor, Vermont, the south end of the Vermont Central, there was a gap, which was filled by the Boston & Maine (B&M), whose Connecticut River route was intertwined with those of CV and its predecessors.

At various points in the nineteenth century, CV and its constituents controlled lines extending into southern Quebec and northern New York State, as well as the Rutland Railroad and a steamship line on Lake Ontario. Yet the railway never prospered, making its securities inexpensive and creating an opportunity for GTR. Given the shortcomings of its route to Portland, Maine, GTR management saw an opportunity to develop long-haul business by using CV's line to New London and coastal vessels beyond to reach the ports of New York City and Boston. By 1885 GTR had gained financial control over CV, and in 1898 the company was reincorporated as Central Vermont Railway under GTR management.

The idea of connecting directly to a major New England port persisted, and in 1912 work began on a new 75-mile (121-kilometer) line from the CV at Palmer, Massachusetts, to the port of Providence, Rhode Island. That year, however, GTR's president, Charles Melville Hays, the chief proponent of the new line, died in the sinking of the *Titanic,* and the Providence extension was never completed.

Following the creation of CN in June 1919, the new parent company's devotion to CV was tested by a disastrous flood in November 1927. The penalty that CV paid for following easy-grade, water-level routes for much of its distance was that rising flood waters wiped out 21 bridges and much of the railway's track structure. Thirty miles (48 kilometers) of CV's mainline were rebuilt at a cost of $3 million, and the line reopened for business in February 1928.

CV's heaviest passenger traffic was north of White River Junction, where trains were interchanged with the B&M. Through service commenced between Montreal and Washington, D.C., in 1924 (the *Washingtonian* and the

In May 1976 a passenger excursion on the Central Vermont crosses the northern end of Lake Champlain at East Alburg, Vermont. *Stan Smaill*

Central Vermont train No. 744 rolls southbound through Leverett, Massachusetts, in December 1978, with three GP9 units—one Grand Trunk and two CV. The two CV units, Nos. 4928 and 4923, are former passenger engines. *Tom Murray*

Montrealer), and between Montreal and Boston two years later (the *New Englander* and the *Ambassador*). The Montreal–Washington trains survived until the end of CV passenger service in 1966.

But CV's route structure never served it well as a freight hauler. In partnership with CN and Grand Trunk Western, it operated a pair of fast freights between Chicago and New London (train Nos. 490 and 491), but the essential problem was that CV didn't serve many locations of commercial importance. It depended on connections—mainly with B&M as well as the New Haven, which was absorbed by Penn Central in 1969—to

CV train No. 324 crosses the White River at West Hartford, Vermont, in October 1993. CN 9401 and 9405 are both from a group of 233 GP40-2L(W) units delivered in 1974 and 1975. GTW 6204, a GP38 built in 1966, was originally DT&I 204. *Brian Solomon*

This CV motive power consist at Palmer, Massachusetts, in December 1987, documents the changing image of the railroad and the changing identities of individual locomotives. CV Nos. 4559 and 4445 were originally GT units. The trailing unit, No. 4917, is one of several engines transferred from GTW to CV. *Brian Solomon*

In the 1970s Grand Trunk locomotives were frequently found on Central Vermont, and vice versa. Here, GT 4906 and 4558 are northbound with CV train No. 511 at Randolph, Vermont. *Tom Murray*

originate or terminate freight. They had their own interests to protect and other connecting lines to choose from. As those carriers slid into bankruptcy (New Haven in 1961, B&M and Penn Central in 1970), they cut back on train service and maintenance budgets, making it harder than ever for CV to keep freight traffic on the rails.

Following the creation of Grand Trunk Corporation as a holding company for CN's U.S. subsidiaries in 1971, management tried to breathe life into CV by investing in distribution centers, where commodities like lumber and cement could be transferred from rail to truck. The company also trimmed operating expenses, put more of an emphasis on local management (such as by moving train

dispatchers from Montreal to St. Albans), and started an innovative intermodal service for lumber customers. It was not enough to make CV profitable.

After trying and failing to sell CV in 1982, CN management put it back on the market in the 1990s. By this time several companies had emerged that specialized in purchasing or leasing financially challenged lines from the major rail carriers. Using a combination of nontraditional labor arrangements, local management, and close attention to customer requirements, they were often able to turn a profit where a larger railway could not. One such company, RailTex, stepped forward to acquire CV, which was reborn as New England Central Railroad.

RailTex was subsequently acquired by RailAmerica, which continues to operate New England Central today.

Grand Trunk in New England

People did not use the term "globalization" in the 1840s, when the idea of a rail line between Montreal and Portland, Maine, was born. However, the builders of the Atlantic & St. Lawrence in the United States and its connecting line, the St. Lawrence & Atlantic in Quebec, were motivated by a similar idea: that international borders should not stand in the way of trade and commerce.

The specific commerce that the backers of these railways were after was grain and lumber traffic destined for Europe and other overseas destinations, much of which moved through the port of Montreal. The winter freezing of the St. Lawrence River made Montreal's port business seasonal, and John Alfred Poor saw an opportunity in this. Poor (the brother of Henry Varnum Poor, founder of what later became Standard & Poor's) led the effort by the city of Portland to secure a rail line to Montreal, in competition with Boston merchants who had similar ideas. The relatively short distance of the land-and-water route between Montreal and London via Portland won the day. The 300-mile (483-kilometer) railway through Maine, New Hampshire, Vermont, and Quebec was completed in 1853 and leased to Grand Trunk Railway of Canada the following year.

For a variety of reasons, the line never prospered to the degree that Poor had envisioned. Since water transport is inherently less expensive than rail, Montreal kept most

A northbound freight on the Grand Trunk, running from Island Pond, Vermont, to Sherbrooke, Quebec, crosses a trestle near Norton, Vermont, in June 1953. GT 2-8-2 Mikado No. 3703 was a 1918 product of Alco's Schenectady, New York, shop. *Jim Shaughnessy*

For more than 70 years this grain elevator was a landmark on the Portland, Maine, waterfront. Yet grain traffic peaked early in the twentieth century, and in 1971, when these three CN GP9 units were preparing to depart with GT train No. 393 for Montreal, the elevator had been unused for decades. It was dismantled a few years later. *Tom Murray*

of its port business during the warmer months. Following Confederation in 1867, and the building of the Intercolonial Railway, political considerations favored all-weather Canadian ports (Halifax and Saint John) over those in the United States.

Long after parent Grand Trunk Railway System had become part of Canadian National, the U.S. portion of the route (between Norton, Vermont, and Portland)

continued to be known as the Grand Trunk, and equipment was painted to reflect this well into the diesel era. To distinguish it from Grand Trunk Western, some tariffs referred to the line as "Grand Trunk (Eastern)," but it was not a separate corporation, nor did it have its own management, as did CN's other U.S. subsidiaries. When Grand Trunk Corporation was formed in 1971 as the parent company for CN's other

MAINE COAST
AND THE WHITE AND
GREEN MOUNTAINS

GRAND TRUNK
RAILWAY SYSTEM

CANADIAN NATIONAL
RAILWAYS

CN promoted tourism on the Grand Trunk through publications such as this one, produced in 1928. *Author collection*

U.S. subsidiaries, the route to Portland stayed under direct CN control.

The biggest single traffic generator was a large paper mill at Berlin, New Hampshire, but it was served by B&M as well as by GT. Other than forest products, the Montreal–Portland line had little local business. The line did enjoy a substantial passenger business during the summer, when residents of Quebec flocked to the beaches along the Maine coast, and New Englanders traveled north to resort towns like Poland Spring, Maine.

The vision of early Canadian railway builders like Francis Hincks, who in the

1850s had dreamed of a commercial route from Portland to Chicago through Canada, was borne out more than a century later when, in the 1970s, the GT route became an important link between Maine's paper producers and customers in the Midwest. Traffic managers at paper mills located on Maine Central could and did route many carloads to customers in the Midwestern United States via Yarmouth Junction and Danville Junction, where Maine Central interchanged the cars to GT. This overhead traffic had long been part of GT's

GT train No. 393 is operating as an extra train, and in accordance with CN operating rules of the time, carries white flags as it arrives at Berlin, New Hampshire, in June 1972. *Tom Murray*

revenue base, but in the 1970s GT and CN traffic volumes benefited from the financial and operational woes of the other outlet for westbound traffic from Maine, the B&M. GT train 393, the daily freight to Montreal, would typically leave Portland with only a handful of cars, but by the time it departed Danville Junction it might have 60 cars in tow.

Even with the overhead traffic, GT remained a light-density line. In the 1980s deregulation and other changes in the rail industry made it harder for John Poor's railroad to compete for business. In 1989 the line from Portland to Island Pond, Vermont, was sold to Emons Development Corporation. Emons later picked up a portion of the connecting line

in Quebec. Today those routes are part of regional rail operator Genesee & Wyoming.

Grand Trunk Western Railroad

In the 1850s achieving access to Chicago was an important objective of Grand Trunk Railway's promoters and builders. It finally attained that goal in 1879, and Chicago traffic was soon generating more than 40 percent of GTR's revenues. GTR expanded its U.S. presence in 1882 with the acquisition of Great Western Railway, an Ontario road that also had a line from Detroit to Grand Haven, Michigan crossing GTR's existing line at Durand; part of this line, from Detroit to Pontiac, had been in operation since 1838.

With the Great Western routes now part of its network, and with a line to Chicago, GTR was in a position to offer robust competition to the Vanderbilt roads (New York Central & Hudson River, Michigan Central, and Lake Shore & Michigan Southern). Yet GTR still depended on ferries to move freight cars across the St. Clair River between Sarnia,

Ontario, and Port Huron, Michigan, and across the Detroit River between Windsor and Detroit. GTR had two steam-powered car ferries carrying railcars between Sarnia and Port Huron, but as traffic grew another solution had to be found. In 1884 the St. Clair Frontier Tunnel Company was incorporated to build and operate a bore under the river.

After two false starts at tunneling through the blue clay under the river, a relatively new technology—shield tunneling—was applied to the job starting on July 11, 1889. The tunnel, lined with cast iron, opened to revenue traffic on October 24, 1891, and four specially built 0-10-0T tank-type steam engines were used to haul trains between Sarnia and Port Huron. After the deaths of 10 employees from asphyxiation in various incidents between 1892 and 1904, however, GTR decided to electrify the tunnel. Six electric locomotives went into service in 1908, and three more were acquired in later years. They continued to operate until electrification was discontinued in 1958.

CN 1953 system pocket calendar depicting GTW F3 No. 9020. *Author collection*

Until 1900 GTR's lines west of the St. Clair and Detroit Rivers were operated as part of the parent company's system but without a unique identity of their own. On November 22, 1900 the Grand Trunk Western Railway was formed as a holding company for the Michigan properties. Historian Don Hofsommer, author of a history of Grand Trunk Corporation, notes that this was a financial arrangement, not a managerial one. But between the operational improvements achieved with the St. Clair Tunnel and the improved financial controls, Hofsommer writes, "the Michigan lines gradually began to pull their own weight, to repay advances made them by the parent, and by midpoint of the first decade in the new century were even prospering."

The prosperity did not last. By the late 1920s, following the creation of Canadian National, the GTW lines had become financial drains on their parent. In 1928 the Grand Trunk Western Railroad was incorporated, with the idea of making this part of the CN system more financially self-sustaining. It was not the last time that CN would reorganize GTW with the objective of improving its profitability.

Like the Central Vermont, GTW hosted several well-known and well-appointed passenger trains that belied the poor financial performance of its freight service. They included the *International Limited,* which had gone into service between Montreal and Chicago in 1900, the *Inter-City Limited* from Montreal to Chicago via Detroit, and the *Maple*

Like parent CN, Grand Trunk Western used a black paint scheme on yard engines. GTW 8204, at Owosso, Michigan, in 1971, is an Alco S4, delivered in 1956. *Collection of George Carpenter*

Leaf between Montreal and Detroit. Prestigious as they were, they were not making money.

There were no dramatic changes in the CN-GTW relationship until 1971, when Grand Trunk Corporation (GTC) was formed as a holding company for GTW, CV, and Duluth, Winnipeg & Pacific (DW&P). All three properties had been managed from Montreal since the formation of CN, or, in the case of GTW, had been managed from Detroit by people sent from Montreal. Putting the U.S. properties in the hands of U.S. managers was one objective of the reorganization, but it was not an end in itself. The idea was to see if these companies could be made profitable. If not, then perhaps they should not remain part of CN.

Heading up the effort was another representative from Montreal, Robert Bandeen.

Bandeen was an agent of change, not a traditionalist. He set out to remake GTC, and in particular GTW, as a stand-alone company, rather than simply as an appendage of CN. A 1972 brochure issued by GTW proclaimed, "We're changing so much we're becoming a new railroad. New Management is applying new, far-reaching philosophies and methods to Grand Trunk's operations everywhere, in every way. New Services are being instituted, to handle shipments faster and more conveniently for our customers."

There was a certain amount of hyperbole in these claims, but also a lot of truth. GTW had to change: its operating ratio, 119 percent in 1971 and 140 percent the year before, was unacceptable. Furthermore, its customers, most notably General Motors, were insisting it change.

St. Clair Tunnel Company No. 1306, shown here at Sarnia, Ontario, in 1908, was constructed by Baldwin Locomotive Works and Westinghouse in 1907 as one of a group of six locomotives that were placed into service in 1908 and retired in 1959. *John Boyd/National Archives of Canada/PA-060704*

Grand Trunk Western, along with Santa Fe and several other railroads, used Chicago's Dearborn Street Station as a passenger terminal. GTW passenger GP9 No. 4919 is shown here at Dearborn Street in September 1966. *Thomas M. Murray. Author collection*

Bandeen did not stay in Detroit long. In 1972 he returned to Montreal as executive vice president of CN (while remaining responsible for the GTC experiment), and in 1974 he became CEO of Canadian National. He continued as president of GTC until January 1, 1976, when he reorganized CN into profit centers. Succeeding him in the top spot at GTC was John Burdakin, a former Penn Central officer whom Bandeen had initially recruited to be GTW's vice president of operations.

By the late 1970s Grand Trunk Western was generating positive operating income. In 1978 GTW filed a proposal with the Interstate Commerce Commission to acquire the Detroit, Toledo & Ironton Railroad (DT&I), which ran from Detroit south through Ohio to Cincinnati. GTW acquired DT&I in June 1980. The following year, GTW bought out Norfolk & Western's 50 percent interest in Detroit & Toledo Shore Line (D&TSL) (GTW already owned the other 50 percent). DT&I was initially treated as a separate subsidiary of GTC, but in December 1983 it was folded into GTW.

Surrounded by ever-larger competitors, GTW looked for ways to expand its reach. An opportunity came along in 1981 when the trustee of the bankrupt Milwaukee Road, which had abandoned its Pacific Coast extension,

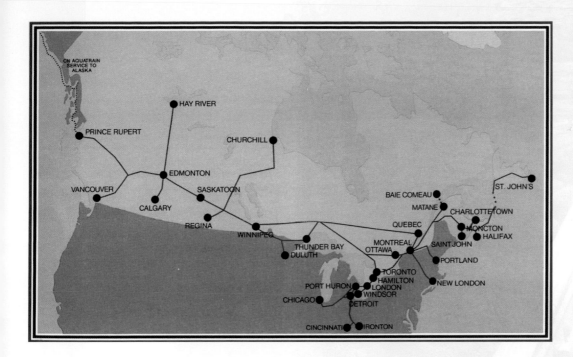

started to look for a potential buyer of the railroad's remaining assets. One of those assets consisted of trackage rights on the Burlington Northern between St. Paul and Duluth, Minnesota. Acquiring the Milwaukee Road would give GTC and parent CN an all-U.S. route south of the Great Lakes.

While a deal to acquire the Milwaukee Road was in the works, the two carriers negotiated a voluntary coordination agreement that made the Milwaukee the preferred U.S. partner for traffic flowing off the CN system into the U.S. Midwest. In 1983 Chicago & North Western made a competing offer for Milwaukee's assets, and early in 1984

Canadian Pacific's U.S. affiliate, Soo Line, also made an offer. The bidding got too rich for GTC, which dropped out of the contest, and in 1985 Soo Line ended up with the Milwaukee Road. The purchase set in motion a chain of events that would lead, 16 years later, to CN's acquisition of the former Soo Line routes in Wisconsin and Michigan, which by that time were part of Wisconsin Central.

Despite its disappointments in the merger game, GTW was making progress financially, and CN was no longer thinking about selling GTW. As the CN annual report for 1990 put it, Grand Trunk Corporation was "strategically placed to play an important role for Canadian

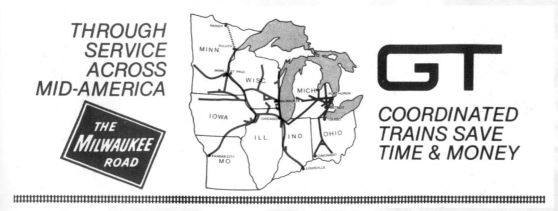

As part of its effort to promote the voluntary coordination agreement with the Milwaukee Road, GTW had scratch pads printed bearing this map. However, Milwaukee Road was not destined to become part of the CN system map. *Author collection*

National in the free trade era." On January 1, 1992 GTC was reintegrated with parent CN as part of "CN North America." GTW, CV, and DW&P retained their identities as operating companies, but there would be a single corporate brand name.

On Dec. 17, 1992 U.S. President George Bush, Canadian Prime Minister Brian Mulroney, and Mexican President Carlos Salinas signed the North American Free Trade Agreement (NAFTA) in separate ceremonies in the three capitals. The trade agreement made it clear to any doubters that CN must have a U.S. presence in order to participate in growing north-south commerce.

CN affirmed its commitment to keeping GTW as part of its network when it decided to invest $155 million in a new St. Clair River Tunnel, one large enough to accommodate high-cube auto-parts cars, multilevel auto racks, and double-stack intermodal equipment. The new tunnel opened in April 1995.

The GTW of today is a slimmed-down version of the railroad it once was. Essentially, it consists of the line from Durand to Chicago, plus the Durand–Detroit–Port Huron triangle and the former D&TSL route to Toledo. DT&I was sold to RailAmerica in 1997, which now operates it as the Indiana & Ohio Railway.

A GTW transfer job with a cut of yellow-door newsprint cars approaches Brighton Park crossing in Chicago in August 1974. GTW 1514 and 1513 were part of a group of eight SW1200 units delivered in 1960. *Tom Murray*

With the acquisition of Illinois Central and Wisconsin Central in 1999 and 2001, respectively, GTW was no longer an appendage of the CN system. It was now a key link in the Canadian National network.

Duluth, Winnipeg & Pacific Railway

Of CN's lines in the United States, the Duluth, Winnipeg & Pacific is the shortest, at 167 miles (269 kilometers), and the youngest. Its predecessor, the Duluth, Rainy Lake & Winnipeg Railway was built in stages from 1901 to 1908, and in the latter it year came under the control of Canadian Northern Railway. CNoR created the Duluth, Winnipeg & Pacific Railway in 1909, and completed the route to Duluth in 1912. At its north end in Ranier, Minnesota, (just east of International Falls), DW&P crosses the Rainy River to connect at Fort Frances, Ontario, with the former CNoR line between Winnipeg and Thunder Bay.

Originally built to carry timber from the white pine forests of northern Minnesota, DW&P carried on in obscurity for many years. It lacked the celebrated passenger trains of GTW or CV, but it gave CN a means of reaching the U.S. Midwest through connections at Duluth with Great Northern and Northern Pacific (later combined into Burlington Northern), Milwaukee Road, Soo Line, and Chicago & North Western.

The DW&P is a pipeline for western Canadian products moving to U.S. Midwestern markets. Here a train composed largely of forest products heads south out of Virginia, Minnesota, in June 1974, with two CN GP9 units in charge. This train, operating as 1st 732, carries green flags to indicate that another section of the same schedule can be expected to follow.
Tom Murray

If DW&P lacked glamour, it at least made money. When Grand Trunk Corporation was formed in 1971, part of the motivation was that by filing a consolidated tax return, the losses at GTW and CV would insulate DW&P's profits from U.S. income taxes. One reason that DW&P was generating income was that it was ideally situated to serve as a conduit for the resources that Canada was sending to the United States in ever-increasing volumes. Forest products, potash, sulfur, and liquefied petroleum gas (butane and propane) all moved from western Canada via the DW&P to consumers in the United States. Historian Don Hofsommer notes that in the second half of the 1970s, DW&P's average operating ratio was a "most agreeable 65.9."

The importance of DW&P was highlighted in the 1980s and 1990s when CN entered into a series of coordination agreements and haulage contracts with U.S. carriers to move traffic south of Duluth. The first was with Milwaukee Road; then, in 1992, a haulage agreement with Burlington Northern gave CN what amounted to single-line service from western Canada all the way to Chicago. A similar arrangement with Wisconsin Central was negotiated in 1998, and its success led to Wisconsin Central becoming part of CN in 2001.

DW&P was again the center of attention in late 2003 when CN announced that it had reached agreement to buy a package of railroads and a fleet of eight Great Lakes vessels from Great Lakes Transportation (GLT). These properties, at one time operated by U.S. Steel, included the Duluth, Missabe & Iron Range Railway (DM&IR). To reach former Wisconsin Central trackage at South Itasca Yard in Superior, Wisconsin, DW&P had been using trackage rights on DM&IR from Nopeming Junction, a distance of 17 miles (27 kilometers).

The GLT transaction would not only give CN ownership of that segment, but also would give it two parallel lines—one DW&P and one DM&IR—between Virginia, Minnesota (roughly at the midpoint of the DW&P) and Duluth. This, said CN, would let it run southbound trains over one line and northbound trains over the other, increasing capacity and helping to avoid costly signaling and track improvements on the DW&P.

The GLT transaction would bring other assets (including the Bessemer & Lake Erie Railroad) into the CN family, but the motivation for the deal was to improve the capacity of the DW&P so that it could continue to provide efficient transportation of Canadian resources into the United States.

DWP 3613, an RS11, switches cars in the yard at Virginia, Minnesota, the midpoint of the railroad, in June 1974. *Tom Murray*

CN 5026, on a DW&P train detouring over the Duluth, Missabe & Iron Range Railway, is shown side by side with DM&IR No. 305 at Iron Junction, Minnesota, in August 1992. *Steve Glischinski*

In 2003 CN entered into an agreement with Great Lakes Transportation to acquire several rail and water carriers. The centerpiece of the deal was GLT's Duluth, Missabe & Iron Range Railway, whose operations are to be coordinated with those of its neighbor, CN's Duluth, Winnipeg & Pacific. Here, DM&IR and DW&P trains meet at Steelton, Minnesota, in March 2000. *Steve Glischinski*

PRIVATIZATION AND EXPANSION

In 1981, Robert Bandeen's last full year as CEO, CN earned an operating profit of $193 million. The company was addressing the rapid growth of bulk commodity traffic (coal, sulfur, potash, and grain) in the West by installing double track, extending sidings, and replacing timber bridges on key segments, particularly between Edmonton and Jasper, Alberta, through the Yellowhead Pass, and into British Columbia.

A westbound CN train to Vancouver at Lasha, British Columbia, in April 1996, makes the railway seem tiny in comparison with the works of nature. *Phil Mason*

CN signed an agreement in 1981 to transport coal originating at mines in northern British Columbia. CN would carry the coal from the BC Rail interchange at Prince George to the port of Prince Rupert. At an expected annual volume of more than 9 million tons, it was, as the 1981 annual report noted, "the largest amount of traffic ever to be contracted for by CN Rail."

Where Will CN Get Its Capital?

However, Bandeen's departure from CN coincided with a recession that turned the black ink on CN's ledger to red. As his successor, the government chose 55-year-old Maurice LeClair, a physician who had come to CN in 1979 after serving in a series of high-level government positions. In early 1983 in his first annual report as CEO,

LeClair talked about the historic role of CN, which had been "to weld a number of railway companies into one strong and commercially competitive enterprise serving the entire nation. Though the world in which CN must function has changed dramatically in the intervening years," he stated, "the mission of the company remains tied to its historic role."

By the following year CN had returned to profitability, but the tone of LeClair's message was different. In one year, from 1982 to 1983, the volume of rail traffic in Canada had increased more than 11 percent. CN had been financing its capital investments partly by generating cash internally and partly by borrowing. Yet the borrowing could not continue. Over the next five years the company forecast capital investments of $5 billion, of which almost half would have to come from sources outside the company. "The most pressing problem facing the Corporation in the short term," LeClair wrote, "is the lack of capital needed to finance the improvement and expansion of a number of nationally-important services, most particularly railway

After the Crowsnest grain rate structure was ended, and consolidation of grain elevators had started to make the grain transport system more efficient, CN was motivated to put more maintenance dollars into its grain-gathering network. This welded rail train is west of Saskatoon in July 1994, on the CN Rosetown Subdivision, part of the former Canadian Northern's Saskatoon–Calgary line. *Phil Mason*

services in Western Canada . . . . Means must soon be found to provide new equity capital for the Corporation."

In 1986 two changes occurred: LeClair resigned and the word "privatization" started to appear in discussions about CN's future. In his outgoing message as chairman and CEO, LeClair said, "Canadian National cannot be both an instrument of public policy *at any cost* and a profitable, commercially sound business. . . . A large portion of the company's debt is attributable to public duties for which compensation is non-compensatory or non-existent." Although privatization was now being considered, he said, "CN must be fit and healthy before it can be offered as a candidate for private-sector investment."

In 1992 CN negotiated a haulage agreement with Burlington Northern: BN would handle CN's trains between Chicago and Duluth using CN power and BN crews. This lasted until 1998, when CN moved its Chicago-Duluth traffic to Wisconsin Central. In April 1996 a westbound CN haulage train operates along the Mississippi River near Savanna, Illinois. *Brian Solomon*

Incoming CEO Ronald Lawless, who had served as president of CN Rail after stints in operations and marketing, noted, "Railways are capital intensive. No matter how efficiently they are run, they need an ongoing reinvestment to perpetuate themselves." Yet without equity capital to support this reinvestment, CN had adopted a strategy of downsizing its physical plant and cutting

CN No. 2437, a General Electric Dash 8-40CM, was making one of its first visits to the West in December 1992, and wearing the "CN North America" map paint scheme as it arrived at Jasper, Alberta, with a westbound train. *Phil Mason*

costs wherever possible. CN, Lawless said, was becoming "a smaller, busier, financially stronger railway." The need to get smaller was captured in a single statistic, repeated often by CN management: two-thirds of the railway carried only 10 percent of its business.

The short-line phenomenon that had been going on in the United States for more than a decade did not catch on in Canada until the late 1980s, when CN finally began spinning off some of the lines that carried respectable volumes of traffic but were not generating an adequate return on capital. Lines in Alberta and Ontario were sold to regional rail operators, as was the GT line between Portland, Maine, and the Canadian border. A

CN line between Montreal and Massena, New York, was taken over by Conrail.

CN was also slimming down as a corporation. Marine operations in eastern Canada became a separate crown corporation. The trucking subsidiary, CN Route, was sold. Hotels, including the crown jewels—the Chateau Laurier in Ottawa and the Jasper

The CN North America logo was applied not just to new locomotives, but also to older equipment as well. Here it adorns Central Vermont GP38AC No. 5806. *Brian Solomon*

In the 1990s traffic volumes on CN's Edmonton-Vancouver corridor made it the railway's second-highest volume route. Here, four westbound trains are ready to depart Boston Bar, British Columbia, in April 1995. Today, Boston Bar sees westbound trains of both CN and CP, due to a paired track arrangement between the two railways. Eastbound trains of both railways pass through North Bend on the opposite side of the Fraser River. *Phil Mason*

Park Lodge—were sold to Canadian Pacific, as was CN's interest in CNCP Telecommunications. Proceeds from the sales were used to pay down debt, which put CN's debt-to-capital ratio into a range that was, once again, comparable to that of other large transportation companies. By 1988 CN's principal non-transportation activities consisted of its oil and gas exploration subsidiary, a real estate unit that pursued both development and land sales, the CANAC consultancy, and CN Tower in Toronto.

Meanwhile, growth on CN's core rail network—the one-third that carried 90 percent of the traffic—continued. The Crowsnest rate issue had been resolved a couple of years earlier, and the grain transportation system was benefiting from new, high-capacity covered hopper cars and from investment in track and support systems. About one-third of the route between Edmonton and Vancouver had been

double-tracked. Domestic intermodal traffic between the Maritimes and central Canada increased 41 percent from 1985 to 1986 thanks to CN's acquisition of new tri-axle trailers.

Grand Trunk Corporation had been formed to focus attention on the financial contribution of the company's U.S. subsidiaries, but effective January 1, 1992, GTC was brought back into the CN fold as part of an effort to project a new image: CN North America. The move, said management, reflected the fact that "the domestic freight transportation marketplace has become continental in scope." Locomotives began to appear with a map of North American integrated with the company's famous "noodle" logo. The new image did not last long, but it foreshadowed the expansion of CN's U.S. presence over the next decade.

In 1992 two events reinforced the image of CN as a North American transportation company. CN began construction on a new tunnel between Sarnia, Ontario, and Port Huron, Michigan, to replace the original St. Clair Tunnel opened in 1891. The new tunnel would be able to accommodate not only the modern cars used to serve the auto industry, which for years had been ferried across the river, but also double-stack equipment, which had become the cornerstone of the intermodal business in North America. CN also negotiated a haulage agreement with Burlington Northern (BN) for the movement of CN trains between Duluth and Chicago, making CN trains a common sight on the BN route along the Mississippi River. This agreement enabled CN to offer single-line service between western Canada and Chicago and reduced its dependence on intermediate carriers.

In CN's 1991 annual report, Lawless noted that, "Despite a 47-percent productivity improvement over the past five years, CN remains a relatively high-cost carrier compared with railway competitors, many of whom matched or exceeded CN's productivity growth during the same period."

Tellier Takes Charge

Lawless retired from CN on June 30, 1992. Prime Minister Brian Mulroney caught CN employees and almost every other stakeholder in the company by surprise when he named a long-time civil servant, Paul Tellier, to succeed Lawless. Most recently Tellier had served as clerk of the Privy Council and secretary of the Cabinet, making him in effect Canada's top government bureaucrat.

Tellier took over on October 1, 1992, and almost from the beginning it was clear that he had a different management style than CN employees were accustomed to. "Urgency" and "impatience" were two of the more polite words used to describe his approach to CN's challenges. "Change must occur more quickly," Tellier stated. "Entrenched habits and attitudes must be replaced by more productive methods

CN SD40 5134 is the leading unit on eastbound train No. 408 crossing the Canso Strait at Port Hastings, Nova Scotia, at the south end of Cape Breton Island, in September 1993. The following month, the Cape Breton & Central Nova Scotia Railway began operating the line between Truro and Sydney. *Phil Mason*

CN 5314 and a Bombardier HR616 lead an eastbound train over the Continental Divide at Yellowhead, British Columbia, in July 1995. (Bombardier took over Montreal Locomotive Works in 1979 and subsequently exited the locomotive business.) The elevation at Yellowhead is only 3,720 feet (1,128 meters), compared with 5,332 feet (1,618 meters) at Canadian Pacific's crossing of Kicking Horse Pass. *Phil Mason*

and a clearer-sighted perspective. In short, CN will have to break with the past—or risk losing the future."

Tellier set out to reduce CN's payroll by 11,000 people over a three-year period. It took him a little longer than that, but by 1996 the company's workforce stood at just over 24,000, versus 35,300 in 1992. The trackage operated by CN was whittled down, too, through abandonments as well as sales and leases to regional operators. In 1992 the company had operated 19,522 route miles

(31,430 kilometers); by the end of 1995 it was reduced to 17,918 miles (28,848 kilometers). CN also set up "internal short lines" in areas where labor unions would agree to modified work rules.

The new CEO also restructured senior management, bringing in new people, obtaining resignations from some long-time employees, and flattening the organizational chart. In the words of one senior executive, "While Bandeen had made major strides in changing the financial structure to enable a profit-motivated, business-like approach, many in senior management still had a crown corporation mentality. Tellier added the final piece to the puzzle by replacing the entire executive team with people who would march to his drum and drive home the bottom-line approach. The strategy was to fix the costs, then the service, and finally grow the revenue."

Privatization

Even though CN was becoming a smaller railway, it was carrying more traffic, and doing so more profitably. From 1992 to 1995 revenue ton-miles increased 9 percent and operating income (excluding special charges) rose from $112 million to $552 million. The stage was set for the privatization of Canadian

National, and in February 1995 the government announced that it would do exactly that. An initial public offering of CN shares was scheduled, and on November 17, 1995 the company's stock was offered to investors on the Toronto, Montreal, and New York stock exchanges.

The privatization of CN was a momentous event in the history of Canadian enterprise. It was the largest initial public offering of stock in the history of the country. But the most shocking thing to Canadians was that CN, which many still thought of as an arm of the government, was being turned into an investor-owned company. Harry Bruce, in his book about the CN privatization, *The Pig That Flew,* writes that Americans "had a stronger faith in CN's future than the

In October 1999 CN train No. 305 has just crossed from New Brunswick into Quebec at Courchesne, on the former National Transcontinental route that now serves as CN's mainline between Montreal and the Maritimes. The 148-car train is slogging through the Notre Dame Mountains and cresting the first of three grades between here and Pelletier, 40 miles (64 kilometers) to the west. *George Pitarys*

CN's acquisition of Illinois Central in 1999 and Wisconsin Central in 2001 meant that locomotives of all three railroads could be found in unfamiliar places. Here, IC SD40-3 No. 6203, a former Burlington Northern unit, leads two Wisconsin Central units at New Brighton, Minnesota, in July 2003. *Steve Glischinski*

Canadians, and were therefore willing to pay a higher price for the shares." When the dust settled after the IPO, U.S. investors owned most of the company's stock.

In the first two years of privatization, CN continued to make gains in efficiency and financial strength. Tellier had set an objective of 85 percent for the operating ratio, which in 1992 stood at 97.5 percent. By 1996 that ratio had, in fact, been reduced to 85 percent, and then to 82 percent in 1996 and 79 percent in 1997. Operating income for 1997 was $927 million. Route mileage shrank to 15,292 miles (24,620 kilometers) in 1997, but revenue ton-miles increased by another 13 percent from 1995 to 1997.

Privatization finally freed CN management from the need to look over its shoulder to see what politicians and bureaucrats thought about its business activities. Though it still operated under government regulations in both Canada and the United States, privatization put CN on the same basis vis-à-vis government as its competitors and connecting lines in the rail industry.

CN to the Gulf: Illinois Central

Tellier knew that the future of North American transportation lay in north-south trade. NAFTA had eased trade restrictions among Canada, the United States, and Mexico. Tellier wanted to ensure that CN got its share of the resulting rail traffic. In

February 1998 CN confirmed widespread speculation that it was negotiating to buy Illinois Central Railroad (IC), which would extend CN's reach to the Gulf of Mexico. Three months later CN and Kansas City Southern announced a 15-year marketing alliance that would effectively give CN access to Mexico.

One of IC's key assets was its CEO, Hunter Harrison, who had implemented an operating plan based on running trains to schedule. IC offered its customers reliable, consistent service, and it also had the lowest operating ratio of any major railroad. CN had already been working toward the objective of running a "scheduled railroad," particularly with the implementation in 1995 of a new

Resplendent in fall plumage, the orange maples east of Tarte, Quebec, nicely match the colors of SD75 CN 5695, leading train No. 148 in October 2001. Midway between Edmundston and St. André Junction, the siding at Tarte was recently lengthened as part of CN's $24 million capital project to improve times on its Halifax-Montreal service. *George Pitarys*

GTW SD40-3 No. 5943 and WC SD45 No. 7506 are on the head end of CN train No. 406 at Shoreview, Minnesota, in December 2003. The WC unit was formerly owned by BN. The GTW unit has a more interesting past. Originally CN SD40 No. 5102, it was rebuilt by Alstom Transport for Kansas City Southern. CN then leased it and renumbered it for GTW. *Steve Glischinski*

computer system called SRS (Service Reliability Strategy). SRS was based on technology acquired from the Santa Fe Railway, but CN had tailored it to meet its own needs and operating conditions.

Tellier wasted no time bringing Harrison on board. In March 1998, more than a year before CN was able to complete its acquisition of IC, Harrison joined CN as its chief operating officer. He, in turn, wasted no time developing a new operating plan for Canadian National aimed at increasing the reliability of CN's service; improving the utilization of cars, locomotives, and train crews; and reducing operating costs. The new plan was put into practice on September 6, 1998.

In July 1999 CN completed its acquisition of IC, but Tellier had bigger ambitions. In December of that year, he announced that CN would merge with Burlington Northern Santa Fe (BNSF). Despite talk about a "merger of equals," and the fact that BNSF's revenues were more than twice CN's, CN was clearly in the driver's seat on the proposed merger. The surviving company, to be called North American Railways, Inc., would be based in Montreal and its top two officers would be Paul Tellier and Hunter Harrison.

The CN-BNSF combination was not to be, however. Four railroads—Canadian Pacific, CSX, Norfolk Southern, and Union Pacific—mounted a vigorous campaign to stop the deal. The Surface Transportation Board (the U.S. regulator of rail mergers) called a time out to examine the larger issue of industry consolidation. In July 2000 CN and BNSF called off the merger.

Completing the Iron Lariat: Wisconsin Central

One of the missing links in the CN network, a gap made all the more noticeable with IC added to the CN route map, was between Duluth (the south end of the Duluth, Winnipeg & Pacific) and Chicago. CN's first attempt to create what some called an "iron lariat" around the Great Lakes had been in the early 1980s when Grand Trunk made overtures to buy the assets of the bankrupt Milwaukee Road. That bid fell short and the Milwaukee Road ended up in the hands of Canadian Pacific's U.S. affiliate, Soo Line.

The Soo-Milwaukee transaction rendered much of the Soo Line's trackage in the upper Midwest surplus. Those routes became

Opposite: CN train No. 406 passes through Arden Hills, Minnesota, with a CN SD60F and two WC SD45 units, in November 2003. *Steve Glischinski*

Maritimes-bound train No. 306 rolls through Ste. Perpetue, Quebec, on the St. Lawrence River plain, in May 2003. Dairy farming is a large part of this area's local economy, and one in which the railway still has a role, serving a nearby feed dealer. *George Pitarys*

the core of a new regional railroad, Wisconsin Central (WC), which began its life in October 1987. WC soon established a reputation for efficiency and customer service. In 1998 CN negotiated a haulage agreement with WC under which WC crews would handle CN trains between Duluth and Chicago, replacing a similar agreement with BNSF.

In January 2001 CN announced that it would buy Wisconsin Central; the transaction was completed in October of that year. However, the WC deal came with some international baggage. WC's president, Edward Burkhardt, had worked to apply the WC management philosophy and business model in countries whose railways were emerging

from government ownership. As a result WC had developed a portfolio of overseas rail investments. Its New Zealand and Australia interests were disposed of within six months of the CN-WC merger. However, a poorly executed privatization plan on the British rail network had reduced the marketability of the WC property there, known as the English, Welsh & Scottish Railway. CN kept the EW&S shares on its books, although it remained hopeful that it could find a buyer for them.

The WC transaction also brought one Canadian property into the CN family: the former Algoma Central Railway from Sault Ste. Marie to Hearst, Ontario, which WC had acquired in 1995.

Scheduled Railroading Makes CN an Industry Leader

The benefits of the new operating plan implemented in late 1998 were evident to anyone who watched CN's operations or read its financial statements. With Illinois Central included, CN had an operating ratio of 75 percent in 1998. The next year, it was down to 72 percent; the following year, just under 70 percent. The company had become the most efficient major railway in North America. By early 2001 Harrison reported that CN had reduced the size of its locomotive fleet from almost 2,000 units to 1,260. The company began to negotiate new labor agreements with its train and engine service employees in the United States, based on hourly compensation instead of the time-honored mileage basis of pay. Harrison said the change could allow CN to reduce its employment in the running trades by as much as one-third.

Thanks to the scheduled railroad, customers were rewarding CN with more of their freight. From 1998 to 2000, the last full year before the merger with WC, revenue ton-miles increased almost 8 percent. By 2002, with WC now part of the CN system, RTMs were up another 7 percent over the 2000 figure.

CN had become an industry leader in efficiency and customer service. Thanks to the effect of these operational improvements on the company's net income and cash flow, CN was also rewarded with gains in its share price that far outpaced most other stocks. From the time it went public in November 1995 through December 31, 2003, the stock generated a return of 507 percent.

Into the Twenty-first Century

The Tellier era at CN came to a close at the end of 2002, 10 years after it began. CN's CEO left to take a similar position with Bombardier, a Canadian manufacturer of railcars, aircraft, and recreational equipment. Chief operating officer Hunter Harrison moved into the top slot, effective January 1, 2003. Although they were different in personality and background, Tellier and Harrison had worked well together over the preceding five years. What they had in common was a sense of urgency and an inability to be satisfied with the status quo.

Soon after Harrison moved up to CEO, CN launched another program aimed at reducing costs while making service more consistent. The "Intermodal Excellence"

The Ultramar refinery at St. Romauld, Quebec, ships a daily tank train of gasoline to Montreal. In May 2003 CN train No. 782 with the Ultramar empties crosses the Nicolet River in St. Leonard D'Aston, Quebec, en route back to the refinery. *George Pitarys*

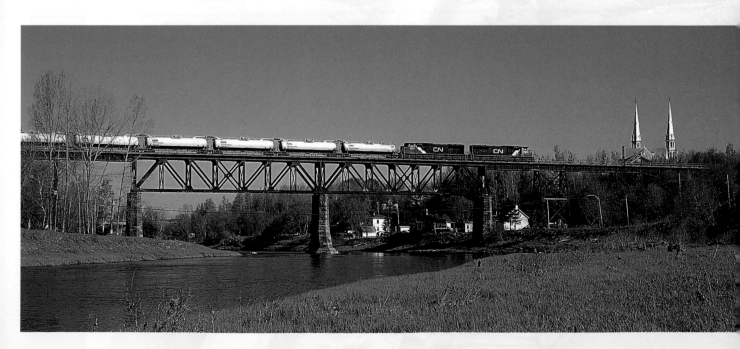

In the fall of 2003, CN announced that it had been selected by British Columbia to operate the provincially owned BC Rail. CN will lease the railway and integrate it with its existing British Columbia operations. *BC Rail*

On Dec 31, 2003, CN train No. 406 rolls across the 185-foot-high St. Croix River Bridge near Somerset, Wisconsin. The bridge was placed into service in 1911 by Soo Line, the U.S. affiliate of Canadian Pacific. In the 1980s this line (between Minneapolis and Stevens Point, Wisconsin) became part of Wisconsin Central, which was acquired by CN in 2001. Writer and photographer David Plowden has called this "one of the world's most beautiful steel structures." *Steve Glischinski*

initiative was intended to smooth out the peaks and valleys of container and trailer shipments, and to keep intermodal traffic moving rather than allowing it to fill up yards and terminals. The initiative involved running fewer, more consistently sized trains, requiring reservations for slots on each train, pricing according to customer demand on various days of the week, and reducing the use of CN facilities for container and trailer storage. Initially implemented in the Halifax–Montreal–Toronto–Windsor corridor, it was subsequently expanded across Canada.

CN continued its search for expansion possibilities under Harrison, although one acquisition that was being negotiated when he took over had to be scuttled. The Province of Ontario was interested in selling the Ontario Northland Railway, and CN was the logical buyer. With an election imminent, the province insisted on labor guarantees that CN could not agree to, and in June 2003 the company said it was walking away from the Ontario Northland transaction.

CN's next deal, announced in October 2003 and completed in May 2004, was the acquisition of several former U.S. Steel rail and water carriers from Great Lakes Transportation. These included a fleet of eight Great Lakes ore vessels, a dock operation in Ohio, and the Bessemer & Lake Erie Railroad. CN's real reason for acquiring this package was that it included the Duluth, Missabe & Iron Range Railway. CN's DW&P unit already used trackage rights over DM&IR as a critical link in its access to Duluth. By combining these two carriers, CN could implement a paired-track arrangement north of Duluth to increase capacity and hold down capital investment.

In November 2003 CN issued another major announcement, this time at Victoria, British Columbia, where the provincial government had selected CN to lease and operate the government-owned BC Rail. CN had competed with Canadian Pacific (and with a partnership between BNSF and regional rail operator OmniTRAX) for the BC Rail franchise. It was a controversial award; labor was fearful of job losses, and some in British Columbia felt that the railway was part of the province's patrimony, not to be given away to an outsider like CN (most of whose owners were U.S. investors). CN tried to mollify the opponents by agreeing to make significant investments in all of its British Columbia rail operations, including a clearance improvement program on the Prince Rupert line.

CN EPILOGUE

Canadian National has come a long way since its inception as a government-run collection of financially troubled railways.

Many of the changes at CN have reflected rail industry trends. Every North American railway has experienced dieselization, the increased use of computers, centralization of dispatching and numerous other functions, as well as dramatic improvements in productivity.

But CN started out in a different place—and has reached a different place—than any of its peers. It started as a collection of capital-starved railways and for several decades its owners, the people of Canada, looked to it to provide social services more than they wanted it to provide efficient transportation.

Through the efforts of one generation of leaders and employees after another, CN was transformed into a modern business enterprise and, most recently, into a standard-setter for the rail industry.

CN was fortunate to have people like Sir Henry Thornton, Donald Gordon, Robert Bandeen, Ronald Lawless, and Paul Tellier lead it during transitional periods, when a clear vision of the future was required. Each of these men left CN a stronger, more capable company than he had found it, even when that strength was not reflected in the cold numbers on the financial statements.

CN has done more than survive. It has prevailed.

SOURCES

Books

Bruce, Harry. *The Pig That Flew: The Battle to Privatize Canadian National.* Vancouver: Douglas & McIntyre, 1997.

Burrows, Roger G. *Railway Mileposts: British Columbia, Vol. I: The CPR Mainline Route From the Rockies to the Pacific Including the Okanagan Route and CN's Canyon Route.* North Vancouver, B.C.: Railway Milepost Books, 1981.

Clegg, Anthony and Ray Corley. *Canadian National Steam Power.* Montreal: Trains & Trolleys, 1969.

Currie, A. W. *The Grand Trunk Railway in Canada.* Toronto: University of Toronto Press, 1957.

Dubin, Arthur D. *More Classic Trains.* Milwaukee, Wis.: Kalmbach Publishing Co., 1974.

Fournier, Leslie T. *Railway Nationalization in Canada: The Problem of the Canadian National Railways.* Toronto: The Macmillan Company, 1935.

Gilbert, Clare. *St. Clair Tunnel: Rails Beneath the River.* Toronto: Stoddart Publishing Co., 1991.

Hastings, Philip R. *Grand Trunk Heritage: Steam in New England.* New York: Railroad Heritage Press, 1978.

Hofsommer, Don L. *Grand Trunk Corporation: Canadian National Railways in the United States, 1971–1992.* East Lansing, Mich.: Michigan State University Press, 1995.

Love, J. A. *Canadian National in the West, Vols. One, Two and Three.* Calgary, Alta.: B.R.M.N.A., 1980, 1981, 1983.

Lowe, J. Norman. *Canadian National in the East, Vols. One, Two and Three.* Calgary, Alta.: B.R.M.N.A., 1981, 1983, 1985.

MacKay, Donald. *The People's Railway: A History of the Canadian National.* Vancouver: Douglas & McIntyre, 1992.

MacKay, Donald and Lorne Perry. *Train Country: An Illustrated History of Canadian National Railways.* Vancouver: Douglas & McIntyre, 1994.

McDonnell, Greg. *The History of Canadian Railroads.* London: New Burlington Books, 1985.

Middleton, William D. *Landmarks on the Iron Road: Two Centuries of North American Railroad Engineering.* Bloomington, Ind.: Indiana University Press, 1999.

——. *When the Steam Railroads Electrified.* Milwaukee, Wis.: Kalmbach Publishing Co., 1974.

Plowden, David. *Bridges: The Spans of North America.* New York: W. W. Norton & Company, 2002.

Stevens, G. R. *Canadian National Railways, Vol. I: Sixty Years of Trial and Error (1839–1896).* Toronto: Clarke, Irwin & Company, 1960.

——. *Canadian National Railways, Vol. II: Towards the Inevitable (1896–1922).* Toronto: Clarke, Irwin & Company, 1962.

——. *History of the Canadian National Railways.* New York: The Macmillan Company, 1973.

Turner, Robert D. *Vancouver Island Railroads.* San Marino, Calif.: Golden West Books, 1973.

Other Publications

Barriger, John Walker. *Sir Henry Thornton, K.B.E. (1871–1933) Pioneer.* New York: The Newcomen Society of England, American Branch, 1948.

Canada on the Move: The Canadian Railroads Modernize for an Expanding Nation. *Modern Railroads*, July 1952.

Canadian National Railways locomotive roster. *Extra 2200 South: The Locomotive Newsmagazine*, issues 48–50, 1974–1975.

CN Lines Special Interest Group, *CN Lines Magazine*, various issues.

Lavallée, Omer. The Grand Trunk Railway of Canada: An Overview. *Railroad History*, Issue 147, Autumn 1982.

The Official Guide of the Railways, various issues. New York: National Railway Publication Company.

Canadian National and Affiliated Company Materials

Annual reports, 1923–2002

Growing Up With Canada, 1987

Growing With Prince Rupert, undated (ca. 1983)

GT Facts: Basic Information About the Grand Trunk Western Railroad, December 1972

Investor fact books, 1997–2003

Maps and travel brochures

Public and employee timetables

Railway Capacity: CN Rail Transcontinental Route, November 17, 1980

Other Resources

Canada Science and Technology Museum web site, www.sciencetech.technomuses.ca

Canadian National web site, www.cn.ca

Canadian Railway Hall of Fame web site, www.railfame.ca

CN Lines Special Interest Group web site, www.cnlines.com

Eisfeller, Richard. *CN's Northern Ontario Mains.* Video. Greenland, N.H.: Big "E" Productions, 2002.

——. *Paired Track in the Canyons, Parts I and II.* Video. Greenland, N.H.: Big "E" Productions, 2002.

CPR INDEX

Algoma Steel, 106, 132, 134
Algonquin Park, 114
Allan, Hugh, 14, 16, 17
Alouette, 98, 121
Amtrak, 115, 126
Angus, R. B., 25, 35
Atlantic Express, 117
Atlantic Limited, 128

Beatty, Edward Wentworth, 9, 79, 80, 82–84, 88
Beaverburn, 88
Belleville Subdivision, 92, 105, 132
Big Hill, British Columbia, 32, 64
Boston & Maine (B&M), 41, 42, 95, 98, 99, 121
Boundary Subdivision, 56, 58, 124
Bowen, Henry, 86
Bredenbury Subdivision, 155, 157
Buck, George, 64, 82
Burbidge, Frederick S., 93, 132
Burrard Inlet, British Columbia, 21–23

Campbell, R. W., 132
Canada Central Railway, 20, 32
Canada Southern Railway, 123
Canadian Atlantic Railway, 142
Canadian International Paper, 132
Canadian Locomotive Company (CLC), 50, 55, 87, 108, 109
Canadian National, 43, 70, 80, 82–84, 103, 104, 121, 123, 128, 129, 132, 135, 137, 143, 155
Canadian National–Canadian Pacific Railway Act, 84
Canadian Northern Railway (CNoR), 25, 67–70, 83
Canadian Pacific Air Lines, 51, 109, 110, 133
Canadian Pacific Hotels & Resorts Inc., 148, 156
Canadian Pacific Investments Limited, 105, 108, 132
Canadian Pacific Navigation Company (CPN), 71
Canadian Pacific Steamships Limited, 73
Canadian Pacific Transport Limited, 105
Canadian Pacific: A Brief History, 14
Canadian, The, 14, 24, 28, 32, 64, 113, 114, 122, 125–129, 136
Chicago & North Western, 120
Chicago Express, 122
Chicago, Milwaukee & St. Paul Railroad, 27, 28

CNCP Telecommunications, 134, 148
Coleman, D'Alton C., 88, 90
Connaught Tunnel, 16, 66, 67, 140
Consolidated Mining and Smelting (Comino), 50, 52, 106, 133
Cooke, Jay, 16, 17
Corbin, D. C., 49, 50, 64
Craigellachie, British Columbia, 36, 37, 79
Crow's Nest Pass Agreement, 50, 103
Crowsnest Pass, British Columbia, 48, 52, 53, 64, 116, 124, 134, 158
Crowsnest Subdivision, 38
Crump, Norris R. "Buck", 9, 91, 93–113, 126, 131, 148
CSX, 130, 151

Dakota, Minnesota & Eastern Railroad, 153
Delaware & Hudson Railway, 45, 142, 149–151, 153, 154
Dominion Atlantic Railway, 69, 121, 122, 133, 143
Dominion, The, 12, 119, 120, 126
Duluth & Winnipeg Railway, 48, 60, 141
Duluth, South Shore & Atlantic Railway, 44, 48, 86

Eagle Pass, British Columbia, 27, 36
Emerson, Robert A., 93
Esquimalt & Nanaimo Railway, 19, 95, 97
Express Airborne, 133

Fairmont Hotels & Resorts Inc., 156
Fleming, Sanford, 21–23, 32, 37, 58
Fording Coal, 108, 148, 149, 156
Fraser River Canyon, British Columbia, 20–23, 118
From Summit To Sea, 64

Grand Trunk, 16, 42, 44, 46, 67, 69, 70, 129
Grand Trunk Pacific, 25, 67–70, 83, 155
Great Depression, the, 86–88
Great Lakes Forest Products, 106, 132
Great Northern Railway, 20, 48, 49, 53, 61, 64
Gull, 121

Hays, Charles M., 67
Hector, James, 28
Heinze, Augustus, 50

Hill, James J., 18, 20, 24, 25, 34, 47–50, 53, 80
History of the Canadian Pacific Railway, 17
Hotels, 73, 74, 84, 85, 116
Hudson's Bay Company, 14, 20
Huron Central Railway, 144

I&M Rail Link, 152
Imperial Limited, 117–119
Indiana Rail Road, 49
Intercolonial Railway, 21, 42, 70
Iowa, Chicago & Eastern Railroad, 152, 153
Iron Road Railways, 144

Kaslo Subdivision, 56
Kellock, R. L., 103
Kettle Valley Express, 125
Kettle Valley Railway, 58
Kicking Horse Pass, 25, 28, 32, 64, 78, 116, 159
King, Mackenzie, 82
Kittson, Norman W., 18
Kootenay Express, 124, 125

Lachute Subdivision, 129
Laggan Subdivision, 14, 140, 159
Laidlaw Transportation Limited, 134
Land sales, 74–77
Laurentian Shield, 20
Lords of the Line: The Men Who Built the CPR, 61

M&O Subdivision, 127
Macdonald, John A., 14, 17–19
Mackenzie, Alexander, 17, 18, 67, 68
MacMillan Bloedel, 106
Macoun, John, 25
Maine Central Railroad, 43, 121
Mann, Donald, 67, 68
Maple Leaf Mills, 132, 133
Marathon Realty, 106, 148
Mather, William A., 91
Maxwell, Edward and William, 75
McPherson, M. A., 103
Michigan Central, 123
Milwaukee Road, The, 49, 118, 141, 142, 152
Minneapolis, St. Paul & Sault St. Marie Railway, *see* Soo Line Railroad
Montana Rail Link, 152
Montreal, Maine & Atlantic Railway, 133, 135, 143
Moosehead Subdivision, 133, 135
Morant, Nicholas, 14
More Classic Trains, 117
Mountain Subdivision, 9
Mountaineer, 120, 126

National Transcontinental, 67
National Transportation Act of 1967, 103

Neal, William M., 90
New Brunswick Southern Railway, 144
New York Central System, 123, 142
Nipigon Subdivision, 10
Norfolk Southern, 130, 154
Northern Pacific, 47
Notch Hill, British Columbia, 137, 139

O'Brien, David, 147–149, 156
Onderdonk, Andrew, 19, 21–23, 27, 36
Overseas, 122

Pacific Express, 117
Pacific Great Eastern, 132
Palliser, John, 77
PanCanadian Petroleum Limited, 77, 147, 148, 156
Passumpsic Railroad, 80, 41
Pembina Branch, 18, 61
Penn Central, 123
Price, Bruce, 73–75

Quebec Central Local, 103
Quebec Gatineau Railway, 144

Red Wing, 121
Ritchie, Rob, 147, 154, 157
Rocky Mountains, 21, 23–32
Rogers, A. B., 25
Rogers Pass, British Columbia, 24, 25, 27, 32, 36, 67, 73, 140
Ross, James, 36
Royal Canadian Pacific, 115, 116
Royal Train, 84
Royal York, 122

Shaughnessy, Thomas G., 9, 28, 29, 58–61, 64, 67, 69, 72, 79, 80, 83
Ships, 70–73, 84, 130, 148, 156
Empress of Australia, 72
Empress of Britain, 72, 84, 88, 110
Empress of Canada, 71, 111, 113
Empress of China, 70
Empress of England, 111
Empress of India, 70
Empress of Ireland, 72
Empress of Japan, 70, 112
Empress of Scotland, 72, 112
Princess Kathleen, 71
Princess Patricia, 136
S.S. *Rossland*, 51
Shuswap Subdivision, 137, 139
Sinclair, Ian D., 9, 93, 94, 132, 148
Smith, Donald, 9, 16, 18, 20, 35–37, 44, 47, 73, 74
Smith Transport Limited, 105

Soo Line Railroad, 44, 49, 43, 61, 62, 86, 118–120, 124, 126, 130, 141, 142, 150, 151
Soo-Dominion, 120
Soo-Pacific Express, 120
South Eastern Railway, 41
Spiral Tunnels, 32, 62, 64, 66, 119
Spokane International Railway, 51, 64, 86, 119
St. Lawrence & Hudson Railway Company Limited, 150, 153
St. Paul and Pacific Railroad, 18, 20, 34
St. Paul, Minneapolis and Manitoba, 34
Stephen, George, 9–11, 18–20, 25, 32, 34–36, 41, 44, 47, 58, 59, 61, 70, 73, 74, 132
Stinson, William, 132, 134, 148
Syracuse China, 132, 133

The Pictorial History of Railroading in British Columbia, 22
The Spiral Tunnels and the Big Hill, 32
Thompson River Canyon, British Columbia, 21–23, 118
Thornton, Henry, 82–84
Toronto, Hamilton & Buffalo Railway, 123
Trans-Canada Airlines (Air Canada), 109, 110
Trans-Canada Limited, 119, 121

Union Pacific, 51, 119, 158

Van Horne, William Cornelius, 9, 11, 27–29, 32, 34–37, 46–50, 58–61, 73, 74, 116, 132
VIA Rail, 115, 128, 129

Wabash Railway, 42
Walker, G. A., 90, 91
Washington, Dennis, 152
Western Grain Transportation Act (WGTA), 137, 139, 140
Windermere Subdivision, 107, 146
Windsor & Hantsport Railway, 143
Winnipeger, 124
Wisconsin Central, 61, 86, 141
Wood Mountain Subdivision, 152
World War I, 80, 85, 88
World War II, 88–89

Yellowhead Pass, Alberta, 21, 23–25

CN INDEX

Acadian, 190, 194
Advertisements, 188, 189, 195, 239, 242, 287
Albert Resources Railway, 268
Alco, 213
Ambassador, 240

Ballantyne, Quebec, 210
Bandeen, Robert, 218, 221, 291, 299, 300, 316
Barriger, John W., 193
Bayview Junction, Ontario, 235
Bennett, R. B., 194
Bessborough Hotel, Saskatoon, 236
Boston, Massachusetts, 180
Bridge Station, Quebec, 198
Brockville, Ontario, 167, 197
Bromptonville, Quebec, 177
Brooks, Ned, 205
Bruce, Harry, 307

Canadian, 242
Canadian Car & Foundry, 242
Canadian economy, 215–217
Canadian General Electric, 175
Canadian Government Railways, 169
Canadian Locomotive Company (CLC), 204, 205, 210, 214
Canadian National Hotel, 236
Canadian Northern Railway (CNoR), 173–176, 194, 202, 262, 270, 272, 274, 295
Canadian Pacific (CP), 173, 174, 192, 194
Cap Rouge, Quebec, 183
Capitol, 230
Caribou, The, 254
Cartierville, Quebec, 227
Cavalier, 230
Central Vermont Railway (CV), 280–285
Centralized Traffic Control (CTC), 197, 212
Chaleur, 229
Charlottetown Hotel, 251
Chateau Laurier, Ottawa, 236
Chaudiére, Quebec, 178
Chicago, Illinois, 177, 179, 180, 190, 237, 279, 282, 287, 289, 290, 293, 302, 305
Churchill, Manitoba, 245, 268, 269
Cisco, British Columbia, 168, 222, 273
Confederation, 190, 194
Continental Limited, 190, 238, 240

Detroit & Toledo Shore Line (D&TSL), 292

Detroit, Michigan, 289, 290
Detroit, Toledo & Ironton Railroad (DT&I), 292
Dewey, British Columbia, 227
Diesel experimentation, 202–206
Dieselization, 208–212
Dubin, Arthur, 242
Duluth, Minnesota, 295–298, 302, 305
Duluth, Missabe & Iron Range Railway (DM&IR), 296, 298, 315
Duluth, Winnipeg & Pacific Railway (DW&P), 291, 294–298, 315

Edmonton, Alberta, 174, 176, 213, 265, 271, 273, 299, 304
Evanston, 228

Fort Erie, Ontario, 190

General Motors Diesel Division, 225, 252
Gordon, Donald, 209, 242, 316
Grand Trunk Corporation (GTC), 218, 284, 291, 293, 296, 304
Grand Trunk Pacific (GTP), 176, 180–183, 261, 268, 270
Grand Trunk Railway (GTR), 170, 171, 172, 176–180, 190, 279, 286
Grand Trunk Western, 211, 212, 280, 282, 286, 289–295
Great Depression, the, 193, 240
Great Eastern Railway, 185
Great Lakes Transportation (GLT), 296, 298, 315
Great Northern Railway, 175
Great Western Railway, 180
Gull, 240

Halifax & South Western Railway, 176
Hanna, David Blythe, 174, 184, 185, 199
Harrison, Hunter, 313
Hays, Charles Melville, 180, 276, 281
Henry House, Alberta, 271
Hincks, Francis, 176, 177, 179, 287
Hofsommer, Don, 290, 296
Hotel Beausejour, New Brunswick, 237
Hotel Ford Garry, Winnipeg, 236
Hotel Macdonald, Edmonton, 236
Hotel Newfoundland, St. John's, 237, 253
Hotel Nova Scotian, Halifax, 236

Hudson Bay Railway, 267
Hungerford, Samuel J., 194, 195

Illinois Central Railroad (IC), 309
Indiana, 179, 279
Inter-City Limited, 234, 290
Intercolonial Railway, 169, 170, 172, 173, 237, 246, 286
Intermodal traffic trailers ("piggyback"), 217
International, 230
International City Limited, 190, 237, 240, 290

Jasper, Alberta, 176, 186, 228, 240, 243, 261, 262, 268, 271, 299
Jasper Park Lodge, 236

King, William Lyon Mackenzie, 185, 194
Kingston, Ontario, 179, 204

La Prairie, Quebec, 177
Lakeshore, 232
Lazare, Manitoba, 181
Le Champlain, 243
LeClair, Maurice, 300–302
London, England, 179
Lowe, Norman J., 202

M. V. Abegweit, 247
MacKay, Donald, 190, 192, 193, 195, 209, 242
Mackenzie, William, 173–176
MacMillan, Norman, 218, 221
Maine, 177, 179, 288
Mann, Donald, 173–176, 183
Maple Leaf, 190, 230, 240, 290, 291
Maritime Express, 240, 251
Maritime Freight Rate Act, 249
Matapédia, Quebec, 211
Michigan, 179, 180, 279, 305
Milwaukee Road, 293, 296, 310
Milwaukee, Wisconsin, 293
Minaki Lodge, Ontario, 236
Minnesota, 174, 175, 188, 279, 293, 308, 310, 314
Moncton, New Brunswick, 180, 183
Monon Railroad, 193
Montreal, Quebec, 175–177, 179, 180, 190, 194, 195, 198, 210, 211, 213, 217, 229, 230, 237, 240, 285–287, 290, 291
Montreal Harbor Commission Terminal Railway, 166
Montreal Locomotive Works (MLW), 167, 181, 211, 213, 223, 224

More Classic Trains, 242
Mount Royal, Montreal, 175, 198, 205

National Research Council, 201
National Transcontinental Railway, 169, 180, 181–183
National Transportation Act, 218
National, 238
Nationalism and consolidation, 183–186
New Englander, 240
New London, Connecticut, 279–282
Newfoundland Railway, 251–254
Niagara River Suspension Bridge, 259
North Bay, Ontario, 180, 210, 211
Northern Alberta Railway, 267
Northland, 230
Norton, New Brunswick, 231, 246, 251
Nova Scotia, 176, 177, 229, 230, 237, 246, 247–249, 251, 254
Nova Scotian Hotel, 251

Ocean, 229
Ocean Limited, 237, 240, 243, 251
Ontario Limited, 240
Ottawa, Ontario 229, 230
Ottawa Car, 193
Owl, 240

Panorama, 228
Passenger service evolution, 237–244
People's Railway, The, 209
Poor, John, 288
Port Arthur, Ontario, 175, 176, 188
Portland, Maine, 177, 180, 285–288
Prince Albert, Saskatchewan, 174, 261, 262
Prince Edward Island Railway, 169, 171, 172, 248
Prince Rupert, British Columbia, 176, 180, 182, 243, 274–277, 300
Privatization, 307–309
Pullman-Standard, 228

Quebec Bridge, 259
Quebec City, Quebec, 183, 248, 257, 258

Rapido, 230, 243
Reid Newfoundland Company, 252
Richelieu River, 186
Riviére-du-Loup, Quebec, 172, 180, 246
Rouses Point, New York, 177, 223

Royal Commission, 194

Sarnia, Ontario, 179
Scenic Canada, 234
Scheduled railroading, 313
Scotian, 229, 257
Sherbrooke, Quebec, 177
Skeena, 243
St. Clair Tunnel, 291
St. John, Quebec, 177
St. John's, Newfoundland, 245, 246, 252, 253
St. Lawrence River, 257, 259, 285
Steam locomotives, 199–202
Stevens, G. R., 174, 183, 194, 270
Stratford, Ontario, 201
Super Continental, 212, 226, 228, 229, 238, 242

Tellier, Paul, 305–307, 309, 310, 313, 316
Tempo, 229
Thompson and Fraser River Canyons, 168, 274, 275
Thornton, Sir Henry, 185, 187, 190, 193, 194, 200, 233, 315
Titanic, 281
Toronto, Ontario, 179, 180, 188, 190, 194, 200, 213, 217, 229, 230, 273
Toronto, 240
Toronto Union Station, 231
Tourism, 251, 287
Traffic Reporting and Control System (TRACS), 214
Trans-Canada Air Lines, 209
Turbo, 241
Tyler, Sir Henry, 179

United Aircraft, 243

Vancouver, British Columbia, 176, 190, 205, 270, 272–274, 300, 304
Vanderbilt, William, 179
Vaughan, R. C., 195

Whitcomb Locomotive Works, 208
Winnipeg Great Northern Railway, 173
Winnipeg, Manitoba, 174, 181, 213, 225, 295–298
Wisconsin Central (WC), 312
Wood, L. L., 192
World War I, 179, 184, 187, 190, 207, 252, 268, 274
World War II, 194–199, 205, 207, 242, 252, 274

Yellowhead Pass, Alberta, 181, 216, 226, 270, 271, 299